SEX AND DIVERSITY IN LATER LIFE
Critical Perspectives

Edited by
Trish Hafford-Letchfield, Paul Simpson
and Paul Reynolds

With a Foreword by
Diana K. Kwok

D1612586

P

First published in Great Britain in 2023 by

Policy Press, an imprint of
Bristol University Press
University of Bristol
1-9 Old Park Hill
Bristol
BS2 8BB
UK
t: +44 (0)117 374 6645
e: bup-info@bristol.ac.uk

Details of international sales and distribution partners are available at
policy.bristoluniversitypress.co.uk

© Bristol University Press 2023

British Library Cataloguing in Publication Data
A catalogue record for this book is available from the British Library

ISBN 978-1-4473-5540-3 hardcover
ISBN 978-1-4473-5541-0 paperback
ISBN 978-1-4473-5543-4 ePub
ISBN 978-1-4473-5542-7 ePdf

Cover design: Robin Hawes
Front cover image: istock-537819435

Bristol University Press and Policy Press use environmentally responsible
print partners.

Printed in Great Britain by CMP, Poole

Sex and Intimacy in Later Life

Series Editors: **Paul Simpson**, Independent Academic,
Paul Reynolds, International Network for Sexual
Ethics and Politics and The Open University and
Trish Hafford-Letchfield, University of Strathclyde

Older people are commonly characterised as non-sexual, or their sexuality is considered a superficial concern in comparison to health, public services and pensions. This is despite evidence of an increase in sexual engagement amongst older people. Little academic attention has been given to this subject, or to the impact that this may have, such as increased rates of sexually transmitted infection or implications for healthy sex lives in care institutions.

This new, internationally-focused series will build on, extend and deepen knowledge of sexual practice amongst older people. Pulling together work by established and emerging scholars across a range of disciplines, it will cover the experiential, empirical and theoretical landscapes of sex and ageing.

Also available

Desexualisation in Later Life: The Limits of Sex and Intimacy

Edited by **Paul Simpson, Paul Reynolds** and **Trish Hafford-Letchfield**

Forthcoming in the series

HIV, Sex and Sexuality in Later Life

Edited by **Mark Henrickson, Casey Charles, Shiv Ganesh, Sulaimon Giwa, Kan Diana Kwok** and **Tetyana Semigina**

Find out more at
policy.bristoluniversitypress.co.uk/
sex-and-intimacy-in-later-life

Sex and Intimacy in Later Life

Series Editors: **Paul Simpson**, Independent Academic,
Paul Reynolds, International Network for Sexual
Ethics and Politics and The Open University and
Trish Hafford-Letchfield, University of Strathclyde

Find out more at
policy.bristoluniversitypress.co.uk/
sex-and-intimacy-in-later-life

The editors extend thanks to all contributors whose hard work and thinking have made this book possible. Thank you to the international advisory board for its help and support concerning this book series. Trish Hafford-Letchfield would like to dedicate this book to her grandchild, Nora Grace, who joined this world during the UK lockdown period of 2020–21. Paul Simpson would like to dedicate this book, by way of thanks, to his husband, Gordon Blows. Paul Reynolds would like to dedicate the book to J.S., A.M. and L.C. for their support over the period this text gestated.

Contents

List of figures and tables

Figures

Tables

Notes on editors and contributors

Editors

Trish Hafford-Letchfield is Professor of Social Work and Social Policy at the University of Strathclyde, Glasgow, Scotland. She is a qualified social worker and nurse. Her research interests lie in the experience of marginalised groups in aged care, sexuality and gender identity issues in social work and social care, leadership, management and organisational development in public services and art-based pedagogies. She has published extensively in these areas with around 100 peer reviewed publications.

Paul Reynolds taught across northern British universities for over 30 years, attaining the position of Reader in Sociology and Social Philosophy. He currently tutors on courses for the Open University, UK. He is currently Co-Director of the international network for Cultural Difference and Social Solidarity, Co-convenor of the International Network for Sexual Ethics and Politics and a member of the Editorial Board of *Historical Materialism: Research in Critical Marxist Theory* among other commitments. His current research interests are sexual ethics and literacy; kink and the construction of perversion; Marxism, sexuality, subjectivities and collectivities, and the role and responsibilities of the intellectual.

Paul Simpson has a PhD in Sociology and lectured in Sociology at the University of Manchester and, more recently, was a Senior Lecturer in Health and Social Wellbeing at Edge Hill University, UK. He has published extensively on gay male ageing (including a monograph, *Gay Men, Ageing and Ageism: Over the Rainbow?*), disadvantaged men, and health and sexuality and intimacy in later life. He has had articles published in *Ageing and Society*, the *British Journal of Sociology*, *Men and Masculinities*, *Qualitative Research*, *Sociological Research Online*, *Sociological Review* and *Sociology of Health and Illness*, among others.

Contributors

Debra A. Harley, PhD, CRC, LPC, is a Provost Distinguished Service Professor in the Department of Early Childhood, Special Education and

Counselor Education at the University of Kentucky. She is coordinator of the doctoral programme in Counselor Education and former department chair, past coordinator of the rehabilitation counseling programme, and past director of the Gender and Women's Studies programme. Her research interests include disability issues, cultural diversity, substance abuse, gender issues, LGBTQ and ethics. She has published books entitled *Cultural Diversity in Mental Health and Disability Counseling for Marginalized Groups*; *Disability and Vocational Rehabilitation in Rural Setting*; *Handbook of LGBT Elders: An Interdisciplinary Approach to Principles, Practices, and Policies*; and *Contemporary Mental Health Issues Among African Americans*. She works collaboratively with Counselor Education programmes and Rehabilitation Counseling programmes at South Carolina State University, North Carolina State A&T University and Langston University, US.

David M. Lee is Reader in Epidemiology and Gerontology, Faculty of Health, Psychology and Social Care at Manchester Metropolitan University. His background is in epidemiology and his academic interest focuses on how multiple biological, psychological and social problems conspire to erode late-life quality-of-life and wellbeing. Human sexuality and intimacy is an important aspect of this, and his current research focuses on how older people prioritise sexual health and the impacts of caring, intimate relationships throughout the life-course. He has published in *The Journals of Gerontology*, *Age and Ageing*, *Archives of Sexual Behavior* and the *Journal of Sex Research*. Research topics have covered quantitative associations between health, hormones, wellbeing and sex and more recently on qualitative analyses using data from the English Longitudinal Study of Ageing.

Ela Przybylo is Assistant Professor in English and core faculty in Women's and Gender Studies at Illinois State University, US. She is the author of *Asexual Erotics: Intimate Readings of Compulsory Sexuality* (Ohio State University Press, 2019) and editor of *On the Politics of Ugliness* (Palgrave, 2018). She is a founding and managing editor of the peer-reviewed, open access journal *Feral Feminisms*.

Karen Rennie, RN BSc (Hons) Nursing and PhD candidate at Queen Margaret University, Scotland. Her research interests consist of the importance of sexual expression and intimacy in older persons and persons living with dementia. Her PhD research is exploring how nurses can provide person-centred care when looking after persons living with dementia who express themselves sexually. Additionally, her methodological interests lie within phenomenological and participatory research approaches.

Peter Robinson (PhD) is a Senior Research Fellow at Swinburne University of Technology, Melbourne, Australia. He has written three books on gay men's life histories, the first of which, *The Changing World of Gay Men* (Palgrave Macmillan, 2008) won the inaugural Raewyn Connell prize for the best first book in Australian Sociology. His research interests include ageing, sexualities and social justice. In 2019, he began work on a fourth book which will examine gay men's end-of-life matters, including will making, estate planning, and funeral plans, as well as their views on life after death and euthanasia.

Laura Scarrone Bonhomme is a clinical psychologist who trained and developed her career internationally, working in Spain, South America and the UK. Although she deals with a variety of issues, she specialises in gender and sexual diversity, working both privately and at the National Health Service (NHS) Gender Identity Clinic, part of the Tavistock and Portman NHS Foundation Trust. She is a Chartered Member of the British Psychological Society (BPS) and an Associate Editor of the BPS *Counselling Psychology Review*. She is part of the BPS Gender Diversity Specialist Register, a member of British Association of Gender Identity Specialists, and a member of the World Professional Association of Transgender Health.

Josephine Tetley is Professor Emerita of Nursing based at the Faculty of Health, Psychology and Social Care, Manchester Metropolitan University, UK. She has been a nurse for over 35 years, undertaking work in practice, education and research. She has over 20 years' experience of undertaking a wide range of international, national and local research work with older people and family carers, with a particular focus on user participation. As a researcher her work is primarily qualitative in nature, which led her to work with Dr David Lee on the English Longitudinal Study of Ageing (ELSA).

Megan Todd (PhD) is Senior Lecturer in Social Science at the University of Central Lancashire, UK. She has been involved in a range of research projects, including a British Academy project investigating educational capital and same-sex parenting, an ESRC-funded project on LGBT+ equality initiatives in local government and LGBT+ service users in Lancashire. Her research focuses on sexualities, gender and violence; she has published on issues relating to health, intimate partner violence, feminisms and homophobic and misogynist abuse online. She is currently developing work on universities' management of their LGBT+ heritage.

Christopher Wells is a PhD student at Leeds University, UK within the School of Languages, Cultures and Societies. His research project investigates the historical formation of bisexual subjectivity and its reciprocal relationship with modernist literature between 1890 and 1939. His research outside of this current project centres on the intersections between literature and the lived experiences of bisexuality in contemporary culture. He is currently working on a monograph that explores the ageing bisexual in 2020. His most recent publication is entitled 'Where Do I Put it? Bisexuality, James Joyce's Buck Mulligan and Contemporary Legislative Practice', published in *The Open Journal of Humanities*.

Series editors' introduction

Paul Reynolds, Paul Simpson and Trish Hafford-Letchfield

This *Sex and Intimacy in Later Life* book series will explore, interrogate and enlighten on the sensual, sexual and intimate lives of older people. The motivation for launching this series was a concern with the relative lack of attention in public, professional and academic/intellectual spheres to sex and intimacy in later life (indicatively, Hafford-Letchfield, 2008; Simpson et al, 2018a, 2018b). The series is intended to contribute to and enrich the development of the field of studies composed of the intersections of age, sex, sexuality and intimacy as a critical and important area of scholarship. It is only beginning to be recognised as an important social, cultural and political domain of study within and beyond the 'Western' academy, from which it has emerged. Its earliest contributions, of which this volume is a part, are motivated by a desire to recognise and reject the pathologies and prejudices that have infused this intersection – what Simpson has termed 'ageist erotophobia' (Simpson et al, 2018b, p 1479) – and fuel the failure to acknowledge older people as sexual agents. This is both an intellectual and a political agenda, to question and evaluate the impact of real rather than assumed losses of cognitive, physical, social and sexual capacity, and to recuperate older people as sexual agents from dismissal, ridicule and trivialisation.

If the latter half of the twentieth century was characterised by challenges to the pathologies of social identities – particularly gender, ethnicity and race, disability, sexuality – and struggles for recognition, rights and liberties, more intersectional struggles and recognitions characterise the twenty-first century (on intersectionality, see indicatively Hancock, 2016; Hill Collins and Bilge, 2016). Significant among these has been the re-evaluation of what it is to age and to be an older agent in contemporary societies. Older people have historically experienced both veneration and respect and neglect and pathology, largely based on differing cultural stereotypes of the value of age (Ylanne, 2012). The most common characterisation is that older people are not sexual, past being sexual or represent a problematic sexuality – or their sexuality is a superficial concern and secondary to concerns of health, care, life course and support by public services and engagement and pensions/resources. Such concerns are mainly those of 'Western' cultures and reflected in the 'Western' influence across the globe in respect of state intervention and provision, but elsewhere they have been subsumed and often rendered invisible into family and kinship structures.

Older people's intimate and sexual lives and experiences have transformed in the last 40 years, as a consequence of a number of significant social changes: new technologies – digital, mechanical and pharmaceutical – and their interventions; the recognition of older people as exploitable markets for consumption; healthier lifestyles, changes and extensions to life course and life expectancy; the erosion of social and sexual pathologies around age and recognitions of different intersections and their importance (LGBTQI older people, older people of different ethnicities, older disabled/neurodiverse and 'able-bodied/minded' people; older men and women).[1] These transformations demonstrate evidence of increase in the sexual relations and intimacies of older people and their impacts, such as increased rates of STD transmission, or implications for healthy sex lives for older people in care institutions (indicatively, Drench and Losee, 1996; Lindau, 2007; Bodley-Tickell et al, 2008; Chao et al, 2011; Simpson, 2015; Age UK, 2019).

The scholarship exploring these developments has only recently begun to catch up. A small but growing literature has focused on age and sexuality (represented in the sources authors draw from in this series), with a principal focus on the erosion of easy pathologies and stereotypes of older people's heteronormativity and heterosexuality. Particularly as the 'baby boomers' of the 1950s and 1960s move into old age, changed sexual attitudes, wants and needs require changed political, cultural and institutional responses. The older generation of baby boomers in the late 1940s and 1950s may have remembered Vera Lynn (an iconic British wartime singer singing patriotic songs during World War 2) and post-war society – retaining traditional stereotypes of older people. However, their horizons will have been formed and broadened more by influences from the 1960s' pop and rock culture (notably with such artists as the Beatles, Rolling Stones, Jimi Hendrix and Janis Joplin), women's and lesbian, gay and bisexual liberation struggles, the proliferation of accessible public representations of sex and the 'pornification' of society in the digital age.

Ageing and becoming 'older', intimacy, sexual identity, relations and practices and sexual pleasure are all contested concepts and subject categories. They are understood as being constituted by different demarcations, distinctions and understandings arising from different intellectual disciplines, conceptual approaches, cultures, geographical contexts and historical conjunctures. While it is neither desirable nor credible to preclude critical and constructive debate on the meanings and demarcations of these intersections, it is necessary to draw some broad conceptual boundaries rather than hard-and-fast definitions.

'Ageing' and 'older' are broad categories that are attached to people considered in their 'third age' or 'later life' – in more affluent countries/regions of the mainly Global North, the threshold is often seen as the age of 50+. This reflects common practice in the literatures of social gerontology, psychology and the sociology of ageing (see Zaninotto et al, 2009; Cronin and King, 2010; Stenner et al, 2011). It is after that, and into their sixth decade, that older people experience a process of de-eroticisation that could be called 'compulsory non-sexuality' (taking our cue from feminist theorist Adrienne Rich [1981], who articulated pressures on women's sexuality towards 'compulsory heterosexuality').

Ageing and being older can be understood mainly in two ways. First, the terms describe ageing as a chronological and physiological process involving key changes, which become particularly marked (and can be stigmatised) in the later stages of the life course. This raises questions around the differential impact of life course experience and physiological change – which *may* include loss and/or reduction of physical and mental capacities for *some* people at different stages in the life course. It is structured both by physiological change and by the (often imperceptible) internalisation and normalisation of orthodoxies describing ageing and being older in cultural and social discourse, and the everyday practice and experience of how older people are perceived and how older people see themselves – often as lacking – and in relation to younger people (Foucault, 1977, 1978). Such is the means by which older people (as much as younger people or social and cultural institutions) both produce and accept the discursive limits to ageing.

Second, ageing and being older could be described as an attribution constituted by ideology and discourse, structural-hierarchical and cultural-discursive influences and material contexts, such as the structure of organisations, public spaces, cultural representations and spaces of connection (for example, labour markets). Ageing is usefully regarded as a product of intersections between the symbolic/discursive and structural/material dimensions of existence. The attribution of a particular age – young, mature or older – is an ideological construct suffused by power relations and composed of cultural attributions, instantiated in material processes and practices. These structural factors impose all manner of constraints on older people's sexual agency (though these can be questioned, challenged and resisted). Put simply, age is a social, cultural and political construct and how older people are perceived and valued – whether prejudicially or with respect – is constituted in the wider character of social values and dominant discourses. While age is an experienced and embodied phenomenon, its meaning is socially, culturally and politically mediated.

'Sex' and 'sexuality' are often distinguished by the former being focused on practices and behaviour, and the latter being focused on identities, relations and orientations. The terms are nevertheless porous and intertwined (Weeks, 2010). Sexuality describes the processes of being sexual (or not) in the world and through self-recognition, expressing (or not) sexual choices and preferences and enjoying (or not) sexual pleasures. It involves the expression of emotions, desires, beliefs, self-presentation and how we relate to others. It most commonly relates to sexual identity – for example hetero, lesbian, gay, bisexual, queer, asexual (Rahman and Jackson, 2010). Sexuality is multidimensional, being co-constituted by the biological (for example bodily sensations interpreted as 'sexual'), the psychological (for example emotions and reasoning) and cultural and socio-economic influences such as dressing up and flirting and so on (Doll, 2012). It is often understood narrowly as genitocentric, itself tied to the heteronormative relationship between genital sex and reproduction. Yet it encapsulates a range of practices that bring sensual pleasure and fulfil wants and desires, such as the agglomeration of practices that are subsumed under the umbrella term BDSM (Bondage and Discipline, Domination and Submission, Sadism and Masochism) (indicatively Weiss, 2011; Ortmann and Sprott, 2013).

'Intimacy' refers to involvement in close and interpersonal relations. It can be a feature of diverse relationships, from those that are sexual, or with strong close personal friendship bonds, or characterised by physical and emotional closeness, to those where a particular relation or facet of life is shared closely, such as close work relationships. It encompasses a spectrum of emotions, needs and activities ranging from feelings of caring, closeness and affection (that can go with long-term companionship) through to 'romance', where an individual 'idealizes' a person(s) (Ehrenreich et al, 1997). Intimacy is to a degree conceived in gendered terms: if men tend to define it more in physical terms, women usually emphasise more its emotional content (O'Brien et al, 2012). It is often conceived as two people sharing intimacy rather than a larger number and is constituted subjectively as a value that is owned or shared with others, although equally it is sometimes seen as an arena that reinforces oppressive conventions of private–public divides and 'compulsory monogamy' (Bersani and Phillips, 2008; Heckert, 2010; Musial, 2013).

These three conceptualisations – age/older, sex/sexuality and intimacies – intersect in complex ways. For example, the prevailing assumption that sexual relationships involve shared intimacy fails to recognise 'fuck buddies' or so-called casual relationships for mutual sexual gratification, though intimacy is sometimes used to describe a particular event without relationship – 'they were intimate' (Wentland and Reissing, 2014). Likewise, sex and age often enmesh in complex ways, though these linkages too often involve mutually reinforcing negative representations. Decline in sexual capacity – often reduced to coital/genital function – is associated with ageing and later life as a standard correlation as opposed to a graduated contingency. Drawing in other intersections, the relationship between sexual capacity and potency is a significant feature of masculinity and therefore sexual capacity is considered more challenging for men, given fears of loss of status and greater reluctance than women to seek help concerning sexual and relationship problems (O'Brien et al, 2012). This reflects gendered assumptions that male sexuality is more active and women's more passive that is rooted in classical sexology (indicatively Davidson and Layder, 1994; Bland and Doan, 1998).

Nevertheless, the sexuality of older women could be constrained by biological changes, understood through cultural pathology as decline and loss of attractiveness. As female sexuality tends to be more associated with youth-coded beauty, older women become excluded from the sexual imaginary (Doll, 2012). In addition, women face the moral constraints of being a good wife/mother/grandmother, where being non-sexual is seen as a virtue and not a deficiency, whereby older women face moral censure for transgressing an approved ageing femininity when not acting their age (Lai and Hynie, 2011). As such the narrative of decline is perpetuated. Since the 1970s, however, women now over 50 will have encountered the countervailing influences of feminism and might challenge such culturally constituted assumptions (Bassnett, 2012; Westwood, 2016).

Even where the idea of older sexual agents meets with approval because of its contribution to well-being and self-esteem, their sexuality has been subject to a medicalised, book-keeping approach that disregards emotions and pleasures and focuses on who is still 'doing it' (Gott, 2004), in the context of declining physical capacity for genitocentric penetrative sex (see Trudel, Turgeon and Piché, 2000, as an example). However, more encouragingly, we perceive the beginnings of challenge to these negative discourses in European, Australian and US contexts and writing, which attempt to recuperate older people, including the oldest citizens (commonly care home residents) and across the spectrum of genders and sexualities, as legitimate sexual/intimate citizens (see Gott, 2004; Hafford-Letchfield, 2008; Bauer et al, 2012; Doll, 2012; Simpson et al, 2016, 2017; Villar et al, 2014).

The purpose of elaborating these brief examples is to underline that a focus on sex and intimacy in later life involves the recognition of intersections both within and beyond the conceptual constituents of the series focus. Lives are not lived in sexual, intimate or aged-based singularities, but in complex differentiated yet overlapping and intertwined experiences with myriad intersections, such as class, race/ethnicity, gender, disability, embodiment and affect (Simpson, 2015). It is this rich patina of experience and knowledge creation that this series seeks to elucidate, working outward from a critical focus on the core concerns of sex/sexuality, intimacy and ageing, and providing the space for innovative and high-quality scholarship that can inform institutions, policy, professional practice, current and future research and older people encountering this focus as lived experience and not simply a subject of inquiry.

The vision behind the series is that it will:

- put the *sex* back in sexuality (and into ageing). This arises from the observation that while sexuality studies has progressed considerably over the last 40 years (Fischer and Seidman, 2016), its development as an intellectual field of enquiry has to some extent dampened the subversive character of a focus on the 'messy physicality' of sexual pleasure. Put simply, there is lots of scholarship about sexuality, but less focus on the pleasures of sex. There is an aspiration that this series might be one avenue by which that can in a small way be corrected. Putting the 'sex' back into 'sexuality' is part of an agenda to enable older people to continue to be recognised as sexual citizens (or more specifically to have the choice to be sexual agents or not). As such, this series can support the vanguard of an intellectual project that will establish sex in later life as a serious yet neglected political issue and thus stimulate and advance debate. If what is at stake in understanding current experience are the impediments and constraints to choice and pleasure, embodied sensual practice and agency must constitute part of the site of scholarship;
- promote and offer an avenue for *critically engaged* work on the subject matter, whether it is empirical and theoretical-philosophical, from across the social sciences, humanities and cultural studies, incorporating scientific and aesthetic insights. An essential part of the project is that assumptions, claims and received knowledge about sex and intimacy in later life are always questioned, challenged and subject to critical review. This is the means by which both extant knowledge is tested, refined and strengthened or rejected, and new knowledge is produced. A critical frame also offers the opportunity

to move beyond traditional academic frames – insofar as a book series allows – in presenting new ideas, evidence and conjectures;

- emphasise the value of *multidisciplinary and interdisciplinary* approaches to sex and intimacy in late life. Though the series is open to critical research studies from specific disciplinary positions, such as sociology, psychology or gerontology, it recognises the value of multidisciplinary studies that draw on more than one discipline or field, and interdisciplinary studies that cut across and suture together different disciplines, perspectives and approaches in understanding the complexity of older people and their sexual and intimate lives. This extends to recognising the value of the interweaving of science, aesthetic and critical approaches across paradigm and disciplinary boundaries;
- recognise the value of different approaches that foreground the *experiential* and/or *empirical* and/or *theoretical* landscapes of sex and intimacy in later life, whether they form layered responses to a question or are presented as discrete levels of analysis;
- have an *international* focus, recognising global differences and inequalities; there is value in both the specificity and depth afforded regional, national and locally based studies but there should be acknowledgement of supranational, international and global contexts to phenomena, trends and developments and political, cultural and social responses. It should be acknowledged that the emergent knowledge on sex, intimacy and later life has been generated mostly within academies of the Global North, but it does not follow that this necessarily implies progress in comparison to other parts of the globe. It also recognises that there are inherent difficulties of resourcing and organisational and common conceptualisation in the development of international projects with a global reach, and these difficulties are unevenly distributed across the globe. In some parts of the globe, researching this focus is not simply difficult but inherently risky to those who might research, be subjects of research or researched with through intolerance, hostility and lack of recognition. Genuine attempts at a global research agenda require properly distributed and balanced strategies for collaboration to meet relevant constraints and challenges. There should be both attention to the seeds of emergent scholarship in the Global South, and sensitivity to the tendency of western scholarship to reflect a bias towards a 'colonial' approach to knowledge production. Notwithstanding the tendency for scholarship to focus on the Global North and particularly North America, Europe and Australasia, the series seeks – in a small way – to promote *international* understandings. This is achieved through the conviction that cross-cultural and spatial perspectives, drawing

from insight and evidence across the globe, can contribute to better understandings of experience and avenues for research, policy and practice and reflection;

- allow for *language, labels and categories* that emerge from particular geographical and cultural contexts in the development of scholarship to be questioned, adapted, resisted and brought into relief with alternatives and oppositions in how age, sex, sexuality and intimacy are conceived;
- recognise and explore the constraints on and complications involved in *expressions of sexual/intimate citizenship as an older person* and across a spectrum of sexual and gender identities, interrogating and challenging stereotypes of older people as prudish or sex-negative and post-sexual. Equally, the series seeks to explore, examine and advocate sex-positive approaches to sex and intimacy in later life that can help empower, enable and support older people's sexual and intimate relations;
- be accessible to readers in order to inform *public understanding, academic study, intellectual debate, professional practice and policy development.*

This is an ambitious agenda to set for any enterprise, and the series hopes only to make modest contributions to it. Nevertheless, the series has been born of a conviction that unless this sort of agenda is adopted, the experience everyone shares of growing old will always be unnecessarily impoverishing and incapacitating. At the core of this series, and what it should exemplify, is the flourishing that arises from older sexual agents making choices, giving and enjoying pleasure and recognising options and experiences that are open to them as they age.

The Editors
March 2021

Note

[1]   The long, full version of what has been called the 'alphabet soup' of sexual identities is LGBTIQCAPGNGFNBA ("Lesbian', 'Gay', 'Bisexual', 'Transgender', 'Intersex', 'Questioning', 'Curious', 'Asexual', 'Pansexual', 'Gender Nonconforming', 'Gender-Fluid', 'Non-Binary' and 'Androgynous'). This list is neither exhaustive nor does it take in non-western sexual identities and cultures that should not be assumed to be equivalent in their conception.

References

AgeUK (2019) *As STIs in older people continue to rise Age UK calls to end the stigma about sex and intimacy in later life,* https://www.ageuk.org.uk/latest-press/articles/2019/october/as-stis-in-older-people-continue-to-rise-age-uk-calls-to-end-the-stigma-about-sex-and-intimacy-in-later-life/

Arber, S. and Ginn, J. (1995) *'Only Connect:' Gender Relations and Ageing*, in Arber, S. and Ginn, J. (eds), *Connecting Gender and Ageing*. Buckingham: Open University Press.

Bassnett, S. (2012) *Feminist Experiences: The Women's Movement in Four Cultures*. London: Routledge.

Bauer, M., Fetherstonhaugh, D., Tarzia, L., Nay, R., Wellman, D. and Beattie, E. (2012) 'I Always Look Under the Bed for a Man.' Needs and Barriers to the Expression of Sexuality in Residential Aged Care: The Views of Residents with and without Dementia', *Psychology and Sexuality*, 4(3): 296–309.

Bersani, L. and Phillips, A. (2008) *Intimacies*. Chicago, IL: Chicago University Press.

Bland, L. and Doan, L. (1998) *Sexology in Culture: Labelling Bodies and Desires*. Cambridge: Polity.

Bodley-Tickell, A.T., Olowokure, B., Bhaduri, S., White, D.J., Ward, D., Ross, J.D.C., Smith, G., Duggal, H.V. and Gould, P. (2008) 'Trends in Sexually Transmitted Infections (Other than HIV) in Older People: Analysis of Data from an Enhanced Surveillance System', *Sexually Transmitted Infections*, 84: 312–17.

Chao, J.-K., Lin, Y.-C., Ma, M.-C., Lai, C.-J., Ku, Y.-C., Kuo, W.-H. and Chao, I.-C. (2011) 'Relationship Among Sexual Desire. Sexual Satisfaction and Quality of Life in Middle-Aged and Older Adults', *Journal of Sex and Marital Therapy*, 37(5): 386–403.

Cronin, A. and King, A. (2010) 'Power, Inequality and Identification: Exploring Diversity and Intersectionality Amongst Older LGB Adults', *Sociology*, 44(5): 876–92.

Davidson, J.O. and Layder, D. (1994) *Methods, Sex, Madness*. London: Routledge.

Doll, G.A. (2012) *Sexuality and Long-term Care: Understanding and Supporting the Needs of Older Adults*. Baltimore, MD: Health Professions Press.

Drench, M.E. and Losee, R.H. (1996) 'Sexuality and the Sexual Capabilities of Elderly People', *Rehabilitation Nursing*, 21(3): 118–23.

Ehrenfeld, M., Tabak, N., Bronner, G. and Bergman, R. (1997) 'Ethical Dilemmas Concerning the Sexuality of Elderly Patients Suffering from Dementia', *International Journal of Nursing Practice*, 3(4): 255–59.

Fischer, N.L. and Seidman, S. (eds) (2016) *Introducing the New Sexuality Studies* (3rd edition). London: Routledge.

Foucault, M. (1977) *Discipline and Punish: The Birth of the Prison*. London: Penguin.

Foucault, M. (1978) *The History of Sexuality Volume 1: An Introduction*. London: Penguin.

Gott, M. (2004) *Sexuality, Sexual Health and Ageing*. London: McGraw-Hill Education.

Hafford-Letchfield, P. (2008) 'What's Love Got to Do with It? Developing Supportive Practices for the Expression of Sexuality, Sexual Identity and the Intimacy Needs of Older People', *Journal of Care Services Management*, 2(4): 389–405.

Hancock, A.-M. (2016) *Intersectionality: An Intellectual History*. Oxford: Oxford University Press.

Heckert, J. (2010) *Love without Borders? Intimacy, Identity and the State of Compulsory Monogamy* http://theanarchistlibrary.org/library/jamie-heckert-love-without-borders-intimacy-identity-and-the-state-of-compulsory-monogamy

Hill Collins, P. and Bilge, S. (2016) *Intersectionality*. Cambridge: Polity.

Lai, Y. and Hynie, M. (2011) 'A Tale of Two Standards: An Examination of Young Adults' Endorsement of Gendered and Ageist Sexual Double Standards', *Sex Roles*, 64(5–6): 360–71.

Lindau, S.T., Schumm, P., Laumann, E.O., Levinson, W., O'Muircheartaigh, C.A. and Waite, L.J. (2007) 'A Study of Sexuality and Health among Older Adults in the United States', *New England Journal of Medicine* 357: 762–74.

Musial, M. (2013) 'Richard Sennett and Eva Illouz on Tyranny of Intimacy. Intimacy Tyrannised and Intimacy as a Tyrant', *Lingua Ac Communitas*, 23: 119–33.

O'Brien, K., Roe, B. Low, C., Deyn, L. and Rogers, S. (2012) 'An Exploration of the Perceived Changes in Intimacy of Patients' Relationships Following Head and Neck Cancer', *Journal of Clinical Nursing*, 21(17–18): 2499–508.

Ortmann, D. and Sprott, R. (2013) *Sexual Outsiders: Understanding BDSM Sexualities and Communities*. London: Rowman and Littlefield.

Rahman, M. and Jackson, S. (2010) *Gender and Sexuality: Sociological Approaches*. Cambridge: Polity Press.

Rich, A. (1981) *Compulsory Heterosexuality and Lesbian Experience*. London: Onlywomen Press.

Simpson, P. (2015) *Middle-Aged Gay Men, Ageing and Ageism: Over the Rainbow?*. Basingstoke: Palgrave Macmillan.

Simpson, P., Brown Wilson, C., Brown, L., Dickinson, T. and Horne, M. (2016) 'The Challenges of and Opportunities Involved in Researching Intimacy and Sexuality in Care Homes Accommodating Older People: a Feasibility Study', *Journal of Advanced Nursing*, 73(1): 127–37.

Simpson, P., Horne, M., Brown, L.J.E., Dickinson, T. and Torkington, K. (2017) 'Older Care Home Residents, Intimacy and Sexuality', *Ageing and Society*, 37(2): 243–65. DOI: 10.1017/S0144686X15001105

Simpson, P., Almack, K. and Walthery, P. (2018a) 'We Treat Them all the Same': the Attitudes, Knowledge and Practices of Staff Concerning Old/er Lesbian, Gay, Bisexual and Trans Residents in Care Homes', *Ageing & Society*, 38(5): 869–99.

Simpson, P., Wilson, C.B., Brown, L.J., Dickinson, T. and Horne, M. (2018b) ' "We've Had Our Sex Life Way Back": Older Care Home Residents, Sexuality and Intimacy', *Ageing & Society*, 38(7): 1478–501.

Stenner, P., McFarquhar, T. and Bowling, A. (2011) 'Older People and "Active Ageing": Subjective Aspects of Ageing Actively', *Journal of Health Psychology*, 16(3): 467–77.

Trudel, G., Turgeon, L. and Piché, L. (2000) 'Marital and Sexual Aspects of Old Age', *Sexual and Relationship Therapy*, 15(4): 381–406.

Villar, F., Celdrán, M., Fabà, J. and Serrat, R. (2014) 'Barriers to Sexual Expression in Residential Aged Care Facilities (RACFs): Comparison of Staff and Residents' Views', *Journal of Advanced Nursing*, 70(11): 2518–27.

Weeks, J. (2010) *Sexuality* (3rd edition). London: Routledge.

Weiss, M. (2011) *Techniques of Pleasure: BDSM and the Circuits of Sexuality*. Durham, NC: Duke University Press.

Wentland, J.J. and Reissing, E. (2014) 'Casual Sexual Relationships: Identifying Definitions for One-night Stands, Booty Calls, Fuck Buddies, and Friends with Benefits', *The Canadian Journal of Human Sexuality*, 23(3): 167–77.

Westwood, S. (2016) *Ageing, Gender and Sexuality: Equality in Later Life*. London: Routledge.

Ylanne, V. (ed) (2012) *Representing Aging: Images and Identities*. Houndsmill: Palgrave Macmillan.

Zaninotto, P., Falaschetti, E. and Sacker, A. (2009) 'Age Trajectories of Quality of Life Among Older Adults: Results from the English Longitudinal Study of Ageing', *Quality of Life Research*, 18(10): 1301–9.

Foreword

Sex and Diversity in Later Life (under the *Sex and Intimacy in Later Life* book series, edited by Hafford-Letchfield, Simpson and Reynolds), explores how ageing, sex, gender, desire and sexuality shape equality and justice in later life from an intersectional and critical perspective. While sexuality is often perceived as being absent from the lives of older adults, research shows otherwise. The ten substantive chapters address a wide range of topics on a diverse ageing population related to sexual desire, sexual behaviours, love, intimacy, gender, ethnicity, race, sexuality, culture, end of life, chronic health concerns, sexual rights and other pressing social issues. Chapter 1 introduces the theoretical and conceptual perspectives of the book, setting the roadmap for the reader to explore sex and diversity in an ageing population through intersectional, multidisciplinary and critical lenses. Chapter 2 offers a perspective on the sexual rights of African American older women as they pursue love, intimacy and sexual pleasure. Such rights, Harley argues, are impacted by intersecting factors of racism, sexual stigma and cultural barriers. Chapter 3 challenges stereotypes about the 'oldest old' and older persons living their final years. Rennie also explores the options of sexual and intimate connections for persons who are at their end of life. In Chapter 4, Hafford-Letchfield reviews some themes on heterosexual desire and sexual expression of solo women in later life within the context of socio-cultural and health-related factors. Chapter 5 discusses sex and ageing of heterosexual men. In the chapter, Tetley and Lee explore heterosexual men's barriers in sexual health and well-being, intersected with perspectives from health professionals on sex and intimacy in later life. In Chapter 6, Robinson explores the narratives from gay men's adventurous stories – sexual encounters with strangers. Their sex and sexuality intersected with the effects of ageism and loss. Robinson argues that the effects of physical ageing or illness can impinge on their making full use of the resources of ageing. In Chapter 7, Todd proposes that, due to hegemonic understandings of gender, sexuality, age and sexual violence, older lesbians with a history of abuse are not sufficiently acknowledged either by professionals or the women themselves. In Chapter 8, Wells reflects on both the sexual intimacies of the ageing bisexual and the limited research on such lived experiences of bisexuality in later life. In Chapter 9, Scarrone Bonhomme uncovers the challenges and resilience of trans people in later life, especially those who suffered from gender dysphoria, focusing on how gender transition and physical intervention impact on their intimacy, sex and sexuality. In Chapter 10, Przybylo draws attention to a highly invisible group – asexual individuals in later life, and in Chapter 11, Simpson discusses how social class creates/reinforces inequalities in sexual validity in later life and theoretical tools that can be used to understand such processes.

The chapters in this book capture the diverse experiences of older persons in varied communities, beyond the heteronormative, gender-binary perspective. The editors capture the survey of this terrain at both the beginning and end of this book. The diverse lived experiences of sexual and gender-expansive individuals in their later lives are presented from an empowerment-based and sex-positive approach, through contesting cultural and institutional barriers/ stereotypes/stigma. This book draws together scholarly work from a multidisciplinary team of researchers and practitioners from Europe, North America and Australia, with diverse academic and practice backgrounds across the social sciences, humanities and cultural studies disciplines. The transnational lens of this book acknowledges both the localities and global character of sex and sexuality in a diverse ageing population. Also, scholarly and practice insights from language study, social work, nursing, sociology and mental health are integrated in this book. Researchers, sexuality educators, practitioners and policy makers will find the multidisciplinary approach of the book valuable, while practitioners and students may find the critical and intersectional framework employed in the book useful in generating knowledge, new ideas, and practice wisdom.

The book will appeal to students, teachers and researchers in the social sciences and humanities, as well as professionals, practitioners and community activists. Hafford-Letchfield, Simpson and Reynolds are to be congratulated for offering a reflective, critical, intersectional, scholarly and above all inspirational approach to prompt dialogues in sex and diversity in later life. They deliver what they promise.

Dr Diana K. Kwok
Associate Professor
Department of Special Education and Counselling
The Education University of Hong Kong
Hong Kong SAR, China

1

Sex and intimacy in later life: a survey of the terrain

Paul Reynolds, Paul Simpson and Trish Hafford-Letchfield

That time of year thou may'st in me behold
When yellow leaves, or none, or few, do hang
Upon those boughs which shake against the cold,
Bare ruin'd choirs, where late the sweet birds sang.
In me thou see'st the twilight of such day,
As after sunset fadeth in the west,
Which by-and-by black night doth take away,
Death's second self, that seals up all in rest.
In me thou see'st the glowing of such fire
That on the ashes of his youth doth lie,
As the death-bed whereon it must expire
Consum'd with that which it was nourish'd by.
This thou perceivest, which makes thy love more strong,
To love that well which thou must leave ere long.
                    William Shakespeare, Sonnet 73

Shakespeare's *Sonnet 73* suggests a recognition of finality, mortality and
the changes that ageing brings, with a plea for love (and respect?) from
those who are younger, through the certain knowledge that they will
miss those who are ageing when they pass, and will experience ageing
and its vicissitudes themselves. This is ageing as natural cycle and self-
aware progression through the life course. It appeals to naturalised and
normalised contours of the process of ageing, which are 'coloured in'
by cultural representations of how we are seen to age. Older people
should 'grow old gracefully', both experience and express that 'slow
journey into the twilight of their lives'.

While the sentiment of the sonnet might be regarded as romantic
in its appeal to the recognition and acceptance of naturalism and
the character of love and respect across generations, it betrays both a
naivety and a danger. Its naivety lies in its 'rose-tinted' characterisation.

Generally, in more economically developed societies, age is more a subject of pathology, prejudice and crude cultural stereotypes – the irrelevant or burdensome rather than the experienced or useful, the decaying rather than the preserved and venerable, the infirm rather than the healthy within the life course, the decrepit or absent-minded rather than the eccentric or the wise. These are real dangers to older people's agency, dignity and (self) respect. Their roles are simultaneously and contradictorily seen as celebrated and wasted, cherished and abandoned, loved and left behind. Late modernity, with its diversification of family and community form and its focus on the twin preoccupations of work and cultural achievement often leaves older people at the margins or with a limited familial role or in the work force. The billion-dollar market in anti-ageing and youth-preserving products suggests that age – and showing age – has diminishing social, economic and cultural power and recognition outside of carefully prescribed roles and characterisations (Zion, 2018; Statistica, 2020). The agenda for today is to simultaneously grow old 'well' and minimise the impact of growing old, by conforming to dominant cultural expectations.

Older people's desire, love and intimacy are commonly stereotyped – and mainly negatively – as not sexual or sensual, progressively dysfunctional and limited. By these representations, sensual pleasures are superseded by friendship, familiarity and the intimacy they bring. Relationships that cross generations are 'May–December' and often regarded as either driven by youth tempted by material wealth or the inappropriate carnality of the older, as if relationships are only meaningful within age bands. Equally, older people's relationships with other older people are viewed with a desexualised reserve, whether they are reified for long-term romantic attachment or diminished as 'companionship'. Older sexual desires and the enjoyment of sexual pleasures are regarded with suspicion, a curious mixture of cultural and moral reserve.

Echoing Shakespeare, convention exhorts that older people should be loved, but only because they embrace their age, their changing place and ultimately their passing. Conforming to the stereotypes afforded to older people becomes essential to their inclusion and respect. This begs the question: what if convention and conformity are not desired? What if the naturalised notion of ageing, and the constraints attached to sexual expression are neither desired nor healthy to a satisfying longevity.

In sociological studies, a dominant feature of the last 70 years, to varying degrees across the globe, has been the retreat from seeing people simply as atomised and unique individuals or as subjects of a nation, ethnicity or sociological class and reducible to its stereotypes. Concerns with gender, ethnicity/race/culture/religion have been joined by (dis)ability and sexuality in being regarded as increasingly significant since the 1960s, within struggles for rights and recognition within a broad shift in critical approaches that focus on the cultural politics of identities (see Honneth, 1995; Fraser and Honneth, 2004 on the conceptual frames of recognition and redistribution). In the twenty-first century, the politics of identity has shifted from focusing on particular social identity constructs to their intersections in the lived experiences of people striving to address multiple oppressions, discriminations and constraints (Jenkins, 2014; Hill Collins and Bilge, 2016). It is within this context that the field of knowledge concerned with the intersections of age and sex/sexuality has emerged.

This text (and its series) is devoted to dispelling prejudices and replacing assumed and prejudicial assumptions with interrogated and examined knowledges. Within this context, it might be surprising to reflect on how resistant stereotypes, pathologies and prejudices about age have been to the critical study of ageing and later life. Age as a meaningful difference has begun to be recognised as significant, particularly as the experience of age has become differentiated in more economically developed and culturally diverse societies. The conception of age (and ageing) has changed for a number of reasons: in many societies people are living longer, working longer and have greater resources, thereby engaging more visibly with consumer society. Older people themselves become a site of consumption and services that occupies a significant proportion of the economy (illustratively, Thorson, 2000; Harper, 2013).

These forms of change also impact upon the prejudicial characterisations of older people that persist in the twenty-first century, that they are homogenised in their conforming to stereotypes. In part, this involves a failure to see them as intersecting *subjects* – constituted *in* class, ethnic, gendered, dis/ability and sexuality social relations and seeking to constitute *themselves within* those relations, rather than singularly constituted *by* their age. This is particularly evident when we consider the intersections of age and sex. The prevailing prejudice is that older people are sexless and subject to 'ageist erotophobia' (see Simpson et al, 2018) – absent of and from legitimate desires, erotic imaginations and want of sexual pleasures. This book, and the series that this book launches, seeks to stand as a resource to turn back the tide of prejudice and pathology, and stimulate critical debate, research, policy and practice (the Series Introduction provides an overview of the project).

This volume explores an array of identity intersections that show the different ways in which older sexual agents are constituted in contemporary cultures and societies. What becomes clear with each successive study is that there are strong common themes that shape the experience and recognition – or invisibility, prejudice and pathology – of older sexual agents. Equally, there are important differences that require attention if the task of elucidating and empowering across one set of intersections does not fall into assumed homogeneity and/or exclusions of others. How ethnic, differently-abled, gendered and class differences (among others) are manifest in the socio-cultural milieu is critical in balancing a focus on sexual agency among older people with a recognition that those agents have very different and distinct life experiences, including their encounters with patinas of oppression and discrimination.

The chapters collected and curated in this text are not intended to be an exhaustive survey of these intersections. What they do, however, is take some dominant intersected identities with the intention of exploring key themes and issues in the nascent development of the field of sex and intimacy in later life. In doing so, they provide valuable digests of the current state of the literature, enlightening case studies that illustrate critical issues, and begin to define part of a critical research agenda. They give the reader the opportunity both to take stock of extant scholarship and consider the next steps in developing the field, articulating more empowering possibilities and informing public and policy debate. This was the explicit intention in curating this collection as a first contribution to this book series.

In the next chapter, Debra Harley focuses on an often-overlooked intersection of age and sexuality – with race and ethnicity – in a focus on older black minority ethnic (BME) women. Harley underlines the importance of the intersection of race and ethnicity in influencing the way the expression of sexuality and pursuit of sexual pleasure are articulated prejudicially, where older BME women are subject to representations that either desexualise or render them as lacking morality and/or taste. This creates powerful prejudices and pathologies that bound and constrain older BME women's sexuality. While she draws from a range of international studies, her primary focus is on the US experience and African American women, where the cultural context of racism, slavery and the persistence of violence and prejudice provides a pervasive and persistent backdrop that BME women struggle against. This struggle impacts on how older BME women neither see themselves nor are seen as sexual agents, and extends to rendering non-hetero, non-monogamous non-gender conforming BME women as doubly invisible or perverse. Harley's chapter elucidates the construction of prejudice and then explores its impact on both sexual health and sexual pleasure. She outlines how further factors, such as living with HIV and receiving sexual health services, only compound the disadvantage to their sexual agency and intimate lives. Yet at the same time, Harley recognises where older BME women are exploring sexual pleasures, even within the context of oppression and pathology.

Karen Rennie considers another underrepresented and under-researched intersection – older people towards the end of life. This is clearly an elusive grouping to describe, but Rennie turns a spotlight on two interrelated but non-exclusive groups, those at the upper end of 'older' and those receiving care signifying the nearing of the end of their lives. Both of these groups are often regarded as non-sexual simply by virtue of their stage in the life course, even by those otherwise keen to dispel pathologies around older sexual agents. Rennie mounts a persuasive narrative against such assumptions, emphasising the sexual and intimate needs of these agents, and takes a critical review of the relevant literature to argue for the special value of sex for 'older' old people and those whose lives are drawing to a close. She draws out the importance of valuing sex and recognising that intimacy takes a range of forms – both inclusive of and beyond genito-centric and penetrative sex – that bring closeness and pleasure, and the way in which these pleasures are subject to 'ageist erotophobia' (Simpson et al, 2018). Rennie manages to retain the value of recognisable sexual pleasures, while recognising that the balance of physical pleasure, emotional satisfaction and sensual practices may vary. A particular variable for older people is their understanding of sexual pleasure and the way narrow genito-centric conceptions may reinforce a normalisation of the assumed relationship between ageing and diminished sexual capacity or pleasure. Rennie recognises that issues such as diminished capacity (Alzheimer's and dementia) and the issue of palliative care and the organisation of older people's care institutions create additional concerns in terms of how older people's sexual pleasure is seen as risk laden. Although – and this is a theme stretching throughout the collection – older sexual agents are beset by constraints, prejudices and limitations, Rennie sets an agenda for a sexier old age, sketching a research agenda that celebrates older and end-of-life sexual agency. This is an important thread through this volume – while invariably the analysis focuses on problems and issues, they should not become a preoccupation at the expense of exploring pleasures and opportunities.

Trish Hafford-Letchfield focuses on solo 'straight' older women's sex and intimacy, and particularly older women's voices that indicate expressions of sexual agency. Once again, there is a focus on barriers, both external and internalised, and particularly on issues around social-cultural constraints and situational limitations. Hafford-Letchfield recognises discursive constructs such as the clumsiness of caregivers around sexual issues to the cultural and medical constraints in managing physiological changes. She draws from her own research participation and an erudite understanding of gendered pathology to explore the way older heterosexual women both pursue and self-limit their sexual agency. Her theoretical framing critically deconstructs older heterosexuality in the context of complexities in gender fluidity, and her synthesis of extant research studies yields a number of key themes: social legitimacy, the impact of health changes and the power of heteronormative assumptions about active and healthy (penetrative) sex. Hafford-Letchfield also explores older women's experience of intimate relationships and the crucial – and contingently, empowering or constraining – factor of relationship status, which has always been a significant feature of gendered experience in socio-cultural analysis. She provides a nuanced review and analysis of the literature that represents fully the maze of limitations constraining older hetero women, while recognising that there are opportunities and possibilities in cultural change and agentic action. She concludes by outlining key challenges that form an agenda for both research and the expression of sexual agency.

Subsequently, David Lee and Josephine Tetley move the focus onto heterosexual men, recognising similar constraints in prejudicial cultural discourses and institutional and relational contexts. While women face qualitatively gendered forms of prejudice and discrimination, it does not follow that older men, under the pervasive power of masculinity (classically, Connell, 1987; Connell and Messerschmidt, 2005), do not experience equivalent (if perhaps not equal) problems. Using large-scale data sets against the extant literature, they explore the way in which heterosexual men are limited by discursive constructions that render their sexual desires perverse, pathological or abnormal in later life. Again, Lee and Tetley make the connection between discursive constructs and the challenges of ageing and extant policy and practice. Their analysis of a large longitudinal study draws out the agenda older men face: concerns about sexual difficulties in performance and sexual health as they age; the way in which sexual relationships changed, were challenged and constrained with age; and their sense of reflecting on their past and understanding the impact of ageing on their sexual desires and performance.

Further, Lee and Tetley emphasise in their analysis that it is in the construction of older men's sense of their own changing sexual selves that issues of health, performance and physiological change are instantiated, as well as in prevailing external discourses. They recognise that in some areas, such as older men's sexual health, there are grounds for seeing constructive change. They also make a critical assessment of the methods and analysis of the longitudinal study that forms the focus of their discussion. Their conclusions aim to promote an opening up of the often 'silenced' narrative of older heterosexual men (as opposed to the construct of masculinity), and the need to build upon research to improve policy and practice.

The focus of the next chapter by Peter Robinson is on older gay men, and draws on narratives of the sexual encounters of a small but international (Anglophone) sample of gay men (contextualised within the extant literature). He draws two main themes from these narratives: the impact of age − and physiological change − on the satisfaction of sexual desires, and the age preferences they expressed. Robinson explores what he takes from Heaphy (2007) as 'resources of ageing' as a counterweight to the constraining impact of ageing. While youth is culturally constituted as the preferential age for sexual desire and pleasure in contemporary societies, Robinson outlines what age might bring in terms of knowledge gains to the older sexual agent. While acknowledging the persistence of prejudicial discourses, he is able to draw from the experiences of men who have improved their sexual esteem and developed strategies for coping with changes in sex drive and fulfilling sexual desires with younger men. The accounts of Robinson's study participants provide a rich sense of how some sexual agents are able to compensate for both personal changes and socio-cultural discourses that constrain other men. Robinson's analysis reminds the reader that, while structural and cultural factors and the intersections that constitute social identities are important, individual sexual agents' personal trajectories and willingness to develop resources that are enabling can lead to significant differences in agentic outcomes. In this respect, Robinson opens up an interesting avenue for further study and reflection.

Shifting the focus to older lesbian-identified women, Megan Todd examines the interrelationship between sex and violence as another significant feature of older sexual agents' lives. Despite a more tolerant social context that includes civil partnerships and marriages as forms of relationship recognition, she discusses the limiting factors for older lesbians that homonormative preconceptions sustain (see Duggan, 2002). Against a youth-oriented 'out' queer culture and persistent negations of lesbian sexuality that encourages invisibility, Todd explores the impacts of sexually abusive relationships. She draws on recent research and feminist methodology to explore the complexities of older lesbians' narratives of their relationships. She provides a rich description of the tensions that lesbian sexual agents experience in the face of a complex conjuncture of progressive change and the persistence of regressive forces, where culturally constituted notions of respectability, conformity to monogamy and the stereotype of intimate relationships persist even among those sexual agents whose recognition is relatively recent. Todd also picks up on another theme that runs through this volume, that there is research that is beginning to unpack and analyse the experiences of different sexual agents, but the gaps and paucity of research speaks to the need for more work in this field. Where sexual violence is concerned, any sense that the cultural constraints to sexual agency produce an invisibility that impedes relief for victims requires urgent redress. Todd concludes by signposting where new research might begin.

In the following chapter, Christopher Wells shifts the focus to older bisexuals, considering the impact of mononormativity and employing the conceptual framing of Foucault's (1967) 'heterotopia' as a means of representing the contradiction of inclusion/exclusion that older bisexuals experience. Wells combines an exploration of the relatively few research studies available with a sophisticated and critical framing that explores how bisexuals experience 'ageist erotophobia' overlaid with the constraining presumptions that older sexual agents will be in settled monogamous relationships (Simpson et al, 2018). The impact of these constructs reinforces the invisibility of older bisexuals, which is itself compounded by the slipperiness with which non-mononormativity is perceived. Where the very terms of bi-identity are often reduced to negative characterisations such as greed and licentiousness (see Udis-Kessler, 1996), it becomes more difficult to constitute the ground for resistance through an identity politics, as with lesbian and gay sexuality. This impacts on both the reflective subjectivity of the sexual agent and the elusiveness yet discursively constrained constitution of bisexual identity. Wells' critical analysis captures the contradictions and complexities of exploring fluidity and plasticity in the self and social identification of sexual agents.

Laura Scarrone Bonhomme explores the experiences of those sexual agents who choose to transition in later life. This introductory chapter explores the context of trans in a gendered hegemonic culture and then draws out the experience of older trans people through the recognition of this intersection, as those in previous chapters, being a space that is composed of overlapping and different pathological discourses. In looking at transitions in older age, the personal trajectories and narratives of transitioning individuals are important to counterpoint against the broader cultural forces that reinforce conformity to cisgenderedness. Scarrone Bonhomme explores these forces, both in their specificity – transitioning as parents, transitioning in established intimate relationships as well as through the opportunities of being an older sexual agent, transitioning regarded as 'second adolescence' – as well as the more generic pressures upon people who transition as a form of sexual agency in later life. Scarrone Bonhomme provides a rich description of the biopsychosocial factors that are relevant to understanding the experiences and positions of older transitioning agents – whether male to female or female to male (each with their own similarities and conformities). It recognises the agency exercised in difficult circumstances as a celebration of self-recognition, while equally recognising the constraints and pathologies they face. Indeed, Scarrone Bonhomme picks up on how this analysis is offered on the basis of limited research into a relatively unexplored intersectional grouping, contrasting the burdens on those who choose to transition and their relative neglect by professionals and healthcare providers, whose cisnormative and heteronormative paradigms render older trans people invisible, unsupported and excluded.

Taking a different route into considering sex and intimacy in later life, Ela Przybylo illuminates the powerful discourses of desexualisation/sexualisation as having an impact on older sexual agents in intimate relationships. Working within the context of a sexualised culture where older people are desexualised and thereby in part limited in their participation and exclusion, she draws attention to asexuality, where intimate relationships, feelings and affections are not accompanied by a desire for expression through sexual pleasure. While desexualisation has been a background feature of all the chapters in the collection, it is here that it is foregrounded and explored for its constituent pathologies – such as disgust, disposability of choices (particularly in institutional contexts such as care homes) and cultural and procedural constraints that impede the pursuit of sexual pleasure. Simultaneously, however, Przybylo is critical of the position that sees a critical response to these limitations as subject to a kind of 'book-keeping', where having more sex signifies progress or 'ageing successfully' and on youth-oriented terms. This constitutes a 'double-bind', within which older people negotiate their sexual and/ or intimate lives. Drawing from both critical disability studies and asexuality studies, she preserves the notion of sexual agency being about choice in how intimate relationships are constituted, and how they are reconstituted in the process of ageing, rather than simply representing an easy binary opposition between desexualisation and resexualisation (selectively see McRuer, 2006 on critical disability studies and Bogaert, 2015 on asexuality). In this analysis, Przybylo provides a powerful corrective to the notion that either a sexualised or a desexualised culture are in and of themselves progressive for older people. Rather they are progressive insofar as sexual agents have choice in constructing their sexual and intimate lives.

In the final substantive chapter, Paul Simpson focuses on an intersection oddly neglected by much of contemporary identity studies – social class. He argues that class is an important factor in exploring issues of entitlement, access, material means and cultural prejudices in how older people practise and 'consume' sexual and intimate lives. He uses the conception of class developed by Pierre Bourdieu (1984, 2005) to provide a framework for thinking about how ageist erotophobia (Simpson et al, 2018) has a particular impact across class stratifications. This involves recognising that class both provides a structure for social experience and is present as relational and cultural processes that have concrete impacts on older people's experiences of intimacy and sexuality. Simpson concludes his chapter with a sketch of a research agenda that might better elucidate class differences as a variable in erotic and intimate lives.

A number of critical themes come from reading across the collection. While they digest an important selection of extant research, a common feature of each chapter is that, in comparison with other intersectional identities and social structures, those characterised by ageing, intimacy and sexuality are under-researched. There is an urgent need for more empirical studies both on and with older people. They need to be tied more clearly to policy, care and welfare provision and professional practice, both in critique and in concrete alternative provisions. They need to deconstruct prejudicial and pathological cultural discourses and recompose them as enabling and enriching. The different contributors use a range of frames of analysis on diverse qualitative, quantitative and mixed data sets to represent the extent to which negative ageing and sexual discourses are compounded when brought together in the older sexual subject. These considerations are compounded with other prejudicial cultural discourses against same-sex relationships, trans, bisexuality or anything that departs from heteronormative/ homonormative and cisgender paradigms. The different chapters in this volume show the mixture of broad socio-cultural discourses that have a common pathological and prejudicial function across different intersected older identities and the specific constraints to sexual agency that these intersections present.

While a strong theme of the collection is the paucity of research studies in this area, the chapters themselves nevertheless provide a range of different approaches, collecting data with different methods and engaging different social and cultural theorists to enable critical thinking. This underlines the opportunities current and future researchers have, in what is a still young field, to bring their methodological and theoretical preferences into play. The sum of these chapters underlines that the exploration of sex and intimacy in later life is deeply complex, requires nuanced responses to the present terrain and sets critical challenges. There is a strong impetus in most chapters towards enabling older sexual agents to take pleasure and express themselves free of constraints, but also a recognition that what choices are made cut across rather than correspond to easy notions of conformity or transgression, traditional or progressive, or repressive or sex-positive paradigms.

The chapters in this volume illustrate the cultural differences within which constraints are experienced, but also strong correspondences across national and cultural boundaries. Part of a developing research agenda might be to explore anthropologically and sociologically different representations and constructions of older sexual agents in different societies. Yet it is clear that there are important communalities as well as differences, which means that there should be value to sharing the different agentic responses that are uncovered and explored across national and cultural boundaries.

While the collection has been curated around a structure that emphasises intersectional identities, it also in varying degrees underlines both the constraints across intersections and the importance of agentic self-reflection beyond such constraints that relate to social identities. Particularly where their identities have less recognition, as with bisexuals, identity formations and belongings, and their intersections, matter. Yet it is necessary to engage with them in a nuanced way that recognises their porous and tendential character, to avoid replacing one form of oppressive and limiting construct with another construct, less or even equally oppressive but nevertheless limiting.

At the beginning of the third decade of the 21st century, notwithstanding arguments varying between unalloyed progress or its superficiality and the persistence of traditional positions (see Weeks, 2007), there is a greater degree of socio-cultural space for sexual diversity and agency in more nations across the globe. Yet the power of conformity and traditional structures such as hetero/homonormativities, monogamy and cisgenderedness remain potent. Dominant discourses that reduce older people to positive or negative social stereotypes and functions (such as the 'sweet' grandparent or the older 'lecherous' delinquent) compound the scope for rendering them invisible and excluded. With an increasing ageing population now reflecting the historically liberating values of the 1960s and 1970s, where traditional values and structures were first substantively challenged and eroded, the agendas for change require important political as well as intellectual work. If this volume encourages both further research and new thinking in policy and practice, while supporting the sharing of ideas, experiences and insights, then it will have fulfilled its function.

References

Bogaert, A.F. (2015) *Understanding Asexuality*, Lanham, MD: Rowman and Littlefield.

Bourdieu, P. (1984) *Distinction: a Social Critique of the Judgement of Taste*, London: Routledge.

Bourdieu, P. (2005) *The Social Structures of the Economy*, Cambridge: Polity.

Connell, R. (1987) *Gender and Power: Society, the Person and Sexual Politics*, Cambridge: Polity.

Connell R.W. (1995) *Masculinities*, Cambridge: Polity.

Connell, R. and Messerschmidt, J.W. (2005) 'Hegemonic Masculinity: Rethinking the Concept', *Gender & Society*, 19(6): 829–59.

Duggan, L. (2002) 'The New Homonormativity: the Sexual Politics of Neoliberalism' in R. Castronovo and D.N. Nelson (eds), *Materializing Democracy: Toward a Revitalized Cultural Politics*, Durham, NC: Duke University Press.

Foucault, M. (1967) 'Of Other Spaces: Utopias and Heterotopias', *Architecture/ Mouvement/ Continuete*, http://web.mit.edu/allanmc/www/foucault1.pdf

Fraser, N. and Honneth, A. (2004) *Redistribution or Recognition?: A Political-Philosophical Exchange*, London: Verso.

Harper, S. (2013) *Ageing Societies*, Abingdon: Routledge.

Heaphy, B. (2007) 'Sexualities, Gender and Ageing: Resources and Social Change', *Current Sociology*, 55(2): 193–210.

Hill Collins, P. and Bilge, S. (2016) *Intersectionality*, Cambridge: Polity.

Honneth, A. (1995) *The Struggle for Recognition: The Moral Grammar of Social Conflicts*, Cambridge: Polity.

Jenkins, R. (2014) *Social Identity*, London: Routledge.

McRuer, R. (2006) *Crip Theory: Cultural Signs of Queerness and Disability*, New York: New York University Press.

Simpson, P., Wilson, C.B., Brown, L.J., Dickinson, T. and Horne, M. (2018) '"We've Had Our Sex Life Way Back": Older Care Home Residents, Sexuality and Intimacy', *Ageing & Society*, 38(7): 1478–501.

Statistica (2020) *Size of the anti-aging market worldwide from 2018 to 2023 (in billion US dollars)* (15 May) https://www.globenewswire.com/news-release/2018/08/30/1563523/0/en/Anti-Aging-Market-To-Touch-US-216-52-Billion-By-the-End-of-2021-Globally-ZMR-Report.html

Thorson, J. (2000) *Aging in a Changing Society*, New York: Brunner Routledge.

Udis-Kessler, A. (1996) 'Challenging the Stereotypes' in Rose, S., and Stevens, C. (eds), *Bisexual Horizons: Politics, Histories, Lives*, London: Lawrence and Wishart.

Weeks, J. (2007) *The World We Have Won: the Remaking of Erotic and Intimate Life*, Cambridge: Polity.

Zion Market Research (2018) *Anti-Aging Market to Touch US$ 216.52 Billion by the End of 2021, Globally: ZMR* (30 August) https://www.globenewswire.com/news-release/2018/08/30/1563523/0/en/Anti-Aging-Market-To-Touch-US-216-52-Billion-By-the-End-of-2021-Globally-ZMR-Report.html

2

Sexual expression and pleasure among black minority ethnic older women

Debra A. Harley

Introduction

Sexual expression and pleasure of black minority ethnic (BME) older women is not a topic of extensive research, and discussion appears to be taboo among these women. In addition, many erroneous assumptions and ageist stereotypes exist about the sexuality of BME older women. In fact, many BME older women themselves believe myths about their sexuality and ageing. The stereotypes and silence about BME older women's sexuality, and their sexual desires and sexual health have both personal (individual) and collective implications (Lagana et al, 2013). For BME older women their 'sexuality is a very delicate and complex topic' because of public accusation of BME women as being sexually immoral and promiscuous jezebels (White and Lagana, 2013, p 1). According to Moultrie (2017), the silence of BME older women's sexuality reflects ageism and sexism through omission as well as the continuation of stereotypes that lead to the sexual silencing of senior black women. Although there is diversity of BME older women's sexual expression, there are some common themes which are presented in this chapter.

Contextualisation of sexuality of African American and BME women

Any discussion about sexual expression of BME older women should occur within the context of the impact of traumatising historical and social events on their predecessors and subsequent generations. BME older women are more closely defined by their sexuality and as their sexuality because of 'black female eroticism as a legacy of colonialism' (Bernard, 2016, p 1). Black women's sexuality is constructed by the system of enslavement in which sexual activity was controlled to enhance and supervise fertility. In turn, for BME older women 'this set the stage for viewing black older women as sexless as they were no longer useful for fertility purposes'. Moreover, 'the commodification of black sexuality through oppression and exploitation can naturally lead to a perception of black older women's sexuality as undesirable, and these women themselves may hold such perceptions' (Lagana et al, 2013, p 1137). For example, a black older woman, after having been in an intimate, exclusive relationship with a long-term sexual partner since they were relatively younger, may see sexual activity as inappropriate or 'nasty' once she is widowed (Lagana et al, 2013).

Historical and contemporary sexual politics in the US and globally continue to acquaint blackness to uncivilised sexuality and BME women as having an animalistic type of sexuality (White and Lagana, 2013). Within the context of racism, BME women's public sense of self-sexuality and private ownership of their personal bodies continue to be influenced by these factors. The black female body is simultaneously hyper-visible (stereotyped and commodified) and invisible (systematic oppression and marginalised; Mowatt and French, 2013). For fear of fulfilling society's implicit expectations about black female sexuality, BME women have been silent (Rose, 2004). Collins (2008) has suggested *all* BME women have seen the necessity to protect themselves from these public assumptions and prescriptions of their sexuality through adopting a stance of silence or non-expression regarding their sexuality in public spaces. See Table 2.1 for examples of sexual stereotypes of black women. For this same reason, self-identification as lesbian and non-binary sexuality is why many BME older women remain silent concerning their sexual expression.

These social stereotypes have damaging effects and play an important role in sexual health outcomes and in many realms of life of black women (Rosenthal and Lobel, 2017). In addition, stereotype threat (when someone is worried or anxious about the possibility of confirming or being judged according to stereotypes about their group) has been found to influence black women's internalisation of sexual stereotypes and is associated with more risky sexual attitudes and behavior (Duvall et al, 2013).

The willingness of BME older women to be open about their sexual expressions and sexual concerns is also influenced by their negative interaction with and mistreatment by doctors, scientists, and researchers. The legacy of medical experimentation and inadequate healthcare along with with social determinants has exacerbated BME older women's complex relationship with healthcare systems (Prather

Table 2.1: Sexual stereotypes of black women

- *Aunt Jemimah* evolved out of the Mammy image but differs in that her duties were restricted to domestic work, especially cooking (her face still can be found on pancake boxes and as collectable (Green, n.d).
- *Breeder* women of slavery were seen to have primary role of reproduction of children by various men.
- *Jezebel* ('sexual siren') is the image of an immoral, sexually promiscuous, and sexually available black woman, the harlot, and more closely resembles the European ideal of beauty than any pre-existing images and was immensely attractive to white males (West, 2008).
- *Mammy* archetype is the image of an unattractive black woman (mother) with pitch-black skin and shining white teeth who is strong and content in her caregiving role for many children, in the service of white slave owners or white employers (West, 2008).
- *Sapphire* (matriarch) is the image of an aggressive, dominating angry, emasculating black woman. 'She is tart-tongued and emasculating, one hand on a hip and the other pointing and jabbing, violently and rhythmically rocking her head' (Pilgrim, 2008).
- *Welfare queen* is an image of an uneducated, poor, single black woman who does not want to work but has many children in order to take advantage of public assistance (West, 2008).

et al, 2018). In addition, BME women over 50 years of age reported they also did not feel comfortable discussing sexual practices with their partners, friends, and physician (Thames et al, 2018). Research suggests that a small number of older women (of all races) report discussing sexual issues with a doctor, and if so, most commonly the patient initiates discussions. For older women who interact with medical providers, doctors should ask regularly and proactively about sexual activity and function of older women patients (Granville and Pregler, 2018). Failure to discuss sexual behaviour with BME older women can also have implications for behaviours associated with HIV risk. Too often BME older women are forgotten or not acknowledged as survivors of sexual violence due to intersectionality which may become more evident by a race, age, and gender gap at the doctor's office, thus creating another level of health care disparity (Prather et al, 2018).

Lagana et al (2013) explored the sexuality of African American older women age 57 to 82, 11 of whom self-identified as heterosexual, one as bisexual, and one as lesbian. They found several emerging themes from participants' interviews about their sexual concerns, sequentially from most to least endorsed: (a) having sexual desire (often unfulfilled); (b) engaging in less sexual activity in older age; (c) experiencing changes in one's sexual life as a function of absence of a spouse; and (d) exercising control over how one's sexual life is conducted. They concluded the common notion that older women are asexual is a myth and lack of a suitable partner is a problem reported by many African American older women who would otherwise enjoy sexual interaction.

Another important contextualisation of BME women's sexuality is the limited room for gender non-conformity in the black community, which often criticises and rejects lesbian and non-binary sexual expression as incompatible with values in the black community. Black lesbians and non-binary BME older women experience their development through three distinct cultural perspectives: race/racism, homo/bi/trans/gender identity-prejudice, and ageing. It is through this intersection that they face multiple oppressions from mainstream society, from mainstream heterosexual society of all races, and from the white LGBTQ community (Crenshaw, 1989; Collins, 2008). If a person does not fit into the dichotomy of traditional male or female sexuality, the rule in the black community of being silent and invisible about their sexual identity may allow the family and community to accept them without having to deal with their sexual orientation or gender expression and issues associated with it (Hunter, 2005; Harley, 2016). A sense of tolerance is extended to them as long as they do not disclose or display their sexual orientation (Savin-Williams, 2001). For example, if a BME lesbian brings her partner home, she is introduced as a 'friend', not as a partner or lover. If the two women participate in the community, the partner is introduced as a 'cousin'. It is similar to the military slogan of 'don't ask, don't tell'. In fact, for many BME older lesbians their lack of disclosure of their sexual identity does not call attention to them within their community (Harley, 2016). BME older women experience minority stress because of intersectional complexities.

In many cultures, black older women have been denied a positive sexuality (Mgadmi, 2009). Ugandan people, for example, still regard sexuality for older people as taboo. Women's sexuality is linked to their ability to reproduce and is expected to change after menopause, whereas men's sexuality is not expected to change in a lifetime. Men feel that it is shameful for ageing women to be sexually active. Women themselves feel that beyond the age of 45, when they start experiencing body changes, sexual activity should be ruled out (Okiria, 2014).

Another perspective of BME women is that they are aggressive in their expression to the point that they are portrayed as 'bitches' and the angry black woman (sapphire) that is considered unintelligent, domineering, and emasculating, behaving in loud and offensive ways (Mowatt and French, 2013). According to Mgadmi (2009), despite the desexualised image of the mammy (usually older), which contradicts that of Jezebel (middle-aged or young), both figures simultaneously underpin societal perception at large. Clearly, at the nexus of race and sex ideologies in the black community, BME older women are doubly discredited.

Sexual health

The sexual health of BME older women is influenced by their general health, health risk factors, mental health (for example depression and anxiety), and cultural expectations regarding sex and performance (Hartman et al, 2004; White and Lagana, 2013). Sexual dysfunction in older women has been found to be strongly associated with chronic conditions such as arthritis, diabetes and hypertension (Hughes et al, 2015), where there is a higher incidence among BME older women (Asiedu et al, 2017). (See Table 2.2 for non-health-related factors impacting sexuality of older women). In addition, older women of all ethnic groups are less likely to seek treatment for physical problems related to their sexual functioning than men, and those who identify as lesbian are marginalised and stigmatised in medical care and are particularly vulnerable with respect to receiving appropriate medical intervention for their sexual concerns (Lindau and Fruin, 2017).

Lindau et al (2006) examined the effects of race and marriage on the sexual attitudes, behaviour, and patient–physician communication about sexuality and HIV/AIDS among older women (aged 58–93). The

Table 2.2: Non-health-related factors impacting sexuality of older women

---

• Lack of available sexual partners*

• Life satisfaction

• Overall well-being

• Cultural norms**

• Lack of privacy to engage in sex in a discreet manner (e.g. living with family)

• Living in sexually repressing settings can lead to issues such as lack of touching (e.g. assisted living)

• Shame over body image

• Prolonged lack of sexual arousal over time due to psychological, social, and physiological reasons

---

*Specific to heterosexual women

**Specific to ethnic minority women

Adapted from Le Gall, Mullet, and Shafighi (2002); Phinney and Flores (2002); Yee and Sundquist (2003).

results showed that over half of the respondents had engaged in sexual activity since their 60th birthday, over half of single women who had been sexually active in the previous ten years had not used a condom, and about 20 per cent of women with a current sexual partner agreed that condom use is not necessary if one can no longer get pregnant. Of the women in the study, African American women were significantly more likely to report changes in their sexual behaviour due to HIV, were more likely to discuss sex with a physician, and more likely to have had a physician initiate such a discussion. Similarly, Foster et al (2012) found single older African Americans (aged 50–74) practised risky behaviours such as having unprotected oral, anal, and vaginal sex, and having multiple sex partners. However, there were significant gender differences, with males using condoms more for vaginal sexual activity and discussing condom use more than females.

In a systematic review of the literature between 2003 and 2013 that focused on HIV sexual risk practices of black women over the age of 50, Smith and Larson (2015) found many black older women are engaged in such practices. These results were similar to those of Conner (2013), who found older African American women (aged 45 and older) participated in unprotected sex out of habit, that impulsivity was associated with risky sex. Black women ages 50 to 64 carry the heaviest burden of HIV diagnosis (Centers for Disease Control, 2012). In general, older black adults in comparison to younger black adults were less knowledgeable about transmission of HIV and were less willing to be tested for HIV, and were less likely to use condoms/ barriers during the past six months and over their lifetime (Kuofie et al, 2019).

BME older women living with HIV/AIDS emphasise how the disease limits their ability to experience sexuality and intimacy as 'damaged sexuality' (reduced sexual activity, challenges to finding suitable partners, and transmission concerns) and 'constrained intimacy' (fear of rejection from potential sexual partners after HIV disclosure; Nevedal and Sankar, 2016). Risky dating behaviour, often leading to risky sexual behaviour, is a growing public health concern for women aged 50 and over because it contributes to the high incidence of sexually transmitted infections (Stepanian et al, 2017). However, BME older women are at particular risk for sexually transmitted infections and diseases as they are more likely to engage in high-risk sexual behaviours and report social isolation and loneliness, depression, and self-esteem issues than their younger counterparts. Moreover, older women who lack power in sexual relationships report less sexual self-efficacy and partner negotiation and are less likely to practise safe sex (Jacobs and

Kane, 2011). Conversely, Lagana et al (2013) found the reason BME older women in their study did not engage or express an interest in interactional sexual activities was a fear of sexually transmitted diseases.

In the UK, those of black African ethnicity carry a disproportionate percentage of HIV, with 38 per cent of new diagnoses among heterosexual black African men and women, including those born in the UK as well as those born in Africa (Public Health England, 2018). Black African women in Britain had a low perception of HIV risk, however distinction by age was not reported (Burns et al, 2005). Similarly, black Caribbean people in England are disproportionately affected by sexually transmitted infections, and black Caribbean women are less likely to seek treatment than black Caribbean men or white British men and women (Aicken et al, 2019). Again, no distinction was made by age.

One recommended method for individuals who are at significant risk of acquiring HIV to stop HIV from taking hold and spreading throughout the body is pre-exposure prophylaxis (PrEP; Centers for Disease Control, n.d.). PrEP substantially reduced the risk of getting HIV from sex among people who inject drugs, heterosexual men and women, and heterosexual couples in which one partner was living with HIV and one was not (National Institute of Allergy and Infectious Diseases [NIAID], 2020). Although PrEP has regulatory approval in 46 countries, different countries are targeting different populations. For example, countries in sub-Saharan Africa are focusing on adolescent girls and young women; the US, most European countries, Australia, Thailand, Brazil, Vietnam, and the Philippines largely focus on gay men and other men who have sex with men (MSM); and South Africa, Kenya, and India have some focus on sex workers (Avert, 2019).

PrEP poses particular challenges for BME women. According to NIAID, in two major studies (that is, FEM-PrEP trial, VOICE study) women did not take the medication as prescribed, and daily pills for HIV prevention were not desirable for women who lived in sub-Saharan Africa, and nor did they fit into their lifestyles. Urban BME women in the US who expressed interest in PrEP preferred a pill formulation to intravaginal gel because of greater perceived privacy and concerns about vaginal side-effects and gel leakage. Women who had taken pills previously advocated daily dosing and expressed adherence concerns about episodic or post-coital PrEP (Flash et al, 2014).

In 2016, of women newly diagnosed accessing HIV care in the UK, 93.4% accesses care in England, 20.4% were aged 50 or older, 46.1% were BME, 50.9% were born in Africa and 26.1% were born in the UK, and 93.3% were likely due to heterosexual contact (Public Health

England, 2017). BME women living in the UK also report low levels of knowledge about the benefits of PrEP to prevent HIV infection. Many of these women considered PrEP as good for others but did not situate it within their own safer understanding, sometimes due to difficulty assessing their own HIV risk. In addition, these women felt that PrEP could undermine intimacy in their relationships. Finally, BME women in the UK assert that interpersonal networks supported their sexual health knowledge and interactions with health services, even though these networks were influenced by prevailing community stigmas (Nakasone et al, 2020).

In a study of BME college women, most had not heard of PrEP and were unsure or apprehensive about initiating use. After participation in an educational module, participants reported being likely to initiate PrEP in the future (Chandler et al, 2020). Barriers to PrEP use among BME individuals in the US include lack of knowledge about PrEP, low self-perceived risk, fewer visits to a health care providers (Ojikutu et al, 2018), stigma from healthcare providers, or family/partners/friends, intimate partner violence, distrust of healthcare providers/systems, access to PrEP, and concerns about side-effects/medication interaction (Mayer et al, 2020). Moreover, these barriers may have different effects on specific populations at risk (Mayer et al, 2020).

With high HIV risk factors because of group membership of age and race/ethnicity, BME older women are not the subject of study with regard to PrEP. Most studies on PrEP and BME women consist of participants with a mean age of 32. Hull and Mompe (2017) evaluated the effectiveness of the Black Women's Health Imperative *#LetsTalkAboutPrep* campaign among BME women living in Washington, DC and the participants ranged in age from 20 to 69 years old. Hirschhorn et al (2020) examined BME cisgender women's PrEP knowledge, attitudes, preferences, and experience in Chicago and the mean age of participants was 28, with a range of 18–57 years old. Poteat et al (2019) examined PrEP in relation to black (62%) and Latina (27%) transgender women aged between 19 and 82 years (median age of 34) and found high PrEP awareness but low uptake. However, 72 per cent of HIV-negative participants said they would be willing to take PrEP if it were available to them. In addition, for the women in this study who had taken PrEP the main concerns were a perception by others that they were taking the medication because they were HIV positive, side-effects, and feeling that they were not at risk of HIV. Conversely, for women not willing to take PrEP the concerns were about interactions with hormones, side-effects, and having to take pills daily. Other studies look at the intersecting disparities of gender, culture, poverty, and poverty of BME women, but not older women (Collieret al, 2017; Willie et al, 2017), and a survey of BME community in the UK awareness of PrEP but only 5 per cent of respondents were female and the age range of the total population was from 15 to 74 years (Ekong et al, 2019). The omission of BME older women in research and conversations about HIV and PrEP in mainstream sexual health campaigns may lead them to believe they are not at risk, thus they remain uninformed about the benefits of the drug (Raymond-Williams, 2019). Thus, we are left to glean from studies about PrEP and BME women that report consistently the same findings regarding limited knowledge and awareness of PrEP, attitudinal beliefs, cultural influences and community stigma, and mistrust of healthcare providers that BME older women are equally impacted.

According to Haire (2015), because of the stigma of PrEP use, being related to high-risk sexual activity (for example homosexuality, sex workers) and HIV in conjunction with stigma that is influenced by specific cultural conditions, social marketing needs to redress this stigma so that people and communities at high risk of HIV might benefit from PrEP access. That is, reframing PrEP access as a positive and responsible option to prevent HIV can help to improve use. For example, in Nigeria being found as someone needing PrEP was suggestive of HIV infection (Idoko et al, 2015).

Cultural context of sexual pleasure

A long-standing influence in the lives of black women is religion. Religion is directly and indirectly active in the teaching of sex-related behaviours for all women. Although religion has long avoided tackling the taboo subject of sexuality, overwhelmingly religion markets to single and married women messages about sex, and furthermore, considering sex for procreation in the context of heterosexual marriage only and discouraging sexual pleasure. For older BME women, religion portrays embracing intimacy as an aspect of sexuality that does not involve intercourse (Moultrie, 2017). Moultrie (2017) provides an example of an older black woman in a relationship with a long-time male friend who was in love with her but had never seen her naked. They were to value their sexual worth from a place of wisdom of their religious understanding of themselves rather than a lack of or diminishing capacity. Of important consideration is that the impact of culture on sexual expression should be understood regarding penalties and sanctions for deviating from what is acceptable, especially as linked to black female sexuality and older adults.

Other practices of religious prescription about sex may involve opposition to forms of self-pleasure such as masturbation because it is seen as a gateway to infidelity or same-sex desire. The influence of religion in sexual expression of some black older women is evident in their use of prayer to keep sex away from their focus (Lagana et al, 2013; Pew Research Center, Religion Public Life, 2014). Historically, and to a certain extent today, religion continues to foster intolerance of sexual diversity. However, religious norms and the way doctrinal beliefs are interpreted into norms are a major determinant of what is considered acceptable behaviour in each individual religion (Stewart et al, 2013).

Overwhelmingly, the literature is somewhat dismissive of discussion of sexuality of BME older straight and lesbian women. Often, the outcome for unattached black older lesbians who desire an intimate companion, the opportunities to find suitable partners in later years become more dismal. Single BME older women aged 55 years and older are more likely to report that they neither have nor desire a romantic relationship for reasons including that the burden of domestic and caregiving responsibilities outweighs the benefits of romantic involvement, and they may be disinclined because they perceive someone less attractive as a potential partner due to health issues (Mouzon et al, 2020). Nevertheless, through the view of queerness, Springer (2008, p 87) offers a perspective of what black women need to do in order to stop being silent and to change the status quo about how black women's sexuality is defined (see Table 2.3).

Table 2.3: Defining black women's sexuality

• Come out as black women who enjoy sex and find it pleasurable.

• Protest the stereotypes of black female sexuality that do not reflect our experience.

• Allow all black women – across class, sexual orientation, and physical ability – to express what we enjoy.

• Know the difference between making love and fucking – and be willing to express our desires for both despite what the news, music, videos, social mores, or any other source says we should want.

• Know what it is to play with sexuality. What turns us on? Is it something taboo? Does our playfulness come from within?

• Know that our bodies are our own – our bodies do not belong to the church, the state, our parents, our lovers, our husbands, and certainly not any media.

Methods of sexual pleasure

For BME women body image and beauty 'can only be truly understood within a framework of interlocking systems of 'isms' – (for example, racism, sexism, classism, heterosexism)' (Awad et al, 2015, p 540). Results concerning body image and BME women are mixed; however, despite higher body mass index (BMI), BME women are more satisfied and confident in body size than other groups of women (Chithambo and Huey, 2013). For example, in general BME women do not place emphasis on their body weight, shape, and size as prerequisites for relationships and intimacy. BME women report lower levels of body image dissatisfaction, maintain a favourable view of larger body sizes, have fewer concerns about dieting, weight fluctuations and fear of fatness, and are less likely to internalise sociocultural standards of beauty (Bancroft et al, 2010; Gordon et al, 2010; Award et al, 2015; Winter et al, 2019).

Thomas et al (2019) has explored how body image relates to sexual function and satisfaction in midlife women (ages 45–60) and found that among all women feeling attractive was an important reason for sexual activity, changes in appearance, especially weight gain and breast changes being common, and that body image affected their sexual satisfaction. Such factors had negative impact especially on women who felt self-conscious; and, in this regard, BME women were more likely to feel confident in their sexual satisfaction than white women, even in the face of bodily changes. Conversely, BME older women in Africa with higher BMI report more concerns about their bodies than their white counterparts (Hewat and Arndt, 2009). Similarly, although older black Caribbean women are keen to embrace their fuller figures, some have concerns over health (for example diabetes, high blood pressure; Appleford, 2016). Clarke and Griffin (2007) in interviews with women aged 50 to 70, found that, regardless of race, mothers are important influences on their daughters' socialisation into body image and beauty, and are perceived to exert accountability across the life course.

The questions that are raised with regard to BME older women are: how have BME older women generated or created depictions of sexuality over time and with age? How have black older women reclaimed their bodies from public gaze? How have black older women defined or redefined sexuality (Green, 2019)? A survey that focused on sex, romance, and relationships during the past six months of adults age 60 years and over looked at sexual behaviour regarding kissing and hugging, sexual touching and caressing, self-stimulation, oral sex, and anal sex (Fisher, 2010). The results indicated that for women aged 60 to 69, approximately half reported they kissed and hugged and used sexual touching and caressing, 8.2% used self-stimulation, 23.9% engaged in sexual intercourse, 11.8% engaged in oral sex, and 3.3% engaged in anal sex. Among women age 70 and older, 32.4% engaged in kissing and hugging, 11.9% engaged in sexual touching and caressing, 1.0% used self-stimulation, 4.8% engaged in sexual intercourse, 3.2% engaged in oral sex, and none engaged in anal sex (Fisher, 2010). This study did not report data based on race or ethnicity. The literature is scarce on sexuality of BME older women (Dickerson and Rousseau, 2009), especially beyond discussion of HIV/AIDS. Because of this scarceness a certain amount of latitude is asserted in the remainder of this section on discussion of methods of sexual pleasure of BME older women.

Self-pleasure/masturbation/sexual touching/solo female sexuality. For women, masturbation can increase sexual pleasure because it helps keep vaginal tissues moist and elastic and boosts hormone levels, which fuels sex drive (Chalker, 2009). Black older women in comparison to their white counterparts were found to be less comfortable and less likely to engage in oral sex and masturbation than their mothers' generation (Zeiss and Kasl-Godley, 2001). Shulman and Horne (2003) found European women reporting greater masturbation frequencies and higher rates of body dissatisfaction than African American women. For African American women, body image was not related to masturbation practice or frequency.

Robinson et al (2003) examined the relationship between several masturbation variables (that is, masturbation guilt, lifetime masturbation, and current masturbation) and HIV-related sexual behaviours and attitudes in a sample of African American women. Results showed that participants who reported masturbating were more likely to report having multiple partners, being in a non-monogamous relationship, and engaging in high-risk sexual behaviours. There was no significant relationship between level of masturbation guilt and HIV risk nor between masturbation and consistent condom use or attitudes toward condoms. Cain et al (2003) examined the sexual practices and function of midlife women (aged 42 to 52 years old) by ethnicity and found BME women report less frequent masturbation than did Caucasian women.

Clitoral stimulation. Fisher (1980) examined various aspects of black women's perceptions about their sexual behaviour (for example orgasm consistency, clitoral-vaginal preferences, intercourse frequency, and masturbation). In responding to the *Edwards Personal Preference Schedule* about preferences for external and internal sources of stimulation, black women's behaviour was more similar to than different from that of white females in the control group.

Oral sex. In a non-random sample of single older African Americans, Foster et al (2012) found that among black older adults aged 50 to 74 older black women engaged in unprotected oral sex less than their black male counterparts. Participants did report practising risky behaviours such as unprotected oral, anal, and vaginal sex (96.5%). Cain et al (2003) found BME women engage in oral sex at lower rates than Caucasian women. In a study of differences in oral sexual behaviour by gender, age, and race (including age cohorts of 20–29, 30–44, 45–59, 60–69) D'Souza et al (2014) found sexual oral behaviour was the primary predictor of oral human papillomavirus infection (HPV), but once this behaviour was adjusted for, age cohort and race were no longer associated with oral HPC16.

Kitchen talk (girl talk). Broadly defined, kitchen talk refers to conversation behind closed doors that cannot be conducted in public but may be in one's own home kitchen. For black women across the age spectrum, kitchen talk often is not about food and hair but about intimate and important issues that affect their lives ranging from mental health to sexuality. It is BME women's talk in their own terms and communities of practice (Jacobs-Huey, 2006). The kitchen offers a sense of freedom to express opinions about any and everything. 'The kitchen table represents physically and symbolically an inclusive space for black girls and women to come together, to be seen, and to just be'. It is a tradition that is passed on from our foremothers and grandmothers who defined the space as something 'beyond gossip and social talk' to one where 'women bared their souls and received healing and affirmation in the company of their sisters' (Haddix et al, 2016).

The discussion of sexuality at the kitchen table is a long-standing and guarded tradition when the audience consists of only (older) women. The explicitness of the discussion can vary from discussion of intercourse with a husband to being too tired to engage in sex. Part of this conversation was to solicit advice from other women, especially the wisdom of BME older women. In addition, BME older women themselves have the opportunity to centre on their sexuality as well. Although there is no pathology present, kitchen talk allows for rich discussion and exploration about the effects of what they are experiencing may be having on their life. Finally, as a result of their desexualisation BME older women often consider the intimacy of kitchen talk and close friendship and family ties as more important and fulfilling than sexual relationships. Because of self-intimacy beliefs, ageism and cultural negativism about older adults' sexual behaviour, BME older women have used their families and community institutions as places where they could develop agency (Lagana et al, 2013).

Music. Sexual references are common in music and these references may influence the behaviours of listeners. Non-white artists were more likely to make more explicit sexual references compared to white artists, who were more likely to reference kissing, hugging, and embracing (Cougar-Hall et al, 2012). The nature of sexual content also varies based on genre. For older adults, music of a specific era (when younger) may be used to relate to mood and memories of sexual activity earlier in life. For example, many older African Americans grew up on the music of Motown and blues that contains many sensual lyrics. In Jamaica, the ebb and flow of sexuality through the music and dance of *mento*, the musical precursor to reggae, abounds in playful double entendre and sexual innuendo, with jokes like 'did dig' or 'big bamdoo'; reggae, Rastafarian; and Mapouka dance (Dannaway, 2012, p 1). Listening to music people consider 'sexy' actually enhances the feeling of being touched by someone else (Fritz et al, 2017). They concluded, 'the sexier we perceive music, the sexier we also perceive touch that is administered simultaneously' (p 1360).

Other strategies employed by black older women in response to sexual desire include seeing friends and family when feeling sexually deprived, denial when sexual desire arose, and doing nothing to cope with feeling sexually deprived (Lagana et al, 2013). Sexual pleasure can be expressed in ways other than sexual intercourse, such as through close physical contact, caressing, and other touching. It is important to remember that pleasure is defined as what makes us feel good, it increases our sense of well-being and creates feelings of enjoyment. In fact, 'we pursue, experience, understand, negotiate, and feel pleasure in many ways – in fantasies, anticipation, ideas, deeds, and thoughts' (Patel, 2006, p 70). The literature did not include information on other topics on methods of sexual pleasure such as emotional sex/ fantasy, sex surrogacy, medications, herbs, and sex aids/toys for BME older women.

Summary

Sexual expression of BME older women is contextualised in social issues such as *isms*, sexual stigma, stereotypes, and cultural boundaries that contribute to what these women feel they deserve when it comes to sex and pleasure. Black older women's sexuality and the ongoing invisibility of their sexuality globally occurs within historical, social, economic, and political contexts. Through 'sexual repression and restraints', BME older women 'got further divorced from their bodies and discourse of female desire, pleasure and empowerment' (Nanda, 2019, p 171). For BME older women it is important to understand that not all expressions of sexuality involve intercourse or another person but also well-being. Key factors influencing BME older women's sexuality include sexual behaviour, health and well-being, availability of a partner, and beliefs about sex outside of marriage. Yet, regardless of marital status, women of all ages have a right to sexual health that intrinsically includes a positive and respectful approach to sexuality and sexual relationships, as well as the possibility of having sexual experiences that are pleasurable and safe and free from coercion, discrimination, violence and disease (World Health Organization, 2013).

The limited coverage if not obvious omission of BME older women's sexuality in the literature calls attention to the need to examine the discourse on sexuality from the intersection and complexities of race, gender, and age. Although there is diversity among black older women's sexual expression, limited research leads to generalisations or assumptions across various groups of BME women. Often, such global expectations of sexual behaviours are reported as being positive or negative rather than culturally expressive. Black older women are dealing with intersectionality in society that is not really thinking about them and the very specific needs of BME older women and sexuality.

References

Aicken, C.R.H., Wayal, S., Blomquist, P.B., Fabiane, S.M., Gerressu, M., Hughes, G,, and Mercer, C. H. (2019) 'Pathways to, and Use of, Sexual Healthcare Among Black Caribbean Sexual Health Clinic Attendees in England: Evidence from Cross-sectional Bio-behavioural surveys', *BMC Health Services Research*, 19, Article number 668, https://doi.org/10.1186/s12913-019-4396-3

Appleford, K. (2016) *'This big bum thing has taken over the world': Considering Black women's changing view on body image and the role of celebrity*, https://eprints.kingston.ac.uk/36145/1/Appleford-K-36145-AAM.pdf

Asiedu, G.B., Hayes, S.S., Williams, K.P., Bondaryk, M.R., Halyard, M.Y., Parker, M.W., Balls-Berry, J., Pinn, V.W., and Breitkopf, C.R. (2017) 'Prevalent Health Concerns Among African American Women Belonging to a National Volunteer Service Organization (The Links, Incorporated)', *Journal of Racial and Ethnic Health Disparities*, 4(1), 19–24.

Avert (2019) *Pre-exposure prophylaxis (PrEP) for HIV prevention*, https://www.avert.org/professionals/hiv-programming/prevention/pre-exposure-prophylaxis

Awad, G.H., Norwood, C., Taylor, D.S., Martinez, M., McClain, S., Jones, B., Holman, A., and Chapman-Hilliard, C. (2015) 'Beauty and Body Image Concerns Among African American College Women', *Journal of Black Psychology*, 41(6), 540–64.

Bancroft, J., Long, J.S., andMcCabe, J. (2010) 'Sexual Well-being: A Comparison of U.S. Black and White Women in Heterosexual Relationships', *Archives of Sexual Behavior*, https://doi10.1007/s10508-010-9679-z

Bernard, A.A.F. (2016) 'Colonizing Black Female Bodies Within Patriarchal Capitalism: Feminist and Human Rights Perspectives', *Sexualization, Media, & Society*, 2(4), 1–11.

Burns, F., Fenton, K.A., Morison, L., Mercer, C., Erens, B., Field, J., Copas, A.J., Wellings, K., and Johnson, A.M. (2005) 'Factors Associated with HIV Among Black Africans in Britain', *Sexually Transmitted Infections*, 81(6), 494–500.

Cain, V.S., Johannes, C.B., Avis, N.E., Mohr, B., Schocken, M., Skurnick, J., and Ory, M. (2003) 'Sexual Functioning and Practices in a Multi-ethnic Study of Midlife Women: Baseline results from SWAN', *Journal of Sex Reserch*, 40(3), 266–76. DOI: 10.1080/00224490309552191

Centers for Disease Control (n.d.) *Pre-exposure prophylaxis (PrEP)*, https://www.cdc.gov/hiv/risk/prep/index.html

Centers for Disease Control (2012) *Diagnosis of HIV infection among adults aged 50 years and older in the United States and dependent areas 2007–2010*, http://www.ced.gov/hiv/pdf/statistics_2010_HIV_Surveillance_Report_vol_18_no_3.pdf

Chalker, R. (2009) *Strategies for staying sexual after menopause*, https://www.nwhn.org/strategies-for-staying-sexual-after-menopause/

Chandler, R., Hull, S., Ross, H., Guillaume, D., Paul, S., Dera, N., and Hernandez, N. (2020) 'The Pre-exposure Prophylaxis (PrEP) Consciousness of Black College Women and the Perceived Hesitancy of Public Heath Institutions to Curtail HIV in Black Women', *BMC Public Health*, 20, 1172, https://doi.org/10.1186/s12889-020-09248-6

Chithambo, T.P. and Huey, S.J. (2013) 'Black/white Differences in Perceived Weight and Attractiveness Among Overweight Women', *Journal of Obesity*, http://dx.doi.org/10.1155/2013/320326

Clarke, L.H. and Griffin, M. (2007) 'Becoming and Being Gendered Through the Body: Older Women, Their Mothers and Body Image', *Ageing & Society*, 27(5), 701–18.

Collier, K.L., Colarossi, L.G., and Sanders, K. (2017) 'Raising Awareness of PrEP Among Women in New York City: Community and Provider Perspectives', *Journal of Health Communication*, 22(3), 183–89. DOI: 10.1080/10810730.2016.1261969

Collins, P. (2008) *Black feminist Thought: Knowledge, Consciousness, and the Politics of Empowerment*. New York, NY: Routledge.

Conner, L.R. (2013) 'Attention HIV: Older African American Women Define Sexual Risk', *Culture Health & Sexuality*, 16(1), https://doi:10.1080/13691058.2013.821714

Cougar-Hall, P.P., West, J., and Hill, S. (2012) 'Sexualization in Lyrics of Popular Music from 1959 to 2009: Implications for Sexuality Educators', *Sexuality & Culture*, 16, 102–17.

Crenshaw, K. (1989) 'Demarginalizing the Intersection of Race and Sex: A Black Feminist Critique of Antidiscrimination Doctrine, Feminist Theory and Antiracist Politics', *University of Chicago Legal Forum*, 1(8), 139–67.

D'Souzza, G., Cullen, K., Bowie, J., Thrope, R., and Fakhry, C. (2014) 'Differences in oral sexual behavior by gender, age, and race explain observed differences in prevalence of oral human papillomavirus infection', *PLOS One*, https://doi.org/10/1371/journal.pone.0086023

Dannaway, F.R. (2012) *Kinky reggae: The agony and the ecstasy of sex in Jamaica*, https://daily.redbullmusicacademy.com/2012/08/kinky-reggae

Dickerson, B.J. and Rousseau, N. (2009) 'Ageism Through Omission: The Obsolescence of Black Women's Sexuality', *Journal of African American Studies*, 13(3), 307–24.

Duvall, J.L., Oser, C.B., Mooney, J., Staton-Tindall, M., Havens, J.R., and Leukfeld, C.G. (2013) 'Feeling Good in Your Own Skin: The Influence of Complimentary Sexual Stereotypes on Risky Sexual Attitudes and Behaviors in a Community Sample of African American Women', *Women and Health*, 53, 1–19. DOI: 10.1080/03630242.2012.750260

Ekong, N., Braunholtz-Speight, J., Mukelabai, N., and Evans, A. (2019) *Awareness of pre-exposure prophylaxis _PrEP) in the black and minority ethnic community: A questionnaire survey in Leeds, UK*, https://www.bhiva.org/file/BITipNrWekDjZ/P71.pdf

Fisher, L.L. (2010) *Sex, Romance, and Relationships: AARP Survey of Midlife and Older Adults*. Washington, DC: AARP.

Fisher, S. (1980) 'Personality Correlates of Sexual Behavior in Black Women', *Archives of Sexual Behavior*, 9(1), 27–35.

Flash, C.A., Stone, V.E., Mitty, J.A., Miniaga, M.J., Hall, K.T., Krakower, D., and Mayer, K.H. (2014) 'Perspectives on HIV Prevention Among Urban Black Women: A Potential Role for HIV Pre-Exposure Prophylaxis', *AIDS Patient Care STDS*, 28(1), 635–642. DOI: 10.1089/apc.2014.0003

Foster, V., Clark, P.C., and Holstad, M.M. (2012) 'The Self-reported Sexual Behavior of Single Older African Americans', *Journal of Health Disparities Research and Practice*, 8(2), 1–11.

Foucault, M. (1980) *The History of Sexuality, Vol. 1: An Introduction.* Translated by R. Hurley. New York, NY: Vintage Books.

Fritz, T., Brummerloh, B., Urquijo, M., Wegner, K., Reimer, E., Gutekunst, S., Schneider, L., Smallwood, J., and Villringer, A. (2017) 'Blame it on the Bossa Nova: Transfer of Perceived Sexiness from Music to Touch', *Journal of Experimental Psychology: General*, 146(9), 1360–5.

Gordon, K.H., Castro, Y., Sitnikov, L., and Holm-Denoma, J.M. (2010) 'Cultural Body Shape Ideals and Eating Disorder Symptoms Among White, Latina, and Black College Women', *Cultural Diversity and Ethnic Minority Psychology*, 16(2), 135–43.

Granville, L. and Pregler, J. (2018) 'Women's Sexual Health and Aging', *Journal of the American Geriatrics Society*, 66, 595–601. DOI: 10.1111/jgs.15198

Green, L. (n.d.) *Negative racial stereotypes and their effects on attitudes toward African-Americans*, https://www.ferris.edu/htmls/news/jimcrow/essays/vcu.htm

Green, T.T. (2019) *Special issues 'Unsilencing Black Sexuality in the African Diaspora'*, https://www.mdpi.com/journal/humanities/special_issues/Africn_Diaspora

Haddix, M., McArthur, S.A., Muhammad, G.E., Price-Dennis, D., and Sealy-Ruiz, Y. (2016) 'At the Kitchen Table: Black Women English Educators Speaking Our Truths', *English Education*, 48(4), 380–95.

Haire, B.G. (2015) 'Preexposure Prophylaxis-related Stigma: Strategies to Improve Uptake and Adherence – A Narrative Review', *HIV AIDS – Research and Pallitive Care*, 7, 241–9.

Harley, D.A. (2016) 'African American and Black LGBT Elders'. In D.A. Harley and P.B. Teaster (eds), *Handbook of LGBT Elders: An Interdisciplinary Approach to Principles, Practices, and Policies* (pp 105–34). Switzerland: Springer International Publishing.

Harley, D.A., Stansbury, K.L., Nelson, M., and Espinosa, C.T. (2014) 'A Profile of Rural Elderly African American Lesbians: Meeting Their Need'. In H.F.O. Vakalahi, G.M. Simpson, and N. Guinta (eds), *Collective Spirit of Aging Across Cultures* (pp 133–55). New York, NY: Springer Science and Business Media Publisher.

Hartmann, U., Philippsohn, S., Heiser, K., and Ruffer-Hesse, C. (2004) 'Low Sexual Desire in Midlife and Older Women: Personality Factors, Psychosocial Development, Present Sexuality', *Menopause*, 11(6Pt 2), 726–40.

Heinemann, J., Atallah, S., and Rosenbaum, T. (2016) 'The Impact of Culture and Ethnicity on Sexuality and Sexual Function', *Current Sexual Health Reports*, 8(3), 144–50.

Hewat, H. and Arndt, M. (2009) 'A Cross-cultural Exploration: Body Image in Older Black and White Women in the Workplace', *Journal of Psychology in Africa*, 19(3), 315–19.

Hirschhorn, L.R., Brown, R.N., Friedman, E.E., Greene, G.J., Bender, A., Christeller, C., Bouris, A., Johnson, A.K., Pickett, J., Modali, L., and Ridgway, J. (2020) 'Black Cisgender Women's PrEP Knowledge, Attitudes, Preferences, and Experience in Chicago', *Journal of Acquired Immune Deficency Syndrome*, 84(5), 497–507. DOI: 10.1097/QAI.0000000000002377

Hughes, A.K., Rostant, O.S., and Pelon, S. (2015) 'Sexual Problems Among Older Women by Age and Race', *Journal of Women's Health*, 24(8), 663–9.

Hull, S.J. and Mompe, A. (2017) *An evaluation of the effectiveness of the Black Women's Health Imperative (BWHI) #LetsTalkAboutprep campaign among Black women living in Washington D.C.*, https://hsrc.himmelfarb.gwu.edu/gw_research_days/2-17/GWSPH/39/

Hunter, S. (2005) *Midlife and Older LGBT Adults: Knowledge and Affirmative Practice for the Social Services*. New York, NY: Routledge.

Idoko, J., Folayan, M.O., Dadem, N.Y., Kolawole, G.O., Anenih, J., and Alhassan, E. (2015) '"Why Should I Take Drugs for your Infection?": Outcomes of Formative Research on the Use of HIV Pre-exposure Prophylaxis in Nigeria', *BMC Public Health*, 15(1), 349.

Jacobs, J.J. and Kane, M.N. (2011) 'Psychosocial Predictors of Self-esteem in a Multi-ethnic Sample of Women Over 50 at Risk for HIV', *Journal of Women and Aging*, 23, 23–39.

Jacobs-Huey, L. (2006) *From the Kitchen to the Parlor: Language and Becoming in African American Women's Hair Care*. New York, NY: Oxford University Press.

Kuofie, A.A., Bauer, A., Berkley-Patton, J., and Bowe-Thompson, C. (2019) 'HIV Knowledge and Risk Behaviors Among Older Church-affiliated Black', *Gerontology and Geriatric Medicine*, https://doi.org/10.1177/2333721419855668

Lagana, L., White, T., Bruzzone, D.E., and Bruzzone, C.E. (2013) 'Exploring the Sexuality of African American Older Women', *British Journal of Medical Research*, 4(5), 1129–48.

Lee, M.G. and Quam, J.K. (2013) 'Comparing Supports for LGBT Aging in Rural Versus Urban Areas', *Journal of Gerontological Social Work*, 56(2), 112–26.

Le Gall, A., Mullet, E., and Shafighi, S.R. (2002) 'Age, Religious Beliefs, and Sexual Attitudes', *Journal of Sex Research*, 39(3), 22–44.

Lindau, S.T. and Fruin, K. (2017) 'Sexuality, Sexual Function, and the Aging Woman'. In J.B. Halter, J.G. Ouslander, S. Studenski, K.P. High, S. Asthana, M.A. Supiano, and C. Rithcie (eds), *Hazzard's Geriatric Medicine and Gerontology* (7th ed.) New York, NY: McGraw-Hill.

Lindau, T., Leitsch, S.A., Lundberg, K.L., and Jerome, J. (2006) 'Older Women's Attitudes, Behavior, and Communication About Sex and HIV: A Community-based Study', *Journal of Women's Health*, 15(6), 747–53.

Mayer, K.H., Agwu, A., and Malebranche, D. (2020) 'Barriers to the Wider Use of Pre-exposure Prophylaxis in the United States: A Narrative Review', *Advances in Therapy*, 37, 1778–1811. DOI: 10.1007/s12325-020-01295-0

Mgadmi, M. (2009) 'Black Women's Identity: Stereotypes, Respectability and Passionlessness (1890–1930)', *Revue LISA/LISA e-journal*, 7(1), http://journals.openedition.org/lisa/806

Moultrie, M. (2017) *Passionate and Pious: Religious Media and Black Women's Sexuality*. Durham, NC: Duke University Press.

Mouzon, D.M., Taylor, R.J., and Chatters, L.M. (2020) 'Gender Differences in Marriage, Romantic Involvement, and Desire for Romantic Involvement Among Older African Americans', *PLOS One*, https://doi:10.1371/journal.pone.0233836

Mowatt, R.A. and French, B.H. (2013) 'Black/female/body Hypervisibility and Invisibility: A Black Feminist Augmentation of Feminist Leisure Research', *Journal of Leisure Research*, 45(5), 644–60.

Nakasone, S.E., Young, I., Estcourt, C.S., Calliste, J., Flowers, P., Ridgway, J., and Shahmanesh, M. (2020) 'Risk Perception, Safer Sex Practices and PrEP Enthusiasm: Barriers and Facilitators to Oral HIV Pre-exposure Prophylaxis in Black African and Carribean Women in the UK', *Sexually Transmitted Infections*, 96(5). DOI: 10.1136/sextrans-2020–054457

Nanda, S. (2919) 'Re-framing hottentot: Liberating Black Female Sexuality from the Mammy/hottentot Blind', *Humanities*, 8(4), 161, https://doi.org/10.3390/h8040161

National Institute of Allergy and Infectious Diseases (2020) *Pre-exposure prophylaxis (PrEP) to reduce HIV risk*, https://www.niaid.nih.gov/diseases-conditions/pre-exposure-prophylaxis-prep

Nevedal, A. and Sankar, A. (2016) 'The Significance of Sexuality and Intimacy in the Lives of Older African Americans with HIV/AIDS', *The Gerontologist*, 56(4), 762–71.

Nusbaum, M.R.H., Singh, A.R., and Pyles, A.A. (2004) 'Sexual Healthcare Needs of Women Aged 65 and Older', *Journal of American Psychiatric Society*, 52, 117–22.

Ojikutu, B.O., Bogart, L.M., Higgins-Biddle, M., Dale, S.K., Allen, W., Dominique, T., and Mayer, K.H. (2018) 'Facilitators and Barriers to Pre-exposure Prophylaxis (PrEP) Use Among Black Individuals in the United States: Results from the National Survey on HIV in the Black Community (NSHBC)', *AIDS and Behavior*, 22(11), 3576–87. DOI: 10.1007/s10461-018-2067-8

Okiria, E.M. (2014) 'Perspectives of Sexuality and Aging in the African Culture: Eastern Uganda', *International Journal of Sociology and Anthropology*, 6(4), 126–9.

Patel, N. (2006) 'Talking about Pleasure: How Does Language Make a Difference?', *Women in Action*, 1(3), 66–74.

Payer, P.J. (1985) 'Foucault on Penance and the Shaping of Sexuality', *Studies in Religion/Sciences Religieuses*, 14(3), 313–20.

Pew Research Center, Religion Public Life (2014) *U.S. religious landscape study [data file]*, https://www.pewforum.org/dataset/pwe-research-center-2014-u-s-religious-landscape-study/

Phinney, J.S. and Flores, J. (2002) 'Unpacking Acculturation: Aspects of Acculturation as Predictors of Traditional Sex Role Attitudes', *Journal of Social Work and Human Sexuality*, 4, 47–65.

Pilgrim, D. (2008) *The sapphire caricature*, https://www.ferris.edu/HTMLS/news/jimcrow/antiblack/sapphire.htm

Poteat, T., Wirtz, A., Malik, M., Cooney, E., Cannon, C., Hardy, W.D., Arrington-Sanders, R., Lujan, M., and Yamanis, T. (2019) 'A Gap Between Willingness and Uptake: Findings from Mixed Methods Research on HIV Prevention Among Black and Latina Transgender Women', *Journal of Acquired Immune Deficiency Syndromes*, 82(2), 131–40. DOI: 10.1097/QAI.0000000000002112

Prather, C., Fuller, T.R., Jeffries, W.L., Marshall, K.J., Howell, A.V., Belyue-Umole, A., and King, W. (2018) 'Racism, African American Women, and Their Sexual and Reproductive Health: A Review of Historical and Contemporary Evidence and Implications for Health Equity', *Health Equity*, 2(1), 249–59. DOI: 10.1089/heq.2017.0045

Public Health England (2017) HIV testing in England, 2017 report, https://www.gov.uk/government/uploads/system/uploads/attachment_data/file/666478/HIV_testing_in_England_2017_report.pdf

Public Health England (2018) *Progress towards ending the HIV epidemic in the United Kingdom*, https://assets.publishing.service.gov.uk/government/uploads/system/uploads/attachment_data/file/821273/Progress_towards_ending_the_HIV_epidemic_in_the_UK.pdf

Raymond-Williams, R. (2019) *We need to do a better job of including black women in conversations about HIV and PrEP*, https://www.independent.co.uk/voices/black-women-hiv-sti-terrence-higgins-trust-a8972241.html

Robinson, B.B.E., Bockting, W.O., and Harrell, T (2003) 'Masturbation and Sexual Health', *Journal of Psychology & Human Sexuality*, 14(22–3), 85–102.

Rose, T. (2004) *Longing to Tell: Black Women Talk About Sexuality and Intimacy*. New York, NY: St. Martin's Press.

Rosenthal, L. and Lobel, M. (2017) 'Stereotype of Black American Women Related to Sexuality and Motherhood', *Psychology of Women Quarterly*, 40(3), 414–27.

Savin-Williams, R. (2001) *Mom, Dad, I'm Gay: How Families Negotiate Coming Out*. Washington, DC: American Psychological Association.

Shulman, J.L. and Horne, S.G. (2003) 'The Use of Self-pleasure: Masturbation and Body Image Among African American and European American Women', *Psychology of Women Quarterly*, 27(3), 262–9.

Smith, T.K. and Larson, E.L. (2015) 'HIV Sexual Risk Behavior in Older Black Women: A Systematic Review', *Women's Health Issues*, 25(1), 63–72.

Springer, K. (2008) 'Queering Black Female Heterosexuality'. In J. Friedman and J. Valenti (eds), *Yes Means Yes! Visions of Female Sexual Power and a World Without Rape* (pp 77–91) Berkeley, CA: Seal Press.

Stepanian, N.A., Davidson, M.R., and Rosenberger, J.G. (2017) 'Risky Dating Behavior Among Women aged 50+: A Growing Public Health Concern', *Women's Healthcare*, 5(4), 24–8.

Stewart, J.M., Sommers, M.S., and Brawner, B.M. (2013) 'The Black Church, Sexual Health, and Sexuality: A Conceptual Framework to Promote Health Through Faith-based Organizations', *Family & Community Health*, 36(3), 269–79.

Thames, A.D., Hammond, A., Nunez, R.A., Mahmood, Z., Jones, F., Carter, S.L., Bilder, R.M., Fisher, S., Bivens-Davis, T., and Jones, L. (2018) 'Sexual Health Behavior and Mental Health Among Older African American Women: The Sistahs, Sexuality, and Mental Health Well-being Project', *Journal of Women's Health (Larchmt)*, 27(9), 1177–85.

Thomas, H.N., Hamm, M., Borrero, S., Hess, R., and Thurston, R.C. (2019) 'Body Image, Attractiveness, and Sexual Satisfaction Among Midlife Women: A Qualitative Study', *Journal of Women's Health*, 28(1), https://doi.org/10.1089/jwh.2018.7107

West, C.M. (2008) 'Mammy, Jezebel, Sapphire, and Their Home-girls: Developing an "Oppositional Gaze" toward Images of Black Women'. In J. Chrisler, C. Golden, and P. Rozee (eds), *Lectures on the Psychology of Women, 4* (pp 286–99) New York, NY: McGraw Hill.

White, T. and Lagana, L. (2013) 'Factors Influencing Older Black Women's Sexual Functioning and Their Disclosure of Sexual Concerns', *OA Women's Health*, 1(1), 1–10, www.oapublishinglondon.com/images/article/pdf/1390264115.pdf

Willie, T.C., Kershaw, T., Cambell, J.C., and Alexander, K.A. (2017) 'Intumate Partner Violence and PrEP Acceptability Among Low Income, Young Black Women: Exploring the Mediating Role of Reproductive Coercion', *AIDS Behavior*, 21(8), 2261–9. DOI: 10.1007/s10461-017-1767-9

Winter, V.R., Danforth, L.K., Landor, A., and Pevehouse-Pfeiffer, D. (2019) 'Toward an Understanding of Racial and Ethnic Diversity in Body Image Among Women', *Social Work Research*, 43(2), 69–80.

World Health Organization (2013) *Gender Inequities and HIV*. Geneva: WHO, http://www.who.int/gender/hiv_aids/en

Yee, L.A. and Sundquist, K.J. (2003) 'Older Women's Sexuality', *Medical Journal of Australia*, 178(12), 640–2.

Zeiss, A.M. and Kasl-Godley, J. (2001) 'Sexuality in Older Adults' Relationships', *Generations*, 25, 18–25.

3

Sexual desires and intimacy needs in older persons and towards the end of life

Karen Rennie

Introduction

The need for touch, intimacy and sexual pleasure does not diminish with age, nor should it be dependent on how long we have left to live. For too long, the sexual desires and intimate connections of older persons have been, like some embarrassment, swept under the carpet or have been subject to misunderstanding (Zordan, 2009), based on myths concerning a natural or inevitable non-sexual status. Such stereotypical thinking seems deeply ingrained and affects how we perceive older persons in general (Zordan, 2009). In this chapter, I aim to challenge such stereotypes about older people and sexuality, especially focusing on the 'oldest old' and older persons experiencing their end of life. I start the main section of this chapter by focusing on the significance of sex and intimacy for older persons. I will address how older persons view sex and intimacy and will draw upon the literature regarding sexual satisfaction and older people. This section will also address the sexual needs and desires of older persons who are living with dementia and those who are living in care homes. I will then develop this chapter further by moving onto sexual and intimate connections for persons who are at the end of life. I begin this chapter by looking at the *specialness of sex* in terms of its significance for older persons in order to provide a context for discussion of the sensitive subjects of sex and intimacy and persons living with dementia and older persons who are at the end of life.

For the purposes of this chapter, when using the term 'older persons' or 'older people', I am specifically referring to those aged 75+, which is regarded by the World Health Organization (WHO, 2018) as 'older old' or distastefully as 'late elderly'. Additionally, I aim to demonstrate that older persons can, and do, enjoy a satisfying sex life and their need for intimacy and closeness often persists. I will explore the neglected, sensitive, counter-intuitive if not still taboo subject of sex towards the end of life and in relation older people. This chapter is predicated on the notion that sex is not just about the physical acts of sex, or whom we have or might want to have sex with, although it undoubtedly does encompass that. Sex and intimacy comprise emotions, feelings and desires about how we perceive and experience love, intimacy, touch, pleasure and passion. Sexual expression could be described as:

> ... a general term used to describe the ways human beings communicate and present ourselves to the world as sexual beings. Our sexual expression is unique and includes the expression of our sexual activities, thoughts, feelings, desires, hopes and dreams. Sexual expression is connected to sexual activity, sexual orientation, identity and gender, bodily expressions and can range from how we move, walk and talk, how we relate to others and the extent to which humans connect with each other. (Adapted from Rennie et al, 2017)

Essentially, I will argue that sex and intimacy are still important for many experiencing the end of life and I hope, contrary to common myth, to extend knowledge in terms of the value of sex and intimacy to older persons.

Literature search strategy

As publications on sex and intimacy in older persons and towards the end of life are sparse, the search strategy for this chapter aimed to identify and critique relevant literature and materials from diverse sources. A collection of the publications and resources used in this narrative are not to be found through the traditional academic route of database searching. Including papers from a range of sources can encourage a deep analysis and synthesis of the material in order to offer a different perspective and to arrive at new insights (Grant and Booth, 2009), which correlates with the intentions of this chapter.

Searches for literature began with, but were not limited to, academic databases to find relevant research publications on sex and intimacy in later life. The databases that were used to locate some of the articles included in this chapter were CINAHL, ASSIA and SCOPUS. The key terms used for the database searches were 'older people', 'older person', 'ageing', 'end of life', 'palliative care', in combination with 'sex', 'sexual desires', 'sexual practice', 'sexuality' and/or 'intimacy'. A total of 28 research articles were found through searching the online databases. Articles which did not include or discuss persons aged 75+ were excluded from this chapter. As there is a significant knowledge gap regarding older persons and sexual desires and intimacy needs, other publications were accessed through Google Scholar and press and broadcast media. This yielded a further nine publications that are included in this chapter. In total, 37 sources have been used in this chapter to explore sexual desires and intimacy needs in older persons and towards the end of life.

Sex and intimacy in older persons: the specialness of sex

This section will address the particular significance of sex and intimacy and older persons (in terms of health, well-being and enjoyment/pleasure), including those who are living with dementia and living in residential care. Since the 1960s the way we think about sex has dramatically changed (Hills, 2014). Availability of 'the Pill' in the 1960s helped legitimate premarital and recreational sex, though largely for younger people! However, the various liberation struggles from the late 1960s onwards tended to forget about the sexual needs of older people, an issue that persists today. In general terms, we continue to shy away from the sexual needs of older persons, and research focused on health problems and sexual dysfunction in later life encourages the stereotype that older people do not want, are incapable of, or are not interested in sexual relationships (Maataoui et al, 2017). However, Benbow and Beeston (2012) have argued that sex and intimacy continue to provide individuals with a better quality of life but are still largely ignored by healthcare professionals, academics researchers and the general public.

Yet, it is still common that engagement in sexual activities can induce feelings of shame and guilt. Gewirtz-Meydan et al (2018) found that socialisation and social legitimacy impacted on how older adults viewed their sexuality in later life. There is evidence indicating that older persons who want to establish romantic relationships try to adapt to social norms by acting younger and distancing themselves from the use of the term 'old' or by finding a younger partner (Gewirtz-Meydan et al, 2018), which is suggestive of 'ageist erotophobia' (Simpson et al, 2018). 'Ageist erotophobia' is a term used to describe anxieties concerning older people that fail to acknowledge them as sexual beings (Simpson et al, 2018). Similarly, various studies (Drummond et al, 2013; Yun et al, 2014; Gewirtz-Meydan et al, 2018; Simpson et al, 2018) have shown that older people themselves report and internalise assumptions about their non-sexual status. This endemic silence regarding sex and intimacy can make raising such issues with friends, families or service providers feel uncomfortable (Drummond et al, 2013). The invisibility of older people as sexual beings reflects dated traditions in which sex is viewed as only for two individuals who were bound together in matrimony and for the purpose of procreation (Dumpleton, 1992). Yun et al (2014) found that sexual desire in later life was mediated by wider concerns about older people engaging in sexual activities rather than focusing on what the person or couple may want for themselves. The lack of discussion about health-related sexual issues can negatively affect ability to have a satisfying sex life, to manage changes in sexual functioning, identity and expectations concerning a diminished sex life (Gewirtz-Meydan et al, 2018).

From the research that has been conducted, older persons have tended to emphasise how the ageing process has affected their sexual lives (Gewirtz-Meydan et al, 2018). Contrary to wider beliefs, older people have indicated how maintaining a sex life can be an integral part of healthy ageing and perceived as a symbol of vitality and longevity but that it is dependent on physical health and well-being, which in turn reflect intersecting differences of class, gender and ethnicity. Interestingly, some older people do not view age itself as preventing sexual experience or satisfaction (Malta, 2007; Gewirtz-Meydan et al, 2018).

Another strand in the literature has observed that older people agentically develop alternative views of sex beyond genitocentrism and penetration. This suggests a challenge to youth-oriented views of sex and a challenge to dominant norms about what 'real' sex should consist of. Indeed, some people have extended what counts as sex by referring to caressing and so on. Many older persons have found alternative ways of viewing sex and sexuality and have emphasised relationships beyond genital functionality and penetration (Malta, 2007). Some men and women have spoken openly about achieving sexual satisfaction through the alternative sexual knowledge and skills they have learned that do not depend on erection and penetration. According to Freak-Poli et al (2017) sexuality is an important aspect of active ageing and is increasingly important to older adults. Addressing sexual activity among older adults and even having open discussions can contribute to maintaining and improving quality of life and reducing misconceptions (Freak-Poli et al, 2017). By including physical contact, such as hugging, kissing, cuddling and caressing into the equation, many older people speak of experiencing a satisfactory sexual experience and men were able to successfully reconstruct their sexual identity despite erectile dysfunction (Drummond et al, 2013). As people grow older, they may develop a more enhanced sense of entitlement to sexual pleasure that involves reappraisal of sex/intimacy, questioning of inhibitions and better understanding of both one's self and others. Sex in later life was described by some older people as greater and improved, perhaps due to the growing knowledge of one's own body, the ability to derive pleasure from it (alone or partnered), feeling more comfortable with a partner, with changing sexual practices and with less concern about fertility (Trudel et al, 2010; Ménard et al, 2015). Relative freedom from wider social pressures and the fear of unplanned pregnancy in later life have allowed some older people to re-evaluate their understanding of sex and intimacy, to attempt new sexual practices and to enjoy better sex lives compared to when they were younger (Ménard et al, 2015). Some older people have claimed that sexuality in later years involves deeper feelings than those experienced earlier in life and have reported more pleasure from a wider range of practices such as cuddling, foreplay, masturbation, and so on (Drummond et al, 2013; Ménard et al, 2015). Additionally, the emotional aspects of sexual activity and sexual expression have been more satisfying later in life (Trudel et al, 2010; Drummond et al, 2013).

It is important that such dominant if restricted ways of thinking of sexual pleasure are counter-balanced. Those wishing to continue with penetrative sex but experiencing challenges may need sensitive information about erectile dysfunction and vaginal dryness (as well as physical health, for example cardiology and respiratory complications, arthritis) or their psychological and social well-being (for example loneliness, depression, isolation). Nevertheless, older people may benefit from support concerning sexual alternatives and with feelings of disappointment, self-recrimination and a sense of hopelessness. Such feelings may represent the legacy of second wave (of the 1960s and 1970s) sexology (for example of Masters and Johnson, 1966) that perpetuates the notion of real sex as bound up with genital stimulation and intercourse. Such approaches have helped marginalise other forms of pleasure and satisfaction such as trust, intimacy, sensuous touching, affection, caressing, kissing and communication (Tiefer, 1991; Leiblum, 1998). However, research has also demonstrated that despite the decline in frequency of sexual activity (mainly penetrative sex), many older persons have learned to approach sex in a more sensual way, for example by resignifying activities such as kissing, touch, physical closeness and what was regarded as 'foreplay' but is now central to the sexual/intimate repertoire.

In exploring the literature on older people and sex, it soon becomes clear that older persons habitually assume that sexual intercourse is *the* means to 'have sex' and the benchmark for pleasure (Loe, 2004). The hegemony of penetrative sex reveals the narrow definition of sexual activity that many older persons imbibe: sex means intercourse; intercourse means vaginal penetration; and vaginal penetration requires penile erection (Malta, 2007). This ideology has the potential to be accompanied by feelings of distress, disappointment, frustration, shock and fear of failure, which could lead to despair, devastation and a sense of hopelessness (Loe, 2004). Most participants in the studies concerned spoke of the significance of romantic relationships, which included penetrative intercourse as normative, definitive, important and desirable (Gewirtz-Meydan et al, 2018). Older women also identified penetrative intercourse as being the 'gold-standard' of sexual activity. One study documented the impact of physical limitations in a new relationship that led to disappointment when sex was attempted but failed (Gledhill and Schweitzer, 2014). It also appears that some older women expect male partners to function and assume that penetration rather than by forms of sexual pleasuring (such as oral sex) are seen as the means for securing this. For older men, penetration remains an essential signifier of manhood and other forms of physical contact such as kissing, hugging and caressing were not considered 'sexual' but more as romantic or expressions of love (Gledhill and Schweitzer, 2014).

Comparatively, this particular issue has been ignored because it poses potentially sensitive problems and moral dilemmas. Sex and intimacy with regard to older persons living with dementia is arguably a much more neglected issue. Understandings of sexual expression in persons living with dementia are rudimentary and often situated in behaviouristic and medicalised orientations, where sexual expression is viewed as problematic and unnatural and is thought of as a symptom of the dementia itself (Rennie et al, 2017). To emphasise, dementia is not a natural process of ageing, although the risks of developing dementia increase as we get older. As regards sex, persons living with dementia have to face ageing and cognitive impairment. This can be problematic given the value placed on attributes such as abilities in memorising, forming judgements and using problem-solving skills, all of which are characteristics that can decline with dementia (Noguier et al, 2017). Thus, decline in cognitive ability can often result in diminution of value and greater dependency for fulfilment of day-to-day activities. Such a paternalistic position can be detrimental to older persons who are living with dementia and especially in terms of their sexual/intimacy needs and desires.

Based on interviews with couples where one was affected by Alzheimer's Disease (AD), Dourado et al (2010) concluded that the frequency of sexual activity in couples where at least one partner was living with AD significantly decreased, which resulted in individuals feeling dissatisfied with their sex lives. Interestingly, evidence suggests a reduction in sexual satisfaction among people living with dementia and their spouses is strongly correlated with feelings of sadness, loss and increased anxiety levels (Dourado et al, 2010; Bauer et al, 2013; Noguier et al, 2017). Indeed, Dourado et al (2010) found that men living with AD and spouses generally associate sexual dissatisfaction with unhappiness compared to women, who were more likely to report greater concern with a lack of intimacy and increased anxiety. These findings support the view that sexual activity and intimacy, whether kissing and cuddling, oral sex or sexual intercourse remain important with age and greater attention to sexuality and intimacy has the potential to contribute to the quality of life of people living with dementia and their caregivers.

The need and wish to continue intimate relationships and to express one's sexuality also applies to people living in residential care. In an Australian context, it has been observed that older residents still see themselves as sexual beings with a continuous need and desire to express sexual desire (Bauer et al, 2013) whether that be physical intimacy, companionship, sex or how one is represented, irrespective of whether they lived in a residential care facility or not (Bauer et al, 2013). Similarly, Simpson et al (2018), in an English context, have found that older care residents reported missing 'being touched' in an intimate way. The majority of the participants, with dementia or otherwise, longed for intimacy and welcomed opportunities for closeness. In the Australian study just cited, there was a widespread view that people living in aged care facilities still thought about sex, and moreover, it was recognised that this was perfectly 'normal'. Even when residents may not have been interested in sexual intercourse, it was clear that other expressions of sexuality were very important to them (Bauer et al, 2013; Simpson et al, 2018).

Some of the extant academic literature has, though, started to challenge the myth that older persons are non-sexual and undesirable (see Hafford-Letchfield, 2008; Simpson et al, 2018). Also, more recently, there has been an increase in media attention (Telegraph, 2012; BBC, 2018; Telegraph, 2018). Rare headlines such as 'The taboo of sex in care homes for older people' (Weymouth, 2015) and 'Majority of over-65s would like more sex' (BBC, 2018) have featured in the BBC. These articles were drawing upon several studies, one of which claimed that over half of people over the age of 65 feel they do not have enough sex and the same proportion of over-65s stated that one of the only reasons they would stop having sex would be a lack of opportunity. Bringing this topic into the spotlight challenges assumptions not only that sex is for the young, but also the unrealistic notion that 'good' sex is only for the young. However, these headlines remain rare and are often stereotypical and very pathologically focused. Nevertheless, while the evidence base behind and the validity of these articles remains questionable and up for debate, and much more needs to be done to tackle the topic around ageing and sexuality, there is no doubt that what is published in newspapers and displayed on websites raises awareness, public interest and conversations, and has the ability to challenge taboos.

I want to conclude this section by discussing the work of Jean Malek, a photographer and filmmaker based in Montreal. Specifically, I want to focus in on one of his projects, which shines a new light on older persons. The photograph titled 'The Photo That Proves Older People Having Sex is Beautiful', taken by Montreal-based photographer and filmmaker Jean Malek, offers a challenge to the belief that sex in later life is distasteful and ugly (Brenoff, 2015). The photograph was a piece of commissioned artwork for a calendar on challenging taboos: old people having sex was one of them. The image offers a counter-narrative concerning the aesthetics of sex in later life, which can be sensual, beautiful and a very real prospect. The two volunteers in the image (a man aged 92 and a woman aged 74) show that older people still have sexual desires. This photograph conveys sensuality, passion, romance and sexual desire and demonstrates that sexual activity is important to many older persons, no matter what challenges life presents. Contrary to dominant assumptions, the image conveys that sex and intimacy are important and relevant at any age and indicates evidence of resistance and challenge to ageism and ageist erotophobia. Contrary to dominant expectations, the image claims sexual validity for older persons and indicates that they should be included in the sexual imaginary (Sabsay, 2016).

This is an incredibly rich photograph, with a mix of various elements and messages. There is a humorous element, with the couple's pet dog minding its own business and appearing to be searching for something to chew on while the couple are in the throes of passion. Malek took great care in styling the photo. He set a dish of peppermints in the scene because he felt that peppermints were symbolic of being an older person and he always considered older people to carry peppermints with them (Brenoff, 2015). For me the wallpaper, which is made up of clocks, symbolises time passing in this photograph. The artist also created the suggestion that even couples who have been together a long time can feel passion. This is represented in the photo frame that gets knocked over during the older couple's intimate moment. Additionally, the lighting on the skin (particularly on the back of the man) is incredibly rich and textured and shows off the contours of the ageing body in a very generous way. Despite the effects of ageing being shown on the bodies of the older persons, for example wrinkles, lentigines (age spots), this piece of art shows their skin in a glowing and sensitive light and conveys tenderness and intimacy, which is rarely captured in art, television, media or education.

Sexual and intimate connections at the end of life: the spark that never dies

So far, I have discussed several ways of thinking that shape how we view sex in later life. I have also argued that sexual and intimate relations we engage in throughout our lives represent connections that we can come to define as special. Further, I have shown that sexual intimacy and activity can be just as fruitful and extraordinary as we grow older. Arguably, and even more contrary to dominant thinking, I want to challenge the view that older persons, including those with dementia, are non-sexual by focusing on sex and intimacy in relation to older people approaching the end of life that is in their last years, months or days.

Evidence asserts that sexual and intimate expressions are still important to people approaching end of life (Stahl et al, 2017). However, the desire for sexual activity and intimacy is often ignored during this period (Bowden and Bliss, 2009) and often because hospice staff do not generally consider sexual expression and intimacy as a priority, overshadowed by concerns with nutrition (Taylor, 2014). Sexual intimacy remains an unmet care need in up to 75 per cent of people with advanced cancer in palliative care, and thus presents an essential quality-of-life concern (Mah, 2019). Assumptions were made about persons towards the end of life being 'too old' or 'too sick' (Matzo and Hijjazi, 2009). People receiving care may also be exposed to the attitudes and beliefs of workers who consider various types of sexual expression inappropriate for multiple reasons, including moral and/or religious ones and due to misunderstandings of age and health status (Taylor, 2014). Even when healthcare professionals are critical about later life/end of life as a non-sexual state and avoid defining sex and intimacy in limited terms (as genitally focused and penetrative), they may still fail to address sexual expression due to their own discomfort and fear that they will embarrass the people they are looking after

(Taylor, 2014). It is crucial to point out that not all people nearing the end of life are the same or have the same needs. Our sexual expression and intimacy needs are unique, and factors such as diverse cultures, ethnicity, religious beliefs, gender and sexual orientation influence our own personal values around sex and intimacy (Wiskerke and Manthorpe, 2018). Thus, it is fundamental that when thinking about sex and intimacy we have a clear understanding about these differences and many persons experiencing their end of life may have different needs and face different challenges.

Health differences and inequalities can affect sex and intimacy throughout life, including end of life. Age-related health changes, such as in the hormonal system, vascular system, illness and psychological factors can impact on sexual desire and expression. These can also include limited access to sexual information, being exposed to negative attitudes towards sexual expression, and changes in mental health (Stahl et al, 2017). A variety of health factors can impede both sexual appetite and expression. One could also have a high sexual appetite but find opportunities for sexual expression limited by structure of the care environment (lack of double rooms) or beliefs of caregivers. For example, someone who is experiencing end of life may be sleeping in a single bed as single beds are often more convenient for healthcare professionals to provide care but provide a barrier for the person to sleep and lie down with a partner. There could be a lack of privacy if the person is in a hospice, care home or hospital, or even their own home could be crowded with healthcare professionals, family and visitors. The presence of medical equipment (for example syringe drivers) may prevent physical contact or could reinforce the belief that older persons should not engage in any sexual activity. Additionally, poor pain relief and nausea control can also impact on individuals' sexual appetite and ability to engage in sex.

Intimate partnerships can be supportive and deeply valuable to people at the end of their lives. Because there are many changes occurring, both physically and emotionally, during the end-of-life process, individuals' and couples' attitudes about sexuality are likely to change (Mah, 2019). The sense of emotional connection and intimacy derived from sexual activity with one's partner is particularly valued by many people with advanced cancer (Mah, 2019). Sexual intimacy and the derived emotional connection can take on new significance in the context of terminal illness. The sense of specialness that can come from being close to someone both physically and emotionally, desiring another and being desired in return can be a life-affirming act for those who are dying (Taylor, 2014). Therefore, it is important for practitioners to consider that sex and intimacy may be a part of care planning for those with dementia and/or at the end of life. Family members and close friends could also play a role in supporting their loved one and providing them with the opportunity to have intimate moments at the end of life. This could be achieved simply by ensuring privacy for sexual expression or by investment in staff development and time to open up sensitive conversations about how to support residents' choices in this respect (Wright, 2019).

Individuals with advanced cancer and other long-term illnesses who are approaching end of life have reported that they would like clinicians to initiate sexual health discussions and especially about their intimate relationships (Redelman, 2008). This indicates that older people are generally more prepared, in appropriate circumstances and with due sensitivity and respect, to talk about their sexuality and intimacy needs. Indeed, nearing the end of life may prompt questioning that sees reluctance to address sex and intimacy (or tiptoeing around such issues) as being over-cautious/over-protective practically to the point of infantilisation and denial of autonomy. Indeed, we might ask whose sensitivities are being protected and whether this, again, reflects another form of ageist erotophobia? While advanced illness can impose significant constraints on sexual activity, especially intercourse, individuals might still welcome reassurance that not only is sexual activity possible but also that it can still pleasurable. There needs to be an understanding that if there is a decline in sexual activity and sexual intimacy, feelings of emotional disconnection, sense of separation and loneliness may then escalate, as sexual intimacy is often seen as an important aspect of emotional connectedness. Additionally, during the end-of-life process, couples may become nervous or assume the other does not want to discuss sexual activity during this phase of their relationship (Lemieux et al, 2004).

In the previous section I argued for the need to move beyond myths that sex is not really for older people. The same could be said concerning people facing the end of life. The specialness of sex may involve new approaches such as appreciating physical and emotional closeness and cuddling, handholding, kissing, caressing, massage, sexual touch without intercourse, and conversations about intimate feelings. Indeed, nearing the end of life may mean that that the need for closeness is deepened and sexuality may be transformed from sexual intercourse to include a broader understanding of it. Towards the end of life, individuals and couples may look for shared meaning in their lives and relationships. Lemiex et al (2004) found that couples who spoke of experiencing such a change reported it as very satisfying. However, it is important to consider that many individuals who are at the end of life will not be in a committed relationship and may be unpartnered. Overall, we should never forget that sexual intercourse and other forms of sexual activity such as oral sex are important for many people at this time too, and they need to be reassured that it is perfectly 'normal' to experience these feelings. The end of life can also be experienced as a time when relationships, intimacy and human connections reach a new level. Sensuality and love for a partner may be at their most vital, whether this involves enjoying the passions of intercourse, oral sex or intimate connections.

Taking research, policy and practice to a new and sexier level

It has been argued that meeting needs for sex and intimacy in later life requires a holistic approach that takes into account various lifestyle factors, needs, preferences and cultural differences (Wright, 2019). A change in health status may be only one of many other factors influencing sexual activity and satisfaction in later life but research on sexual activity and relationships in later life has maintained its focus on issues of decline, dysfunction and dissatisfaction. Despite the importance of sexual activity and satisfaction to well-being and quality of life, this aspect of older people's health has received inadequate public and professional attention, though, as noted earlier, the time is ripe for change in this respect, especially as post-war baby boomers now in later life have grown up and grown older in a social and moral climate that more positively sanctions talk on bodily and sexual autonomy (Zordan, 2009).

Sex and intimacy in later life should be addressed within social policy, sex education and ageing policies. Sexual intimacy needs to be made more integral to healthcare assessment and provision by giving attention to older people's wishes to maintain a healthy sexual life as one of their human rights. Sexuality should be viewed and treated from a broad perspective, addressing its biological, psychological and social aspects, as well as the diverse range of sexual desire, preferences and intimacy needs of older persons. Further, and considering effects of intersectional identities, all those involved in needs assessment and provision could take stock of how needs will differ. For instance, a black lesbian-identified working class older woman/resident will need different support concerning sexuality and intimacy compared to a white middle-class older man/resident.

If we are to advance thought and practice on later life sexuality, it is important for carers, healthcare professionals, family members, academics and people more generally to familiarise themselves with the sexual and intimacy issues encountered by diverse older people, to examine their own values and beliefs with respect to this 'taboo' topic and to ensure that they are open to consultation and discussion when appropriate. Older persons will benefit from sensitive, trained support to avoid concealing sexual problems and embarrassment and to ensure that deep-rooted cultural issues are accepted and addressed. There is a need for more positive perceptions of older people's sexuality, recognising the diversity of late-life sexual desire and legitimising other ways in which older adults can express this. Indeed, it is vital that the voices of older persons are included in research and as co-producers of research about *their* lives as one way of influencing policy and practice. Developing awareness will depend as much on care providers and the general public taking stock of how their assumptions about who counts as sexual and what counts as sex in relation to diverse older people to avoid the pitfalls of a homogenising, one-size-fits-all approach to meeting sexuality/intimacy needs.

Conclusion

In this chapter I have called for recognition of the overlooked special significance of sex in later life and that we recognise and celebrate the intimate connections of older persons. In general, ageist myths have led the general public and older adults themselves to believe that sexual desire ceases in later life. Contrary to pervasive stereotypes, the need for physical closeness, intimacy and sexual contact does not diminish with age or because of co-morbidities, loss of capacity or when we are experiencing the end of life. Ultimately, sexual desires and intimate connections are essential to identity and being and 'doing' human. Sexual expression and intimacy are fundamental aspects of who an individual is and their overall well-being, throughout the life course.

Older people commonly speak of sexual intimacy as important but also value it for the maintenance of relationships and expression of love. Sexual activity and physical intimacy are, nevertheless, important to many older persons and the oldest old. As older persons encounter health issues that affect their sexual function, many adopt a wider definition of sexual activity. In general, older men and women are not without agency and can establish their own pathways to intimacy and making space for the views and concerns of a population that otherwise might not be heard. While some older people report understanding sexuality beyond genitocentric intercourse, expression of their sexuality is often delegitimised and thus subject to constraints. Myths and stereotypes that deny rights to sexual desire are attributable to lack of knowledge about the realities of older people's lives, which is itself animated by a widespread ageist erotophobia. Additionally, those living in long-term care facilities – generally the oldest and many affected by dementia – are likely to be influenced by wider social attitudes as well by the context of the long-term care environment. It is important, therefore, to ensure that residents' rights to intimacy and to express their sexuality are not neglected. However, the good news is that some older persons and their allies are beginning to resist ageist erotophobia. Finally, the existing literature has largely overlooked sexuality and intimacy in those who are experiencing their end of life. If palliative care professionals and scholars are to provide holistic care, supporting one's sexual expression is essential. This requires us to challenge our values and beliefs about what is significant to every individual and any assumptions we might have about differences for example of gender and old age and infirmity as equating with lack of agency and desire.

References

Bauer, M., Fetherstonhaugh, D., Tarzia, A., Nay, R., Wellman, D. and Beattie, E. (2013) '"I Always Look Under the Bed for a Man". Needs and Barriers to the Expression of Sexuality in Residential Aged Care: the Views of Residents with and Without Dementia', *Psychology and Sexuality*, 4(3): 296–309.

BBC (2018) 'Majority of over-65s would like more sex', BBC, [online] 14 February, https://www.bbc.co.uk/news/health-43044912.

Benbow, S.M. and Beeston, D. (2012) 'Sexuality, Aging and Dementia', *International Psychogeriatics*, 24(7): 1026–33.

Bowden, G. and Bliss, J. (2009) 'Does a Hospital Bed Impact on Sexuality Expression in Palliative Care?' *British Journal of Community Nursing*, 14(3): 122–6.

Brenoff, A. (2015) 'The Photo that Proves Older People Having Sex is Beautiful', HuffPost UK, [online] 3 September, https://www.huffingtonpost.co.uk/entry/old-people-sex-photos_us_5

Dourado, M., Finamore, C., Barroso, M.F., Santos, R. and Laks, J. (2010) 'Sexual Satisfaction in Dementia: Perspectives of Patients and Spouses', *Sexuality and Disability*, 28(3): 195–203.

Drummond, J.D., Brotman, S., Silverman, M., Sussman, T., Orzeck, P., Barylak, L. and Wallach, I. (2013) 'The Impact of Caregiving: Older Women's Experiences of Sexuality and Intimacy', *Affilia: Journal of Women & Social Work*, 28(4): 415–28.

Dumpleton, H. (1992) *Sex: A Four Letter Word? An Intriguing Look at the Relationship between Sex and Spirit*. New South Wales: Southwood Press.

Freak-Poli, R., Kirkman, M., Lima, G.D.C., Direk, N., Franco, O.H. and Tiemeier, H. (2017) 'Sexual Activity and Physical Tenderness in Older Adults: Cross-sectional Prevalence and Associated Characteristics', *The Journal of Sexual Medicine*, 14(7), 918–27.

Gewirtz-Meyden, A., Hafford-Letichfield, T., Ayalon, L., Benyamini, Y., Biremann, V., Coffey, A., Jackson, J., Phelan, P.V., Zeman, M.G. and Zeman, Z. (2018) 'How Do Older People Discuss Their Own Sexuality? A Systematic Review of Qualitative Research Studies', *Culture, Health & Sexuality*, 21(3): 293–308.

Gledhill, S. and Schweitzer, R.D. (2014) 'Sexual Desire, Erectile Dysfunction and the Biomedicalization of Sex in Older Heterosexual Men', *Journal of Advanced Nursing*, 70(4): 2093–103.

Grant, M.J. and Booth, A. (2009) 'A Typology of Reviews: an Analysis of 14 Review Types and Associated Methodologies', *Health Information and Libraries*, 26(2): 91–108.

Hafford-Letchfield P. (2008). 'What's Love Got to Do with It? Developing Supportive Practices for the Expression of Sexuality, Sexual Identity and the Intimacy Needs of Older People', *Journal of Care Services Management* 2(4): 389–405.

Hills, R. (2014) 'What Every Generation Gets Wrong About Sex', *Time* [online] 2 December, https://time.com/3611781/sexual-revolution-revisited/

Leiblum, S.R. (1998) 'Definition and Classification of Female Sexual Disorders', *International Journal of Impotence Research*, 10(2): S102–S106.

Lemieux, L., Kaiser, S., Pereira, J. and Meadows, L.M. (2004) 'Sexuality in Palliative Care: Patient Perspectives', *Palliative Medicine*, 18(7): 630–7.

Loe, M. (2004) 'Sex and the Senior Woman: Pleasure and Danger in the Viagra Era', *Sexualities*, 7(3): 303–26.

Maataoui, S.L., Hardwick, J.S., and Lundquist, T.S. (2017) 'Creating Space for Relationships', *Psychological Services*, 14(3): 347–51.

Mah, K. (2019) 'Existential Loneliness and the Importance of Addressing Sexual Health in People with Advanced Cancer in Palliative Care', *Psycho-Oncology*, 28(6): 1354–6.

Malta, S. (2007) 'Love Actually! Older Adults and Their Romantic Internet Relationships', *Australian Journal of Emerging Technologies and Society*, 5(2): 84–102.

Masters, W. and Johnson, V.E. (1966) *Human Sexual Response*. Boston, MA: Little, Brown.

Matzo, M. and Hijjazi, K. (2009). 'If You Don't Ask Me … Don't Expect Me to Tell', *Journal of Hospice Palliative Nursing*, 11(5): 271–81.

Ménard, D., Kleinplatz, P.J., Rosen, L., Lawless, S., Paradis, N., Campbell, M. and Huber, J.D. (2015) 'Individual and Relational Contributors to Optimal Sexual Experience in Older Men and Women', *Sexual and Relationship Therapy*, 30(1): 78–93.

Noguira, M.M.L., Neto, J.P.S., Sounsa, M.F.B., Sanos, R.L., Lacerda, I.B., Baptista, M.A.T. and Dourado, M.C.N. (2017) 'Perception of Change in Sexual Activity in Alzheimer's Disease: Views of People with Dementia and Their Spouse-caregiver', *International Psychogeriatrics*, 29(2): 185–93.

Redelman, M.J. (2008) 'Is There a Place for Sexuality in the Holistic Care of Patients in the Palliative Care Phases of Life?' *American Journal of Hospice and Palliative Medicine*, 25(5): 366–71.

Rennie, K., Dewing, J. and Banks, D. (2017) 'Sexual Expression by Persons Living with Dementia', *Journal of the All Ireland Gerontological Nurses Association*, 4(1): 20–5.

Sabsay L. (2016) 'Diversity and the Sexual Imaginary'. In: *The Political Imaginary of Sexual Freedom. Studies in the Psychosocial*. London: Palgrave Macmillan, pp 31–38.

Simpson, P., Wilson, C.B., Brown, L.J.E., Dickinson, T. and Horne, M. (2018) ' "We've Had Our Sex Life Way Back": Older Care Home Residents, Sexuality and Intimacy', *Ageing & Society*, 38(7): 1478–501.

Stahl, K.A., Bower, K L., Seponski, D.M., Lewis, D.C., Farnham, A.L. and Cava-Tadik, Y. (2017) 'A Practitioner's Guide to End-Of-Life Intimacy: Suggestions for Conceptualization and Intervention in Palliative Care', *Journal of Death and Dying*, 77(1): 15–35.

Taylor, B. (2014) 'Experiences of Sexuality and Intimacy in Terminal Illness: a Phenomenological Study', *Palliative Medicine*, 28(5): 438–47.

Telegraph (2012) 'Sex gets better with age says scientist', *The Telegraph* [online] 4 January, https://www.telegraph.co.uk/news/science/science-news/8992519/Sex-gets-better-with-age-say-scientists.html

Telegraph (2018) 'The truth about intimacy for older couples', *The Telegraph* [online] 30 November, https://www.telegraph.co.uk/health-fitness/living-with-erectile-dysfunction/why-sex-is-better-when-older/

Tiefer, L. (1991) 'Historical, Scientific, Clinicical and Feminist Criticisms of "The Human Sexual Response"', *Annual Review of Sex Research*, 2(1): 1–23.

Trudel, G., Turgeon, L. and Piche, L. (2010) 'Marital and Sexual Aspects of Old Age', *Sexual and Relationship Therapy*, 15(4): 381–406.

Weymouth, A. (2015) 'The taboo of sex in care homes for older people', BBC [online] 27 June, https://www.bbc.co.uk/news/magazine-33278117

Wiskerke, E. and Manthorpe, J. (2018) 'New Relationships and Intimacy in Long-term Care: The Views of Relatives of Residents with Dementia and Care Home Staff', *Dementia*, 17(4): 405–22.

World Health Organization (2018) 'Ageing and Health', The World Health Organization [online] 5 February, https://www.who.int/news-room/fact-sheets/detail/ageing-and-health

Wright, J. (2019) 'Addressing Sexuality and Intimacy in People Living with Parkinson's During Palliative Care and at the End of Life', *British Journal of Nursing*, 28(12): 772–9.

Yun, O., Kim, M. and Chung, S.E. (2014). 'The Sexuality Experience of Older Widows in Korea', *Qualitative Heath Research*, 21(4): 474–83.

Zordan, D. (2009) 'Too Old for That Kind of Thing? Sexuality and Unshareable Desire in Dresen's Cloud 9', *Theology and Sexuality*, 15(3): 283–92.

4

Heterosexual sex, love and intimacy in later life: what have older women got to say?

Trish Hafford-Letchfield

Introduction

The current epistemology of heterosexuality, love and intimacy in later life has highlighted how older women's sexual desire and sexual expression have been subject to highly gendered socio-cultural restrictions, an emphasis on relationship status and problematisation of physical health. These are associated with dissatisfaction and discomfort for older heterosexual women when talking about their own sexuality with a lack of social legitimacy for doing so. Poor engagement of care professionals with their issues and concerns makes the situation more complex (Hafford-Letchfield, 2008; Gertwitz et al, 2018), for example in terms of the unproblematic acceptance of the consequences and compromise in sexual function that may be constructed when an older woman has pelvic floor weaknesses including incontinences (Mota, 2017).

This chapter reviews some themes on heterosexual desire and sexual expression in later life within the context of socio-cultural and health-related factors. I draw on several sources. First, selected theoretical concepts on heterosexuality in terms of how these speak to the sexual identities of women in later life, or indeed, throughout the life course. Second, I review further some relevant themes from a systematic review I was involved in (Gerwitz et al, 2018) of international empirical research about sexuality and ageing. This review included subjective views of older heterosexual women on their sexuality. Third, heterosexual sex, love and intimacy in later life are illustrated through the case study of women ageing solo, where relationship status has been a key factor in mediating desire and expressions of intimacy in later life (Hafford-Letchfield et al, 2017; Lambert et al, 2018; O'Reilly et al, 2020). These sources will enable focus on factors that differentiate between expression of sexual desire and subsequent pursuance of sexual relationships in later life. I will consider how gender norms and performativity pertinent to existing heterosexual women's sexuality are impacted by external and internalised stigma that accompany ageing and/or are made complex in situations where health is affected. These key themes are examined from a standpoint that highlights discrimination and oppression by placing the voices of heterosexual older women at the centre of a relational analysis of sexuality. This is in opposition to those ageist social practices that pose barriers to older people, especially older women, being able to speak about and make the best decisions concerning their sexual and intimate lives and to access more appropriate responses in support (Hafford-Letchfield, 2008; Lee and Tetley, 2017).

The overall aim of this chapter is to continually centre women's experiences, and bring them into critical discussion with the hegemonic structures highlighting both their historic roots and contemporary expressions. This chapter also highlights the sidelining of women's desires and bodies particularly in relation to sexual functioning, and draws on empirical work to underpin these concepts on agency and power.

Theoretical concepts concerning heterosexuality

Heterosexuality has been described as a 'given' or 'silent term' (Kitzinger and Wilkinson, 1993, p 3) in which everyday sexuality is barely realised, implicit and embodied. This is unlike the labelling of other sexual and gender identities where *differences* are emphasised and made to explain themselves. Within the history of feminist theorising on sexual identities, the gay/straight divide occupies a pole position and tends to obscure any intersectionalities that relate to sexual identities such as race, class and age. Hockey et al (2007, p 6) suggest that the downplaying of differences and highlighting of heterogeneity is what sustains an individual's judgement of their own experiences against the 'unitary category of heterosexuality'. It is these practices combined with gendered ageism, by which I mean discriminatory actions, whether intentional or non-intentional, that are based on the intersection of gender and age such as in access to health and pensions and other structural forces which impact on heterosexual expressions of sex, intimacies and relationships. Hockey et al (2007) further posit:

> [B]y engaging with heterosexuality as a dominant, pervasive and invisible social category, we begin to understand what is occurring when 'heterosexuality' becomes the implicit

focus for sometimes painful processes of reflexivity. Being 'everywhere and nowhere', heterosexuality resists critical reflection, yet demands conformity, a point which extends to invisible or unmarked identities. (Hockey et al, 2007, p 4)

Theorisation by Butler (1990, 1993) of the social construction of (hetero)sexuality emphasises the repeated performances that imitate its own idealisations, norms and social practices. With regard to sexual practices, some scholars (Rich, 1980; Jenkins, 2004) articulate how an entire system of social organisation can be embodied in private moments of physical and emotional longing which promote relational heterosexual practice as hegemonic in Western societies. The constant reminder of its idealised features concerning lifelong, monogamous, cohabiting relationships are more often than not legally sanctioned through marriage and childbearing. These everyday performances of heterosexuality, and subject to its organising principles (Rich, 1980), provide a wealth of images, narratives and representations against which individuals evaluate their own experiences, including those of their partners, parents, children and grandchildren (Hockey et al, 2007). Where these do not fit, according to Hockey and James (2003), are the silences which remind individuals of the instability of heterosexuality as an institution and 'of the social, emotional and economic implications of transgressing its contours and boundaries' (Hockey et al, 2007, p 124). Further, the absence of positive and powerful counter-narratives, where any deviation from heterosexual performativity can become disparaged and stigmatised, constrains the possibilities of identity for all women. Academic research, for example on older heterosexual women's relationship status, is surprisingly sparse and relatively underdeveloped, with few empirical investigations, most of which are coming from a feminist discursive analysis (Lahad and Hazan, 2014; Hafford-Letchfield et al, 2017). Further, such research is usually conducted within the context of long-term marriage, rather than among single, dating older adults (Bulcroft and Bulcroft, 1991), who may, arguably, have different sexual profiles.

The different ways of theorising heterosexuality within social and political theory as just illustrated have brought an historical approach to the diversity of heterosexual practices. These ways of thinking are underpinned by feminist epistemology, life course and ageing theories, thus giving rise to a diversity of conceptualisations of heterosexuality between and within these different theoretical positions. These are useful in finding new ways of speaking about it (or against it, in terms of heteronormativity) and illustrate how later life female heterosexuality itself works intersectionally along axes of class, ethnicity, disability and so on. A focus on sexual experience for women in later life regarding sexual pleasure cannot be separated from an analysis of male power symbolised through emphasis on penile penetration and robust gendered patterns of sex and intimacy, with strong traditional and patriarchal versions of how things are or should be in a heterosexual relationship. More recently, there has been attention to structure and agency and sexual fluidity in relationships (Hafford-Letchfield and Dunk-West, 2018). However, the prevalence of domestic abuse and sexual violence in its various guises indicates that many men have retained their right to enforce their domination of women through sexual relationships even as these relationships evolve and mature in a changing society. Some older women may have grown up in an era in which they lacked an appropriate language to talk about sex and where gender, class and age militated against the seizing of body autonomy. They also may have lacked the means or resources to make decisions that supported their decision-making and choice around subsequent relationships such as in marriage and having children (Hockey, 2007).

One significant achievement of feminism has been to challenge the notion of 'compulsory heterosexuality' (Rich, 1980) as implicit in the previous paragraph, and has opened up space for critical exploration of ageing lesbian, bisexual and transgendered women whose experiences are only just beginning to be systematically researched (Ribbens McCarthy and Edwards, 2011; Traies, 2016). More generally, the study of gender and sexuality within ageing populations has been growing and is more urgent given our need to understand the different life trajectories, diversity and their wider implications for society and culture. This is particularly important in the context of an ageing population and one in which the welfare state is rolling back its provision with disproportionate impact on women (Lambert et al, 2018). Women's changing circumstances, attitudes and behaviours affect their experience of ageing at both an individual and societal level and need to be addressed by governments, policy makers and service providers in terms of any rethinking of appropriate policies and provision. At the same time, gendered ageism is being better articulated within research and draws attention to the importance of socio-cultural, spatial and temporal contexts in which it occurs and the dynamics involved in the creation and reproduction of social reality, including social inequalities (Hockey et al, 2007). In this chapter and in this text generally, it is asserted that sex, love and intimacy are intrinsic to contemporary debates on gender.

Influences on older women's sexual and intimate relationships

Some recent trends observed in later life relationships have challenged aspects of the institutions that shore up heterosexuality. Writing from the UK, a snapshot of data from UK National Statistics, for example (ONS, 2017), shows that older people in England and Wales are getting married and divorced in greater numbers (taking into account the ageing population). These so-called 'silver splicers' and 'silver separators', and baby boomers who are doing things differently and challenging the norm, reveal that 'brides' and 'grooms' aged 65 and over went up by 46 per cent in the last decade (the population grew by 20 per cent in the same period and as a proportion of the single, divorced or widowed population). This meant that there was still an increase for both sexes after 2009. Men are tending to marry younger women (56%) and women aged 65 and over married a man under 65 (22%). Almost all (92%) of these marriage partners aged 65 and over in 2014 were divorcees, widows or widowers, with only 8 percent getting married for the first time (ONS, 2017).

Likewise, research into the sexual health and well-being of men and women in later life equally demonstrates increasing expectations concerning sexual fulfilment (PHE, 2019). A higher proportion of men (50+) than women of this age reported being sexually active in the past year (ONS, 2017). These findings are thought to reflect how women are more likely to be living without a partner because of widowhood or divorce and not having a new partner. Given this diversification of the sexual health and well-being needs of people across the life course, it is now clear that sexual health policy and services to older people need to step up. These are particularly limited given the increasing rates of sexually transmitted infections (STIs), with the largest proportional increase in gonorrhoea (42%) and chlamydia (24%) seen in people over 65. Public Health England (PHE, 2019) conversely suggest that the substantial changes in sexual lifestyles in the UK in the past 60 years seem to be greater in women than men. The continuation of sexual activity into later life emphasises that attention to sexual health and well-being is needed, including a better understanding of the barriers and support needed to maintain, achieve and fulfil heterosexual goals. This might address women's embarrassment about seeking advice from health professionals due to sexist and ageist stereotypes. Services are likely to be challenged by particular cohorts of ageing populations who will continue more 'liberal' sexual attitudes from the boomer generation. As far back as in 1998, Jamieson highlighted that seeking sexual pleasure now incites a more varied sexual repertoire than conventional heterosexual sex. Giddens' (1992) theorising on the shift towards 'plastic sexuality', which is sexuality freed from the needs and demands of reproduction, has also been associated with greater equality and disclosure about intimacy between sexual partners. This is not to say that the concept of plastic sexuality has not been critiqued, given that such a transformation would call into question many other gendered and oppressive institutions in which love and sexuality remain embedded (Jamieson, 1998). A question to ask of the research literature, then, concerns whether there are routinely produced links and separations between intimacy and sexual relationships or behaviours in the everyday lives of heterosexual older people that help us understand how these statistical factors are affecting their sexual lives. Giddens' thesis has been critiqued by feminists who insist that the personal is social and, according to Jamieson (1998), feeds into a therapeutic discourse that *individualises* personal problems and, by not getting behind the statistics, tells us very little about the intersection of a multiplicity of discourses by which bodies, pleasures and powers are circulated and exchanged. By saying yes to sex, older women are not always saying no to power. We will go on to look at some of these nuances in the research which highlights heterosexual women's voices about sex in later life.

What does research tell us about older heterosexual women's sex lives?

Research suggests that remaining sexually active contributes to the quality of life and well-being of heterosexual older people (Hinchliff and Gott, 2011; Hinchcliff et al, 2016; Lee and Tetley, 2017). Less is known about sexuality from the subjective viewpoints of people in later life as opposed to quantitative studies, which mainly focused on sexual behaviour, sexual health and sexual dysfunctions (for example, Lindau et al, 2007; Lee et al, 2016). Research has focused on the perspectives of staff and family members regarding later life sexuality, rather than those of people themselves (for example, Bauer et al, 2015; Villar et al, 2016). Given this apparent dearth, a systematic review that I was involved in (Gertwitz-Meydan et al, 2018) placed older people's voices at the centre of analysis to provide an opportunity to understand their views about their own sexuality and how these perspectives might meet their needs and shape services and support. Thematic synthesis from 20 studies (spanning 1987–2015) were used to generate 'analytical themes' which summarised this body of literature. The methods used to conduct the review have been reported elsewhere (Gertwitz-Meydan et al, 2018). Here I have returned to the original contributory literature to reiterate and consider some of the insights offered into the experiences of heterosexual women in three key themes reported in the review as outlined in the following subsections.

Theme one: social legitimacy for sexuality in later life

This theme concerned the impact of the socialisation and legitimacy on how women viewed their sexual selves in later life. Many study participants included women reporting how they were perceived as asexual (de Oliveira Silva et al, 2015) or sexually invisible (Bayler-Levaro, 2011). Women described a social silence regarding their sexuality and intimacy, which made raising these issues with friends, family, or service providers uncomfortable (Drummond et al, 2013). Their invisibility as sexual beings also reflects a 'western' orientation (in consumer societies) toward youthfulness and beauty, which could make women feel less inhibited by personal sexual expression but more inhibited by social norms and perceived social legitimacy (Rowntree, 2014). Negative attitudes towards expressing sexuality in later life compelled women to further conceal their sexuality and adopt more modest sexual dress and to avoid attracting attention as a 'cougar', a term used to describe 'older' women who assertively pursue sexual partners where they are seen as predatory on hapless younger males (Montemurro and Siefken, 2014). Social norms and delegitimisation were not always direct barriers to sexual expression in later life but accepting these norms could inhibit sexual expression. Yun et al (2014), for example, found that sexual desire in later life was mediated by concerns of societal opinions of older people engaging in sexual activities or new romantic relationships. It was more socially accepted that men would still wish to engage in penetrative sex, while women would be satisfied with 'cuddling' (Fournier, 2000, p 100). The availability of drugs for treating erectile dysfunction provided a more legitimate basis accepted by society (Loe, 2004). Older women did not have these options to the same degree, albeit Hormone Replacement Therapy (HRT) has addressed some issues about comfort and ease in relation to penetrative sex. However, where women did not support their partners using Viagra, some saw expectations of diminished sexual interest with age as a welcome relief and as a legitimate means of escaping this 'oppressive' aspect of their lives (Rowntree, 2014). This was also an opportunity to experiment and to engage in practices which are not focused on penetration (Loe, 2004).

Despite these constraining messages, age did not always prevent women from enjoying satisfying sexual experiences (de Oliveira Silva et al, 2015). Freedom from social norms that inhibited them when younger allowed the person to re-evaluate their understanding of sex and sexuality, to attempt new sexual techniques and to enjoy a better sex life than experienced earlier in life (Menard et al, 2015). Yet, engaging in sexual activities or expressing sexuality still caused many, particularly women, to feel shame and guilt and demanded secrecy between generations, making sex a very private matter (Nyanzi, 2011). Some turned to online communication (for example cybersex) to express their sexuality (Malta, 2007) and establish new romantic relationships, which included acting younger and distancing themselves from the term *old* (Bayler-Levaro, 2011), or by finding a partner younger than themselves (Loe, 2004). These actions facilitated *greater* social legitimacy for expressions of sexuality.

Theme two: sexuality and health

The review highlighted how the ageing process affected people's sexual lives, and the mutual relationship between sexuality and health. Maintaining a sex life was seen by older people in several studies as an integral part of healthy and positive ageing (Loe, 2004; Bayler-Levaro, 2011; Yan et al, 2011; Menard et al, 2015). In one study, they articulated active sex lives as a symbol of vitality and longevity (Yan et al, 2011), but which was dependent on physical health and well-being (Sandberg, 2013; de Oliveira Silva et al, 2015). Within these studies there were rich descriptions of how maintaining an active sexual life promotes psychological health (see Ravanipour et al, 2013). Women who were physically active and who were taking little or no medication, reported higher levels of sexual desire (Malta, 2007). At the same time, this could present new pressures and expectations of ageing, one which sits alongside or rivals the narrative of a sexless older age.

Sexual activity, sexual intimacy and sexual desire were limited by physical impairments or medical conditions (Bauer et al, 2013; Roney and Kazer, 2015). Declining physical functioning of a partner or concerns over a partner's medical condition constituted a primary reason to stop having sex (Drummond et al, 2013; Roney and Kazer, 2015). Women reported concerns about male partners with enlarged prostates and vascular conditions such as heart problems and high blood pressure where both the condition, and the medication taken for it, contributed to erectile dysfunction (Fournier, 2000).

There were intersecting realities of caregiving and ageing, which together undermined women's self-actualisation separate from their role as caregivers and challenged self-perceptions of being sexual or desirable (Drummond, 2013). Losing control over bodily functions, such as incontinence associated with prostate surgery, can alter relationships and day-to-day functioning (Lowe, 2004). For women, declining oestrogen levels can result in lower levels of sexual desire, vaginal dryness and atrophy, and painful intercourse (Fournier, 2000; Ravanipour et al, 2013). Again, these challenges have the potential to impact on hegemonic constructions of what 'sex' actually is.

Healthcare providers were often referred to as not being willing to ask about or discuss older people's sexual needs, even where these were potentially treatable (Drummond et al, 2013; Roney and Kazer, 2015). This stereotyping of older people as asexual prevailed in medical consultations, which was very disappointing for the older person and lacked any reflection of their needs and realities (Bauer et al, 2013; Drummond et al, 2013) to be able to function sexually. Women in particular reported a negative impact on their expectations of being sexually fulfilled and their ability to cope and ultimately on their identities (Bauer et al, 2013; Drummond et al, 2013). Further, women were rarely consulted when treatments were offered to their male partners.

Despite being highly correlated with health, the biomedicalisation of sex can be a disappointing experience. This was particularly true when changes in sexual function as a result of medical conditions or ageing were conceptualised via biomedical terms and in relation to hormones or pathology (Gledhill and Schweitzer, 2014). Some treatments for enhancing performance created further anxiety and were described as interfering with health by 'putting up a brand-new flagpole on a condemned building' (Fournier, 2000, p 898). Whether or not male partners chose to use pharmaceuticals, they were frequently offered (in various forms of pills, pumps and injections) instead of other interventions (Fournier, 2000; Gledhill and Schweitzer, 2014).

In short, Gewirtz-Meydan et al (2018) talk about the hegemony of penetrative sex in the way they describe the progression of definitional components for sexual activity. According to theorisations by Malta (2007), sex means intercourse; intercourse means vaginal penetration; and vaginal penetration requires penile erection. This schema accompanied by sexual desire and loss of sexual function gave rise to feelings of distress, disappointment, frustration, shock and fear of failure, which led to despair, devastation and a sense of hopelessness (Loe, 2004) striking deep into the *heart of masculinity* (Gledhill and Schweitzer, 2014, p 899). Conversely, men able to sustain an erection in later life are promoted to 'hero' status (Gledhill and Schweitzer 2014, p 900) as they have preserved a 'normal' sexual life (Menard et al, 2015).

Theme three: penetrative sex in heterosexual relationships as hegemony

Gewirtz-Meydan et al (2018) cited the hegemony of penetrative sex associated with social norms and socially acceptable gender roles. For example, there was very little reference to masturbation as a means of pleasure (Malta, 2007). Within the studies they reviewed, most participants spoke of how penetrative intercourse as normative and definitive was both important and desirable in their romantic and intimate relationships (Malta, 2007). For older women, the desire for sexual intercourse as standard was fully expressed and they lamented the short supply of healthy men who could perform adequately (Loe, 2004). One study documented the impact of physical limitations in new relationships that led to disappointment and sorrow when sex was attempted (Gledhill and Schweitzer, 2014). Men unable to achieve an erection were considered suitable for friendship but not as romantic partners. Some women expected everything in their sexual partner to work and wanted to be satisfied with penetration rather than by other sexual pleasuring, such as oral sex (Loe, 2004). For both men and women, other forms of physical contact such as kissing, hugging and caressing were not considered 'sexual', but romantic or expressions of love (Yan et al, 2011). For women, the availability of Viagra-type drugs was seen as an opportunity to open new conversations about their feelings or about wanting sex (Loe, 2004). Women found themselves having to balance their partners' needs for sexual potency with the health risks and negotiation involved (Loe, 2004) due to side-effects such as heart complications and sudden death. These presented a narrative of mortal danger along with a miracle (Loe, 2004).

Drugs for treating erectile dysfunction were not, however, always welcomed by women, particularly if this meant that their sexual lives were reactivated by such treatments (Loe, 2004). This PDE5i-driven threat of heterosexual penetrative sex constituted an invasion of an emotional safe space after some women decided they no longer needed or wanted sex. This reinforced discourse about what sex is or was expected to be, which emphasised penetrative sex and ejaculation and the male sex drive (Yan et al, 2011).

In summary, the voices of heterosexual men and women described their sexuality in two ways. While penetration remained the gold-standard, alternative ways of viewing sex and sexuality emphasise relationships beyond genital functionality and the imperative of penetration (Loe, 2004). Both sexes spoke openly about achieving sexual satisfaction through alternate sexual skills they learned and developed without the need for erections and penetration (Sandberg, 2013). By including physical contact, such as hugging, kissing, cuddling and holding hands in the equation, many experienced a satisfactory sense of sexuality and men were able to successfully reconstruct their sexual identity despite erectile dysfunction.

Key messages from the literature

The brief overview of thematic synthesis reiterated here (Gertwitz-Meydan et al, 2018) of subjective views about sexuality in later life revealed that the challenges of ageing can enable women to explore and experiment with their sexuality. Cognitive and psychological changes can result in a greater sense of entitlement for pleasure. They can also lead to a reappraisal of what women want, sometimes accompanied by a loosening of inhibitions (Yun et al, 2014). Sex in later life was described as 'greater' (Menard et al, 2015, p 84), perhaps due to the growing knowledge of one's own body, individual agency which comes with the resources of ageing – epistemic and emotional – and enables some older people to question the ageism around their sexuality. Also sex was described as the ability to derive pleasure from it (alone or partnered), feeling more comfortable with partners, with changing sexual practices and with less attention to fertility (Loe, 2004). The quality of the relationships was often of more importance and offered mediation for those women who may feel unhappy with their ageing bodies, which might otherwise have impacted on their willingness to express themselves sexually (Thorpe et al, 2015).

The review reflected thinking that sexuality in later life can be interpreted more broadly and consisting of more than penetrative sex, although this remained a popular discourse reinforced by the dominance of the biomedical view of sexuality in old age. Disability, illness, sexual dysfunction or simply life experience facilitated an appreciation of other aspects of sexuality, such as coexistence, affection and companionship. Again, this may tie into reflexive resources of ageing referred to earlier that transcend the misery narrative of later life as an inevitable slide into sexlessness and decrepitude. Across studies, people specified that sexuality in later years produced richer and deeper feelings than those experienced earlier in life, and reported more pleasure from varied aspects of sexuality such as cuddling, foreplay, masturbation and so on. A recent study confirmed these changes (Hinchcliff et al, 2016).

Research findings revealed the importance of giving attention to health and physical impairments when discussing sexuality. Descriptive themes focused on sexuality in the light of deteriorating health. Researchers often equate problems related to sexuality with health status among older individuals. All three themes from the Gertwitz-Meydan et al (2018) review illustrated the complex and delicate relationship between ageing and heterosexual sexuality. As people encounter health issues that affect their sexual function, they adopt a wider definition of sexual activity. Social constraints and delegitimisation affect their sense of autonomy and well-being and narrow their indicators of how successful they are in remaining sexual and/or expressing their sexuality. All of the studies included in this review referred to people expressing discomfort, anxiety and embarrassment when talking about their own sexuality. This is consistent with the invisibility and delegitimisation of sexuality among older people and as discussed earlier in the chapter, the sociocultural and historical circumstances experienced during their life course. Sex was and still is an even greater taboo, given that exposure to sexual education earlier in their lives was probably limited (Loe, 2004; Bayler-Levaro, 2011). These silences are further enshrined in many areas of government policy and practice in relation to providing support for ageing and can mirror the invisibility of older people, particularly through a gendered lens, that is manifested in other areas of society (Hafford-Letchfield, 2008). Further they hardly address some of the differences within the ageing population in relation to differences between the young old and the older old where different histories and lifestyles will impact on their current expectations and sense of agency.

There was evidence that women are 'forging their own pathways to intimacy' (Marshall, 2012, p 341), eliciting the emotional side of this important issue. There is potential for making space for the views and concerns of a population that otherwise might not be heard. A more nuanced understanding of the needs and sexual realities of people in later life can also help empower their lives (Bauer et al, 2013). These empirical findings have much to offer those responsible for providing support by giving attention to a person's wishes to maintain a healthy sexual life as they age, as one of their human rights. Sexuality should be viewed and treated from a broad perspective, addressing the biopsychosocial aspects, as well as the diverse sexualities of heterosexual women, many of whom may experiment with their sexual and gender identities in later life.

Relationship status and ageing solo

I conclude this chapter with reference to our research into the impact of relationship status on sexuality and intimacy for women in later life, particularly given the silences and pending recent expansion of these themes within the conceptual and empirical literature on heterosexuality (Hafford-Letchfield et al, 2017; Lambert et al, 2018; O'Reilly et al, 2018). A study that I led explored how women who are ageing solo without children and without a partner are multiply marginalised by the heterosexist norm of ageing and sexuality in addition to those themes illustrated so far. The study was based on narrative interviews with 32 women in England and Ireland, of which 24 were heterosexual. We used a voice-centred relational analysis, which is a research method that draws on the woman's voice and how it resonates and puts social relationships at the centre, including how these are embedded in a complex web of intimate and larger social relations. This enabled us to identify stories of counter-norms and solo women's struggle for recognition, intimacy and a meaningful life. These counter-narratives challenged narrow discourses of what it means to be fulfilled in heterosexual intimacy terms and the linear nature of expectations around partnerships and relationships that deny sexual citizenship. Women in this study illustrated further the importance of reflexive resources of ageing and the intersectionalities and inequalities that come with relationship status in later life.

Relationship status has central significance within policy and drives the way in which we frame the design and future provision of quality care and support. For example, those working directly with older people will be concerned to describe the older person's social and economic connections and personal and community networks. Education, health or social welfare policies similarly make many assumptions about family forms, for example in relation to what is expected from its members, living arrangements; work patterns; financial security including inheritance; and subsequent roles taken up in later life. This is particularly relevant to caring and who is considered qualified to make decisions about older women who might become vulnerable in later life (Hicks, 2014). Growing sociological analysis of practices, discourses, display or enactment previously associated with 'the family' have tried to capture and describe contemporary forms of relationality, intimacy and personal life (Edwards et al, 2012). These important observations about gender expectations as part of the fabric of everyday life, and the social nature of expectations of solo women in particular, should facilitate the deconstruction of ageing experiences so as to understand how policy and practices aiming to support successful ageing might need to develop and respond.

Further, it has been observed by Demey et al (2011) that the relationship history of people living alone in mid-life matters for their psychological well-being, and the well-being of those living without a partner is lower than for those living with a partner. Partnership history and psychological well-being are also affected in different ways by relationship breakdowns, with implications for resilience in later life as well as practical impacts such as financial loss for women.

While the term 'solo' for women can be challenging, it is a genuine attempt to describe women's life experiences in a non-pejorative way in the face of language which fails to reflect the shifting political and social circumstances impacting on demography and the impact of gender and sexual inequalities. Such language often lacks sensitivity to a variety of circumstances, that is participants with stepchildren, foster children and even estranged children, while other studies view people with stepchildren or adopted children as parents (cited in Allen and Wiles, 2013). With a lack of consensus, our approach used self-definition which invited women to identify and describe their own status in relation to the phenomenon (Hafford-Letchfield et al, 2017). I focus briefly here on just one of the many themes, concerning how solo women envisioned intimacy in their later lives.

Envisioning intimacy

Women's description of their solo status in terms of their independence versus how they felt being 'alone' was an issue discussed unreservedly reflecting a constant tension that arose in their acknowledgements of the positive freedoms they experienced alongside numerous references to the idealised state that they perceived to come as a result of being in a relationship: "When I have not been in a relationship, it can be feelings of wanting to share quality time with someone ..."

This access to another person was also associated with a desire to have someone to provide support through sharing and practical help, including making decisions. For some women, closeness was associated with their pets – perhaps fulfilling the mad-cat lady myth – and which "filled a great void of loving and being loved". Some women also emphasised the lack of physical contact. Again, within such yearning, there was an idealised version of what a relationship should be: "Well of course, the loneliness. It gets worse as you get older. And I miss closeness, warmth, intimacy, sharing, laughter, loving, compromising ..."

The temporal nature of living solo was present in the metaphors that women used, for example, in the image of coming home in the 'winter to a cold house' and times of the year such as during special festivals, which particularly triggered a keener awareness of one's own solo status and having to lie low about their arrangements if they were spending it alone, or not being seen too keen to people who may invite them over to ensure they were not alone. While sexuality was described along a spectrum from vital to unimportant, intimacy and inversely loneliness were remarked on by most participants. Indeed, women who felt a lack of intimacy described it viscerally in emotional and physical terms. One woman talked about the need for touch and connection as a sensation she called "skin hunger", saying it was accompanied by a longing to avoid what she called "dead time"; and another woman described her lack of intimacy as a "cold and darkness" that could not be breached. The desires solo women expressed were associated with the need to feel closeness; the need for intimacy was at times, but not always, linked to a wish to be in an intimate relationship: "... it can be corrosive. Sometimes I would like a hug!".

Echoing the social legitimacy theme from the literature cited earlier, women felt that their solo status became more visible as they aged, which made them feel different or "on the fringes of life looking in". They were sometimes subject to unsolicited comments from friends, relatives and strangers about their solo status and on occasions even questioned as to why they were on their own at this stage in life, which provoked feelings of anger and resistance.

There were some differences in the stories produced between those who did not choose to be solo and those who found themselves solo as a result of the life course and circumstances. Hostetler (2004) questions whether anyone chooses to be permanently single and what 'choice' means in this context. Many of the participants in the solo study expressed satisfaction and happiness with their lives. It follows that someone who has exercised their choice to remain single may feel differently about being solo than someone who would have liked to be part of a couple and for whatever reason is not. They reframed this choice as exercising active autonomy, particularly in relation to sexism and patriarchy. DePaulo and Morris (2006), however, describe the phenomenon of 'singlism' – that is bias and discrimination against people who are not in partnerships which may exacerbate this issue.

Women noted a lack of a positive public discourse about 'soloness' and how they were seen as failures in terms of the normative relationships and identities that woman are expected to strive for. Indeed, one woman noted the extreme social discomfort she provoked, leading to others conceptualising her as either predatory or tragic. "... because of 'other people's perceptions/assumptions lack of a positive public discourse about it [there is an assumption that] you are either trying to shag anything that moves, or sat in the attic with your cats".

Many solo women were very proactive in seeking connections of all kinds, with memberships of multiple organisations and groups ranging from choirs, faith or cultural communities to educational courses. A vulnerability to the judgement of others also extended to women's own sense of internalised stigma. Di Napoli et al (2013) have suggested that the concerns about the sexuality of older, single women seem to be a response from some sections of society fearful of disruption to established family structures as well as a communal anxiety around loneliness and the need for intimacy in older populations. However, ageism and misogyny do not allow for the many ways in which post-menopausal women can experience sexuality and intimacy and the importance not just for individuals, but for a healthy society, of understanding and celebrating the range of desire and connection humans are capable of. One woman stated: "I have had many good sexual/love relationships. My life as a single woman is wonderful in many ways. I feel very lucky to be living in this time and to have had such a wide range of experiences."

Some women echoed the concern that as their fertility diminished professionals increasingly disregarded their bodies. Again, echoing themes from the review, female health does not appear as high on the agenda as it is in other countries, specifically post menopause. Menopause issues are ignored but impact hugely on ability to manage emotional stresses. Muhlbauer and Chrisler (2012) suggest that while traditional stereotypes and misconceptions still abound, today's older women have reached maturity with a broader range of experiences and social capital in the form of intimate friendships and extensive networks than their forebears. In summary, ageing solo women in this study were well aware of the unappealing nature of the range of personal identities that were socially available to them.

Even as far back as 1986, Copper referred to how western societies elevate the social worth of youth at the expense of older adults. These stereotypes of unnatural ageing in women introduced to us since childhood affect the way we read the bodies of other women. Copper illustrated this with examples of fairy tales built on tropes of wicked witches with unnatural powers which are contrasted with loving, but feeble grannies. But while witches are rarely encountered in current public discourse today certainly the concept of older powerful, deviant woman is still much discussed in the form of the 'cougar'.

Concluding thoughts

This chapter encapsulates some specific issues affecting the heterosexual population, with a focus on women's subjective experiences of sex, relationships and intimacy. I have drawn on examples of my published research to synthesise some of the evidence that highlight the unique issues affecting heterosexual women in later life. While the evidence suggests that they are experiencing sexuality from a broader and richer point of view, its social expression can be delegitimised. They might internalise ageist attitudes and beliefs, such as 'old people are not interested in sex', which is prohibitive and leads to inhibition. Myths and stereotypes that deny their unique sense of sexual well-being and the right to express it are compounded in ageism, heteronormativity, sexism, irrational fears, stereotypical thinking and lack of knowledge. Resultant attitudes and behaviours constitute significant barriers to heterosexual women's sexual expression, enjoying sexuality and achieving a sense of self in later life, which are reinforced by the biomedicalisation of sexuality and the dominant role of the pharmaceutical industry in sexual discourse.

There is a need to challenge ageism where women in later life have faced and continue to face multiple oppressions on grounds of gender, disability, class, sexual and gender identities, race and ethnic origin. The social construction of the ageing body as passive and dependent is conducive to a process of desexualisation, presenting women as inadequate for a full intimate life. The dominant biomedical model reinforces this process, particularly once women start to experience physical health problems as they age. It is, however, important to listen to women's sense of agency, their questioning through the resources of ageing and the subsequent deconstruction of heterosexual ageing stereotypes and potential for resexualisation on their own terms. This latter assertion can be challenging given that women tend not to own their own terms of engagement.

This chapter has drawn on already published selected research evidence from my own work with others and revisited this in the context of engaging with feminist theorising around heterosexuality, a category that has been described as invisible or unmarked (Hockey et al, 2007) and taking for granted ways of being. I have attempted to wrestle women's sexuality in later life away from silence, shame and (male-centric) biomedicalisation through a lens of theories which highlight how the prevailing power structures still place limits on how successful this can be. The meaning of being heterosexual in later life from a life course perspective, and what this means for successful or unsuccessful identities and how heterosexuality transcends our lives, become the organising principles for past, present and future sexual lives.

References

Allen, R.E.S. and Wiles, J. (2013) 'How Women Position their Late Life Childlessness: A Qualitative Study', *Journal of Marriage and Family*, 75(1), 206–20.

Bauer, M., Haesler, E. and Fetherstonhaugh, D. (2015) 'Let's Talk about Sex: Older People's Views on the Recognition of Sexuality and Sexual Health in the Health-care Setting', *Health Expectations*, 19(6), 1237–50.

Bauer, M., McAuliffe, L., May, R. and Chenco, C. (2013) 'Sexuality in Older Adults: Effects of an Educational Intervention on Attitudes and Beliefs of Residential Aged Care Staff', *Educational Gerontology*, 39, 82–91.

Bauman, Z. (2003) *Liquid Love: On the Frailty of Human Bonds*. London, Polity.

Bayler-Levaro, E. (2011) *Theorizing Age and Gender in the Pursuit of Love in Late Life*. PHD thesis presented at Oregon State University.

Bouman W.P. and Arcelus, J. (2001) 'Are Psychiatrists Guilty of "Ageism" When It Comes to Taking a Sexual History?' *International Journal of Geriatric Psychiatry*, 16(1), 27–31.

Bulcroft, K.A. and Bulcroft, R.A. (1991) 'The Timing of Divorce: Effects on Parent-Child Relationships in Later Life', *Research on Aging*, 13(2), 226–43.

Butler, J. (1990) *Gender Trouble: Feminism and the Subversion of Identity*. New York, Routledge.

Butler, J. (1993) *Bodies that Matter: On the Discursive Limits of 'Sex'*. London, Routledge.

Byrne, A. (2008) 'Women Unbound: Single Women in Ireland'. In Yans-McLoughlin, V. and Bell, R. (eds), *Women Alone*. New Brunswick, NJ, Rutgers University Press, 29–73.

Copper, B. (1986) 'Voices: On Becoming Old Women'. In Alexander, J. (ed), *Women and Aging: An Anthology by Women*. Corvallis, OR, Calyx Books, pp 46–57.

Davis, K. (1991) 'Critical Sociology and Gender Relations'. In Davis, K., LeiJennaar, M. and Oldersmar, J. (eds), *The Gender of Power*. London, Sage.

Demey, D., Berrington, A., Evandrou, M. and Falkingham, J. (2011) 'The Changing Demography of Mid-life, from the 1980s to the 2000s', *Population Trends*, 145(1), 1–19.

DePaulo, B.M. and Morris, W.L. (2006) 'The Unrecognized Stereotyping and Discrimination Against Singles', *Current Directions in Psychological Science*, 15(5), 251–4.

Di Napoli, E.A., Breland, G.L. and Allen, R.S. (2013) 'Staff Knowledge and Perceptions of Sexuality and Dementia of Older Adults in Nursing Homes', *Journal of Aging and Health*, 25(7), 1087–105.

Drummond, J.D., Brotman, S., Silverman, M., Sussman, T., Orzeck, P., Barylak, L. and Wallach, I. (2013) 'The Impact of Caregiving: Older Women's Experiences of Sexuality and Intimacy', *Affilia: Journal of Women & Social Work* 28(4), 415–28.

Edwards, R., Ribbens McCarthy, J. and Gillies, V. (2012) 'The Politics of Concepts; Family and Its (Putative) Replacements', *British Journal of Sociology*, 63(4), 730–46.

Fileborn, B., Hinchliff, S., Lyons, A., Heywood, W., Minichiello, V., Brown, G., Malta, S., Barrett, C. and Crameri, P. (2017) 'The Importance of Sex and the Meaning of Sex and Sexual Pleasure for Men Aged 60 and Older Who Engage in Heterosexual Relationships: Findings from a Qualitative Interview Study', *Archives of Sexual Behavior* 46, 2097–110, https://doi.org/10.1007/s10508-016-0918-9

Fournier, S.M. (2000) *Social Expectations for Sexuality among the Elderly*. ProQuest Information & Learning.

Gewirtz-Meydan, A., Hafford-Letchfield, T., Ayalon, L., Benyamini, Y., Biermann, V., Coffey, A., Jackson, J., Phelan, A., Voß, P., Geiger, M. and Zeman, Z. (2018) 'How Do Older People Discuss Their Own Sexuality? A Systematic Review of Qualitative Research Studies', *Culture, Health & Sexuality*, 21(3), 293–308.

Giddens, A. (1992) *The Transformation of Intimacy, Sexuality, Love and Eroticism in Modern Societies*. Cambridge, Polity.

Gledhill, S. and Schweitzer, R.D. (2014) 'Sexual Desire, Erectile Dysfunction and the Biomedicalization of Sex in Older Heterosexual Men', *Journal of Advanced Nursing*, 70(4), 894–903.

Gott, M. and Hinchliff, S. (2003) 'How Important Is Sex in Later Life? The Views of Older People', *Social Science & Medicine*, 56(8), 1617–28.

Hafford-Letchfield, T. (2008) 'What's Love Got to Do with It? Developing Supportive Practices for the Expression of Sexuality, Sexual Identity and the Intimacy Needs of Older People', *Journal of Care Services Management*, 2(4), 389–405.

Hafford-Letchfield, T. and Dunk-West, P. (2018) 'Sexuality, Sexual and Gender Identities and Intimacy Research in Social Work and Social Care: What Does the Lifecourse Lens Have to Offer?' In Dunk-West, P. and Hafford-Letchfield, T. (eds), *Sexuality, Sexual and Gender Identities and Intimacy Research in Social Work and Social Care: A Lifecourse Epistemology*. London, Routledge.

Hafford-Letchfield, T., Lambert, N., Long, E. and Brady, D. (2017) 'Going Solo: Findings from a Survey of Women Without a Partner and Who Do Not Have Children', *Journal of Gender and Ageing*, 29(4), 321–33.

Hicks, S. (2011) *Lesbian, Gay and Queer Parenting: Families, Intimacies, Genealogies*. Basingstoke, Palgrave Macmillan.

Hicks, S. (2014) 'Social Work and Gender: An Argument for Practical Accounts', *Qualitative Social Work*, 14(4), 471–87.

Hinchliff, S. and Gott, M. (2011) 'Seeking Medical Help for Sexual Concerns in Mid- and Later Life: A Review of the Literature', *The Journal of Sex Research*, 48(2–3), 106–17.

Hinchliff, S., Tetley, J., Lee, D.M. and Nazroo, J. (2016) 'Let's Talk About Sex – What Do Older Men and Women Say About Their Sexual Relations and Sexual Activities? A Qualitative Analysis of Data from the English Longitudinal Study of Ageing', *Ageing and Society*, 55(2), 152–63.

Hockey, J. and James, A. (2003) 'Gender, Sexuality and the Body in the Life Course'. In *Social Identities across the Life Course*. London, Palgrave.

Hockey, J., Meah, A. and Robinson, V. (2007) *Mundane Heterosexualities: From Theory to Practices*. Basingstoke, Palgrave Macmillan, p 204.

Hostetler, A.J. (2004) 'Old Gay and Alone: The Ecology of Well-being Among Middle-aged and Older Single Gay Men'. In De Vries, B. and Herdt, G. (eds), *Gay and Lesbian Aging: Research and Future Directions*. New York, NY, Springer Publishing Co. Inc., pp 143–76.

Jamieson, L. (1998) *Intimacy: Personal Relationships in Modern Societies*. Cambridge, Polity.

Jenkins, J. (2004) *Social Identity*. London, Routledge.

Kitzinger, C. and Wilkinson, S. (1993) *Heterosexuality*. London, Sage.

Lahad, K. and Hazan, H. (2014) 'The Terror of the Single Old Maid: On the Insolubility of a Cultural Category', *Women's 520 Studies International Forum*, 47 (Part A), 127–36.

Lambert, N., Hafford-Letchfield, T., Khan, H., Brady, D., Long, E. and Clarke, L. (2018) 'Stories of Intimacy and Sexuality in Later Life: Solo Women Speak'. In Dunk-West, P. and Hafford-Letchfield, T. (eds), *Sexuality, Sexual and Gender Identities Research in Social Work and Social Care: A Lifecourse Epistemology*. London, Routledge.

Lee, D. M. and Tetley, J. (2017) ' "How Long Will I Love You?" – Sex and Intimacy in Later Life, English Longitudinal Study of Ageing, 17. DOI: 10.13140/RG.2.2.34049.45926

Loe, M. (2004) 'Sex and the Senior Woman: Pleasure and Danger in the Viagra Era', *Sexualities*, 7(3), 303–26.

Malta, S. (2007) 'Love Actually! Older Adults and Their Romantic Internet Relationships', *Australian Journal of Emerging Technologies and Society*, 5(2), 84–102.

Marshall, B.L. (2012) 'Medicalization and the Refashioning of Age-Related Limits on Sexuality', *Journal of Sex Research*, 49(4), 337–43.

Mota, R.L. (2017) 'Female Urinary Incontinence and Sexuality', *International Brazilian Journal of Urology*, 243(1), 20–8. DOI: 10.1590/S1677-5538.IBJU.2016.0102

Menard, A., Kleinplatz, P.J., Rosen, L., Lawless, S., Paradis, N., Campbell, M. and Huber, J.D. (2015) 'Individual and Relational Contributors to Optimal Sexual Experiences in Older Men and Women', *Sexual and Relationship Therapy*, 30(1), 78–93.

Montemurro, B. and Siefken, J.M. (2014) 'Cougars on the Prowl? New Perceptions of Older Women's Sexuality', *Journal of Aging Studies*, 28, 35–43, Epub 2013, 15 December, PMID: 24384365.

Muhlbauer, F. and Chrisler, J.C. (2012) *Women over 50: Psychological Perspectives*. New York, Springer.

Muhlbauer, V., Chrisler, J.C. and Denmark, F.L. (eds) (2015) *Women and Aging: An International, Intersectional Power Perspective*. New York, NY, Springer.

Nyanzi, S. (2011) 'Ambivalence Surrounding Elderly Widows' Sexuality in Urban Uganda', *Ageing International* 36(3), 378–400.

de Oliveira Silva, D.N., Pereira Marinelli, N., Marques Costa, A.C., Gomes Santos, R.C., Ribeiro de Sousa, A. and Ribeiro de Lima, J. (2015) 'Perception of Elderly About Their Sexuality', *Journal of Nursing UFPE/Revista de Enfermagem UFPE*, 9(5), 7811–18.

ONS (2017) *Census data*, http://www.ons.gov.uk/ons/guide-method/census/2011/census-data/index.html

O'Reilly, E., Hafford-Letchfield, T. and Lambert, N. (2018) 'Women Ageing Solo in Ireland: An Exploratory Study of Women's Perspectives on Relationship Status and Future Care Needs', *Qualitative Social Work*, 19(1), 79–92.

PHE (2019) *People urged to practise safer sex after rise in STIs in England*, https://www.gov.uk/government/news/people-urged-to-practise-safer-sex-after-rise-in-stis-in-england

Ravanipour, M., Gharibi, T. and Gharibi, T. (2013) 'Elderly Women's Views about Sexual Desire during Old Age: A Qualitative Study', *Sexuality and Disability*, 31: 179–88.

Reilly, E., Hafford-Letchfield, T. and Lambert, N. (2018) 'Women Ageing Solo in Ireland: An Exploratory Study of Women's Perspectives on Relationship Status and Future Care Needs', *Qualitative Social Work*, 19(1): 75–92. DOI: 10.1177/1473325018796138

Ribbens McCarthy, J. and Edwards, R. (2011) *Key Concepts in Family Studies*. London, Sage.

Rich, A. (1980) 'Compulsory Heterosexuality and Lesbian Existence', *Signs*, 3, 631–60.

Roney, L. and Kazer, M.W. (2015) 'Geriatric Sexual Experiences: The Seniors Tell All', *Applied Nursing Research*, 28(3), 254–6.

Rowntree, M.R. (2014) 'Making Sexuality Visible in Australian Social Work Education', *Social Work Education*, 33(3), 353–64.

Sandberg, L. (2013) 'Just Feeling a Naked Body close to You: Men, Sexuality and Intimacy in Later Life', *Sexualities*, 16(3–4), 261–82.

Thorpe, R., Fileborn, B., Hawkes, G., Pitts, M. and Minnichiello, V. (2015) 'Old and Desirable: Older Women's Accounts of Ageing Bodies in Intimate Relationships', *Sex and Relationship Therapy*, 30(1), 156–66.

Traies, J. (2016) *The Lives of Older Lesbians Sexuality, Identity & the Life Course*. Basingstoke, Palgrave MacMillan.

Villar, F., Serrat, R., Celdran, M. and Faba, J. (2016) 'Staff Attitudes and Reactions towards Masturbation in Spanish Long-term Care Facilities', *Journal of Clinical Nursing*, 25(5–6), 819–28.

Yan, E., Wu, A.M.-S., Ho, P. and Pearson, V. (2011) 'Older Chinese Men and Women's Experiences and Understanding of Sexuality', *Culture, Health & Sexuality*, 13(9), 983–99.

Yun, O., Kim, M. and Chung, S.E. (2014) 'The Sexuality Experience of Older Widows in Korea', *Qualitative Health Research* 24(4), 474–83.

5

Sex and ageing in older heterosexual men

David M. Lee and Josephine Tetley

Introduction

The health, well-being and quality of life of older men and women are affected by their sexual and intimate relationships (Lindau et al, 2007; Field et al, 2013; Lee et al, 2016a). However, it has been argued that society most commonly thinks of later life as largely asexual and that sex in later life is a taboo subject (Heywood et al, 2017; Simpson et al, 2018). Against this backdrop the English Longitudinal Study of Ageing (ELSA) wave 6 (2012–13) included a detailed sexual relations and sexual activities questionnaire (SRA-Q) to identify how sex and intimacy interrelates with the health and well-being of older adults. This survey was completed by 7,079 men and women, and over 1,000 respondents provided additional qualitative information which created a unique data set.

An earlier analysis of quantitative and qualitative data illustrated how issues of relationships, perceptions of ageing and gender as well as views on media, culture and pornography impacted on older people's individual contexts and partnered relationships (Lee et al, 2016a; Tetley et al, 2018). Our work has then led us to think more critically about some of the gendered issues around sex and intimacy in later life. While our previous work has focused on the self-reported sexual health and well-being among older men and women in England, this chapter re-examines this data through the lens of older heterosexual men. This chapter further makes an important contribution to the field of sexual health and well-being in later life as we explore how older heterosexual men might be affected by issues of communication with health professionals and their thoughts, expectations and experiences about sex and intimacy in later life.

Background

There is a growing body of literature and evidence-based studies that are focused on sex and intimacy in later life (see, for example Laumann et al, 2006; Field et al, 2013; Lee et al, 2016a). This increasing body of work is starting to 'shift' thinking that characterises later life as non-sexual to a new position where sex and intimacy are seen as potentially contributing factors to successful and positive ageing (Lee et al, 2016b; Štulhofer et al, 2018). Rowe and Kahn (1997) defined successful ageing as incorporating three distinct components; 'low probability of disease and disease-related disability, high cognitive and physical functional capacity and active engagement with life'. It should be stressed, however, that there remains no consensus about the definition or classification of successful ageing. Although not the focus of this chapter, readers should be mindful of the ongoing critical gerontological debate on successful ageing, particularly in relation to intersecting issues of social inequity, health disparity and age relations (see Katz and Calasanti, 2015). Despite this, there is evidence that concepts of successful ageing have been influenced by biomedical models of health and well-being (Bowling and Dieppe, 2005). A more holistic approach to thinking about successful ageing should then take account of education, occupation and income, as these have been found to influence how people adapt to old age (Kok et al, 2016). This is important in the context of this chapter as older men presenting with sexual difficulties are more likely to be overlooked or offered biomedical 'solutions' such as Viagra rather than referred for support to adapt sexual relationships which are not dependent on erections and penile/vaginal intercourse (Potts, 2004).

Given the previously mentioned problems of definition and responses, there are then aspects of sex and intimacy that need further research and critical consideration in the context of successful and/or positive ageing, one of these being the experiences of older heterosexual men (Fileborn et al, 2017). While it is important to develop new work in this area, the wider biological, social and psychological contexts that shape people's lives must also be considered to give a more holistic understanding of the positive and negative factors that impact on the sexual well-being and relationships of men who identify as heterosexual, as they age. DeLamater and Koepsel 2015) proposed moving away from an overtly medicalised perspective of sexual activity and ageing to encompass additional influences on sexual health, that is, psychological factors (knowledge and attitudes about sex) and relational (relationship satisfaction and quality). The key advantage of taking a more holistic, biopsychosocial perspective on later life sex and sexuality is the avoidance of focusing solely on the impacts of illness and treatments on sexual behaviour and, by extension, labelling older men with sexual 'dysfunctions'.

Recognising the need for this wider understanding, we therefore wanted to look at how the ELSA data might give us insights into the extent to which older men in the study reported difficulties and sought help or adapted to changes in their sexual and intimate relationships. From the outset, we prioritised the use of a mixed-methods approach, where the qualitative and quantitative data were initially analysed individually and then linked and compared (see, for example, Sandelowski, 2000) to gain more holistic understandings of the sexual and relationship changes experienced by men as they aged.

Historically, the majority of male sexual health research was carried out in the United States, focussing on men with erectile dysfunction (ED), with little specific focus on population-based studies of non-patient samples (Corona et al, 2010). More recent work has examined the relationship between a wider range of sex hormones and broader aspects of sexual health (O'Connor et al, 2011). Much of this research effort has been driven by the fact that the number of men aged over 65 is predicted to double worldwide from 1980 to 2025 (Mathers et al, 1999), together with an increasing appreciation that a significant proportion of older adults will remain sexually active into their 70s and 80s (Lee et al, 2016a). However, when men do experience difficulties, the typical response has tended towards medical and pharmaceutical interventions that focus on restoring penetrative and heteronormative sexual activities (Gledhill and Schweitzer, 2014).

From an overtly biological perspective, the key sex hormone involved with moderating and maintaining sexual drive and function in men is testosterone (T). Typically, blood serum levels of T average around 16 nmol per litre in 50-year-old men (Wu et al, 2008), with previous literature describing in detail how this hormone declines progressively by approximately 0.5–2 per cent per year from around the age of 30 (Orwoll et al, 2005). Attempts to clarify the relationship between declining circulating T and the ageing phenotype have proved inconclusive, with only weak associations found (Bhasin et al, 2006). It is well established that T is important for the maintenance of normal sexual function in young, healthy men (Corona et al, 2010). What has remained particularly controversial is the role of circulating T in the sexual health and functioning of older men aged 50 and over (Boloña et al, 2007). Clinical guidelines, although not universally agreed upon, suggest that circulating T levels below around 8–10 nmol per litre are 'potentially' diagnostic of late-onset hypogonadism (diminished functional activity of the testes) among older men (Bhasin et al, 2006; Wang et al, 2008), and such individuals may benefit from the use of testosterone therapy. However, there are complicating factors that make such clear-cut diagnoses problematic.

First, T levels are only one part in an ensemble of other potential changes in the male endocrine reproductive axis, that is, the plethora of hormones and factors that interact with each other to, in part, control a man's sex drive. While beyond the scope of this chapter, other hormones, within what is known as the hypothalamic-pituitary-testicular (HPT) axis, include gonadotrophin-releasing hormone, luteinising hormone and follicle-stimulating hormone. These hormones, in addition to T, are tightly regulated by feedback and feedforward relationships, potentially leading to distinct forms of hypogonadism (low levels of T) in older men (Tajar et al, 2010). Those readers interested in the finer points of the HPT axis and its potential dysregulation in later life are directed to explore the pertinent literature (Keenan et al, 2006).

Second, there are a number of long-term conditions and co-morbidities common in later life that further complicate the relationship between circulating levels of T and sexual function and health. The best-studied example is obesity and T, where a number of studies have documented decreased levels of circulating T following weight gain, particularly among obese older men with or without diagnosed type 2 diabetes (Camacho et al, 2013). The problem lies in unpicking these various patterns of association, given that chronic conditions such as obesity, type 2 diabetes and cardiovascular diseases have been shown to have direct, detrimental impacts on male sexual function in later life (Lee et al, 2016a). For example, ED is around three times more prevalent in men with diabetes than those without and the onset of ED typically occurs 10–15 years earlier in men with diabetes as compared to those without (Edwards, 2016). There are, however, limitations to the biomedical response to maintaining and supporting sex and intimacy in later life for older men, which are now explored.

In addition to biological ageing changes, responses to issues of sex and intimacy in later life have been seen not only as taboo, but also as a joke, embarrassing and irrelevant (Bytheway, 1994). Older bodies are similarly seen as sagging and when a man is no longer able to engage in penile penetrative sex with an orgasm, this can challenge heteronormative perceptions about sex and intimacy (Hughes, 2011). It has been argued that the masculine lives of younger and older men differ and that social norms around men's experiences of sex and intimacy can put their health at risk (Anderson and Fidler, 2018). In taking a more critical stance on the factors that can impact on older heterosexual men, further consideration also needs to be given to social class and ethnicity as it has been argued that research that does exist tends to overlook the role that social oppression plays in explaining sexual inequality in our everyday lives, although the thought structures that support our everyday sexual attitudes and behaviour indeed reflect patterns of dominance and inequality (Gonzales and Rollinson, 2005, p 716).

This chapter now moves to explore how data from one study can be used to understand sex and intimate experiences of older heterosexual men and the lessons that can be learnt for future policy, practice, research and education.

Methods

The English Longitudinal Study of Ageing is a nationally representative panel survey of community-dwelling men and women aged 50 years and older in England. Full details on the study design and methods have been described previously (Steptoe et al, 2013). Briefly, ELSA is a panel survey of a representative sample of men and women living in England aged ≥50 years. It is multidisciplinary and involves the collection of economic, social, psychological, cognitive, health, biological and genetic data. The study commenced in 2002, and the sample has been followed up every two years. The original sample consisted of 1,1391 members ranging in age from 50 to 100 years. ELSA is harmonised with ageing studies in other countries to facilitate international comparisons and is linked to financial and health registry data. The data sets are openly available to researchers and analysts soon after collection (https://www.elsa-project.ac.uk/data-and-documentation).

However, in wave 6 (2012–13), a new instrument was included which aimed to capture data on sexual relationships and activities in later life. Out of a total of 10,601 individuals who participated in wave 6, 7,079 (67%) completed and returned the paper-based ELSA SRA-Q. The SRA-Q included questions on attitudes to sex, frequency of sexual activities and behaviours, problems with sexual activities and function, concerns and worries about sexual activities, function and relationships, and details about current sexual partnerships. Wave 6 participants completed the SRA-Q in private and sealed the questionnaire in an envelope upon completion. There were male and female versions of the SRA-Q, which are available from the ELSA website (http://www.elsa-project.ac.uk). At the end of the questionnaire there was a free text box and participants were invited to provide any additional comments. The specific prompt asked: 'If there is anything else you would like to tell us, please write in the space below. We shall be very interested to read what you have to say.' A total of 1,084 men and women completed this section. The majority of men identified themselves as being in a partnered relationship (80%) and heterosexual (95%) (Lee et al, 2016a).

Preliminary analyses of the overarching SRA-Q quantitative data have previously been described (Lee, Nazroo et al, 2016a; Lee, Vanhoutte et al, 2016b). Moving on from these two initial papers, more specific sub-analyses of the quantitative data revealed more negative sexual health outcomes among older people experiencing chronic pain (Wade et al, 2018), urinary incontinence (Lee et al, 2018), poorer sleep quality (Lee and Tetley, 2019) and gender-divergent associations between sexual expression and cognitive function (Wright et al, 2019). The ELSA data include sampling weights to enable correction for sampling probabilities and differential non-response to calibrate back to the 2011 Census population distribution for sex and age, and these were used where appropriate in the quantitative analyses of the SRA-Q data.

The qualitative data were analysed using Template Analysis. Template Analysis, an established method of analysing qualitative data (Crabtree and Miller, 1999; Cassell, 2008; King, 2012), was used as it offers a pragmatic approach for analysing a wide range of textual data. More specifically, Template Analysis was appropriate for the qualitative data generated by ELSA as it is allows for: analysing open ended question responses on a written questionnaire; coding template on subset of data, flexible and iterative approach; and more than one person to be involved in the analysis (King, 2004; Brooks and King, 2012; http://www.hud. ac.uk/hhs/research/template-analysis/). The use of Template Analysis then enabled qualitative and quantitative researchers to work together with the qualitative data to develop themes from the qualitative data and consider them against the findings from the preliminary analysis of the quantitative data. Papers that illustrates how the qualitative data gave us insights into the ways in which people's health, relationships, experiences and perceptions of ageing, along with sexual satisfaction, impact on sexual relationships and activities have been published in other key areas captured by the SRA-Q (see Hinchliffe et al, 2017; Tetley et al, 2018).

ELSA wave 6 received ethical approval from the NRES Committee South Central – Berkshire, and all participants were provided with a letter and leaflet to allow them to give informed consent. All the qualitative comments were anonymised and reviewed by the data holders to ensure that no disclosive statements were included in the final dataset released to the research team.

Findings

As researchers from different backgrounds (an epidemiologist and a nurse-academic) and traditions we have worked to bring the qualitative and quantitative data together. We believe this gives a more rounded overview of the issues that impact on the sexual and intimate lives of older adults (see, for example, Lee and Tetley, 2017). For this chapter, we revisited both quantitative and qualitative data reported by male ELSA participants. Building on our analysis of the qualitative and quantitative data, we worked iteratively, identifying common themes and issues reported across the two data sets. In the first instance, we worked collaboratively with the whole qualitative data set on 'Post-It' notes to create themes and categories. Subsequently, when exploring the data for more specific reasons, such as looking at the reported data from heterosexual men, we took the male qualitative data and reanalysed it to see what specific themes and issues could be identified. The key issues highlighted by the male data were: sexual difficulties, health and ageing, relationships, and reflections on ageing. These themes were then mapped against the quantitative data more fully to explore the men's self-reported attitudes, beliefs and experiences. These are now presented and later discussed.

Sexual difficulties, health and ageing

The initial analysis of the quantitative data found that sexually active men aged 50 and over reported more concerns about their sexual activities and function than women and, with increasing age (see Lee et al, 2016a). In terms of sexual function, an analysis of the quantitative data illustrated the extent to which men over 50 experienced erectile and orgasm difficulties (see Figure 5.1).

The qualitative comments gave some insights into the factors that older men thought had impacted on their erectile and orgasm difficulties or their thoughts on managing these. One man wrote: "How can I solve erectile problems, I suffer from blood pressure and diabeti[es]" (Male aged 60–70). Others reported a loss of "… sexual drive mostly attributable to medication for hypertension and prostate problems" (Man, aged 70–80).

In terms of managing erectile difficulties to remain sexually active, another man noted: "I have been having problems keeping an erection

Figure 5.1: Prevalence of erectile and orgasmic difficulties among men in wave 6 of ELSA: by 10-year age band (weighted percentages)

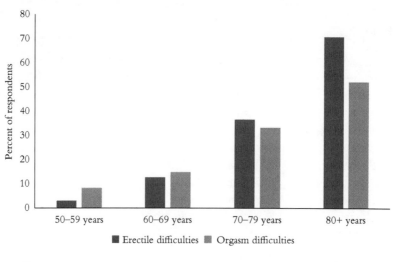

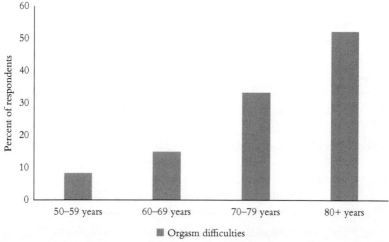

and am considering trying Viagra, as I would like to keep my sexual life going as long as I can" (Man aged 70–80). When seeking help for sexual difficulties, the response of health professionals was not always seen as positive: "Doctors and health care professionals do not seem to give any help re sexual health problems: in my case, erectile dysfunction" (Man aged 70–80).

While men reported their sexual difficulties, participants also described how changes to their partner's sexual health impacted on them: "My wife and I have had a very good sex life, regular sex until

Figure 5.2: Prevalence of men reporting feeling 'obligated to have sex', 'not sharing sexual likes with their partner' and 'not feeling emotionally close during sex' in wave 6 of ELSA: by 10-year age band (weighted percentages)

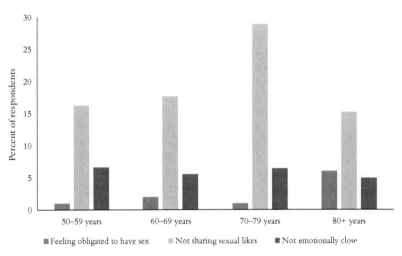

she went through the change, over the last five years approximately her desire has totally gone" (Man, 50–59 years).

Relationships and sexual intimacy

As noted earlier, the data generated from ELSA wave 6 was captured from participants who were or had predominantly been in a partnered relationship. In an earlier analysis we had noted that more women commented on relationships in the qualitative comments (Tetley et al, 2018). The quantitative data gave some indication of male views on sexual intimacy in the context of their relationships, see Figure 5.2.

From the qualitative data it was interesting to note that while the quantitative data identified that a significant proportion of men of all ages (15–30%) reported that they did not share sexual likes with the partners, for some men, broader aspects of their current intimate relationships were of greater importance than sex per se, as one man commented: "I think it would be nice to have more sex with my wife but sometimes you get tired in the evening, which puts you off. But love keeps you together and happy sex is not everything. Love is" (Man, 60–69 years). Another said: "Now too old but my wife and I sleep in the same bed, and kiss and cuddle each other before settling down to sleep. We enjoy each other's company" (Man aged 80–90).

Figure 5.2 interestingly shows how men reported 'not sharing sexual preferences' was a key issue in their sexual relationships. Again, the qualitative data gives insights into what these might be. In terms of sexual intimacy one man wrote that: "My wife doesn't seem to want sex. When we do, I manually bring her to a climax, but found it difficult to eject [ejaculate] when we have intercourse. If I masturbate I eject okay" (Man aged 60–70). Differences in sexual preferences were illustrated in the following comment: "Would like other forms of sex e.g. anal and oral but my wife will not engage in them" (Male aged 70–80).

Sexual activities and preferences also appeared to be affected by the sexual relationship with their partner as a man noted that he "enjoy[ed] mild porn on internet 2–3 times a month, masturbation, interested in keeping things working although nothing possible with wife these days, chance would be a fine thing" (Male aged 80–90).

Reflecting back

While the quantitative and qualitative data gave insights into the men's current sexual activities and relationships, for others there was a reflection (looking back and forward) on their sexual activities, difficulties and physical changes to the body.

From the quantitative data, drawing on the attitudes and beliefs questions, more of the older male participants responded that sexual changes during ageing were not particularly important to older people (Figure 5.3). Just over a fifth of those 65 years and under reported that they agreed with the statement that 'sexual changes that occur with age are not important to older people', as compared to almost half of those aged over 75. Figure 5.4 further illustrates the men's attitudes and beliefs regarding the ability to have sex as a person grows older, with the proportion of men agreeing that 'the ability to have sex decreases as a person grows older' clearly increasing with age.

While the changes that the men were reflecting on were not stated, the qualitative data gave some insights into some of the changes that the men had experienced or anticipated happening.

One man commented on potential future changes and the impact of these: "Some time, maybe soon, maybe not I shan't be able to do it anymore and will that be a source of regret or relief to know that, biologically speaking, my life will no longer serve any purpose?" (Man, aged 60–70). Another man reflected on his sexual activities in the context of his younger self: "As I am getting older sexually, I am reverting back to my teenage years, always ready and wanting sex. Masturbation has become a hobby now" (Man, aged 50–60).

For others, there was a comment about how the thinking about sex as a younger man was still relevant: "Don't forget: the mind is still in its

Figure 5.3: Sexual changes that occur with age are not important to older people

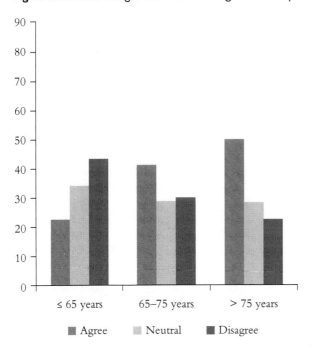

Figure 5.4: The ability to have sex decreases as a person grows older

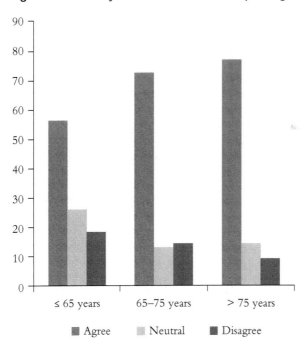

20s even when you get old" (Male 80–90). The physical changes to the body, though, particularly the penis, were noted by participants: "Penis shrunk with age" (Man, aged 70–80); "I have a collapsed circumcision and I have had no visible penis since approx 2005!!" (Man, aged 60–70).

Overall, the quantitative and qualitative data in combination gave us an insight into how issues of health, relationship and physical changes impacted on the sexual and intimate relationships of males in the ELSA study. These are now discussed through a critical consideration of the intersection of biological, sociological and psychological impacts on older heterosexual men.

Discussion

Our findings illustrate some of the issues that heterosexual men experience for themselves and in the context of their partnered relationships. In terms of the theme Sexual Difficulties, Health and Ageing raised some interesting issues about the key sexual difficulty reported by older men. More specifically, those aged 65 and over reported erection and orgasm difficulties. The prevalence of ED has appeared to increase over recent decades, possibly related to the rise in obesity and vascular diseases and also reflecting improved reporting and data capture (Shamloul and Ghanem, 2013). The public recognition of ED as a sexual difficulty associated with ageing has certainly increased markedly over the last decade, thanks in large part to the ubiquitous presence and advertising of the phosphodiesterase type 5 inhibitor group of drugs, of which Viagra remains the best known. However, any causal associations between low levels of circulating T and ED remains poorly defined as compared to other outcomes such as sexual desire and nocturnal erections (O'Connor et al, 2011).

There has been relatively little research exploring the association between sex hormones other than T and a wider range of sexual health outcomes such as sexual satisfaction or concerns about sexual function. Circulating T is metabolised into other key sex hormone in men, for example, oestradiol (E2) and dihydrotestosterone (DHT), and these hormones in turn have been implicated in age-related declines in sexual functioning (Corona et al, 2010b; O'Connor et al, 2011). Cross-sectional data from the European Male Ageing Study (EMAS) (Lee et al, 2009), a community-based study of middle-aged and older men, showed that lower levels of T, and not E2 or DHT, were associated with poorer overall sexual function, as assessed by a composite measure of frequency of sexual thoughts, sexual intercourse, fondling and petting, waking erections and orgasm (O'Connor et al, 2011).

In extending our understandings beyond the biological changes, issues of later life masculinities are important as the participants commented on issues such as 'keeping their sex lives going' and 'keeping things working'. However, both the qualitative and quantitative data illustrated that the men in the ELSA study recognised change and decrease in the ability to have sex as they aged. Sandberg (2016) has noted that, while changes in sexual activities and desire might be seen as natural and inevitable, older men, sex and intimacy present conflicting issues. She argues that for older heterosexual men, on the one hand, there is the risk of being labelled a 'dirty old man', despite the fact that, in reality, continued sexual desire should be seen as natural and that sexuality in later life is a positive, life-enhancing experience. Building on the biological changes already discussed, there were also comments about the size and visibility of the penis, the possible use of Viagra to maintain sexual activity and other ways of being sexually intimate as sex lives changed over time. These observations raise several issues in terms of older men's sexual identity, of which one is the rise of a consumer market. Calasanti and King (2005) note that consumerism and marketing promote successful sexual ageing around the promotion of penetrative sex. They further argue that phallic ads value men only to the extent that they act like younger, heterosexual (and wealthy) men (p 17). So, achieving the consumerist view of successful sex and intimacy in later life is then only available to a certain few. It is also suggested that the size of a man's penis also has a psychological effect, with a small penis seen as humiliating and embarrassing in social public situations such as changing rooms (Franken et al, 2002; Wylie and Eardley, 2006). Wylie and Eardley further argue that the penis is also seen as a sign of masculinity associated with 'attributes such as largeness, strength, endurance, ability, courage, intelligence, knowledge, dominance over men, possession of women; a symbol of loving and being loved' (p 1449). Such thinking resonates with the work of Connell (2005) on hegemonic (dominant) forms of masculinity. Such expressions of masculinity are undergirded by socio-economic status and high social esteem that few men actually achieve though many internalise it as a benchmark by which they may subconsciously judge themselves. Indeed, Connell points out that ability to achieve, claim or even display anything like hegemonic masculinity can diminish with age. Further, we cannot say that for the male ELSA participants who identify as heterosexual that there is one way of understanding their worlds or the knowledge and power that they can claim or not in relation to their sexual health, well-being and relationships. However, an analysis of the ELSA wave 6 quantitative data identified that poorer health was clearly associated with lower levels of sexual activity and a higher prevalence of problems with sexual functioning, particularly among men (Lee et al, 2016a).

In terms of their relationships, in the second theme identified, the men reported their views on their intimate relationship with their partner. The quality of their relationships, particularly when penetrative sex was not a key to intimacy with their partner, has been reflected in other studies. Fileborn et al (2017), in their study of older men who engage in heterosexual relationships, noted that accounts of intimacy, even when men lacked 'drive' or a 'functional penis' (p 2107), enabled men to acknowledge that they were still sexual beings. The relationships data further identified that not sharing sexual preferences was an issue for some men. As noted in one of our earlier papers (Tetley and Lee, 2018)) while the qualitative comments from participants focused on anal sex, pornography and masturbation were from a small number of male participants, these findings were reflected in a study by Kontula and Haavio-Mannila (2009) who found that sex without love and use of pornography were more common in men. Our previous work also identified that 'the expressed desire for anal and oral sex from a man aged 70–80 is significant, as the literature suggests that there is an under reporting at all ages of "taboo" sexual behaviours such as heterosexual anal sex (McBride and Fortenberry 2010; Tetley and Lee, 2018, p 514)'.

Our theme of 'Reflections' illustrates that having a sexual and intimate relationship with a partner is important, but for men issues of health, changes and thoughts about the past and present can challenge their experiences. Moreover, Figure 3 in the findings illustrate that men, as they age, increasingly agree that sexual changes that occur with age are not important. We have strongly argued that sex and intimacy in later life should not be seen as a time of decline. However, there are real changes, a point made in this chapter, particularly considering the literature on testosterone and other sex hormones. Sexual function will then change across the life course and impact on the health and well-being of older men. There is then a need for more practical and psychological support for older men. While not all of the older men in the ELSA survey were in poor health, Bytheway (2011) argues that despite the presence of ill-health, adaptation, resilience and social engagement can still lead to successful ageing. We would argue that support for adaptation, resilience and social engagement would also promote a more positive experience for same-sex couples in relation to sex and intimacy in later life.

In moving towards a more positive perspective on sex and intimacy, particularly for older heterosexual men, it is important to recognise that there are health gains. For example, Liu et al found that

> older men are more likely to being sexually active, having sex more often, and more enjoyably than are older women. Results cross-lagged models suggest that high frequency of sex is positively related to later risk of cardiovascular events for men but not women, whereas good sexual quality seems to protect women but not men from cardiovascular risk in later life. We find no evidence that poor cardiovascular health interferes with sexuality for either gender. (2016, p 276)

Support for the sexual health and well-being of older men can also be problematic. Male heterosexual sexual health can be overlooked and we suggest that older heterosexual men, unlike older heterosexual women, do not have the same opportunities to engage in sex-focused health and advice because of differing health care responses across the life course to issues of fertility and screening. For example, the HPV vaccine was not given to boys in England until 2018, (https://www.gov.uk/government/news/hpv-vaccine-to-be-given-to-boys-in-england), 10 years after it was given to girls. It is also argued that psychologists and health professionals miss opportunities to help older people patients improve their sex lives because they do not ask, or are embarrassed (Clay citing Syme, 2012, p 42). In this feature, Syme further posits that education of staff about sex and intimacy is also crucial, as barriers to successful sex and intimacy in later life can be overcome with the right help.

Before we draw our final conclusions and recommendations, we also feel that it is important to recognise that while the male participants in the ELSA study primarily identified themselves as heterosexual, heterosexual men may also have sex with other men (Public Health England, 2016). A heteronormative discourse on sex and intimacy at any age may then exclude some men from important health messages. However, from our analysis of the ELSA wave 6 data, we recognise that notions of successful ageing, particularly in the context of sexual and intimate relationships, are multifaceted and have to take account of individual preferences and experiences. Moreover, we recognise that the experiences of older heterosexual men's relationships and sexual intimacy are impacted on by issues such as socio-economic class, ethnicity, individual experiences and biological changes that can impact on sexual 'performance' and physical changes to their ageing bodies. Building on this thinking, Griffith (2012, p 106) argues that consideration of how multiple characteristics come together and impact on, in this case men's sexual relationships and intimacy, is important as

> An intersectional approach suggests that socially-defined and socially meaningful characteristics are inextricably intertwined and experienced simultaneously. Thus, intersectional approaches help men's health researchers to examine how the blending of identities and experiences create a new understanding of these factors, and arguably a more accurate reflection of the determinants of men's health.

Our conclusion now summarises and makes recommendations as to how men's sexual and intimate relationships can be more fully understood and appropriately responded to.

Conclusion

This chapter has revisited the ELSA wave 6 data but drawing on self-reported data and qualitative comments from older heterosexual men. As we previously noted (Tetley and Lee, 2018, p 516), in discussing the findings generated by the qualitative ELSA data it is important to highlight that people's responses were given in the context of responding to a structured questionnaire (the SRA-Q) described earlier in this chapter. People's responses were limited to a short comment box. We also had to take the comments as 'truthful' reports; this was an anonymised survey, and, in the main, the comments were sensitive and insightful. Moreover, to date, ELSA has not attempted to over-sample sexual minorities and the results presented here may not accurately reflect the specific circumstances pertinent to older LGBT people in relation to ageing and sexual activity. Despite this limitation, the findings do illustrate diversity of sexual activities in heterosexual relationships and identify that, while physical and sexual intimacy change as people age, older people are still sexually active into their 70s, 80s and 90s. However, the findings that sexual activities in later life encompass more than penile-vaginal intercourse also challenges more heteronormative ideas about sexual relationships (Allen and Roberto, 2009).

We believe there are some important points for research, practice, education and policy that can be drawn from the male ELSA data. First, more research that looks critically at the views and experiences of older heterosexual men is required. Second, health care professionals need more education, particularly around the issues and challenges men may experience as they age. Health care professionals also need information and resources to manage these needs. Third, peer and online support can provide opportunities for men to engage in conversations with other men about their experiences and difficulties; see, for example, resources from Age UK (https://www.ageuk.org. uk/information-advice/health-wellbeing/relationships-family/sex-in-later-life/), NHS guidance on sex as you get older (https://www. nhs.uk/live-well/sexual-health/sex-as-you-get-older/, and Men in Sheds (Milligan et al, 2015). Fourthly, relationship services, such as Relate, can provide important support for older people; see, for example, https://www.relate.org.uk/relationship-help/help-older-people/common-problems-older-people. Finally, policy and public engagement activities need to continue and develop. Examples include the UK-wide campaign group Sex and Intimacy in Later Life Forum (SILLF) and its Manchester-based sub-unit, the Sexual Health and Older People (SHOP) group. These groups include members from the public sector, academia, older people, care providers, medical practitioners, voluntary groups, faith communities, sexual health networks and Public Health England. Their ultimate aim is to coordinate the knowledge among different stakeholders and translate it into impactful policy and practice.

To ignore the needs of older people's sexual well-being and intimate relationships risks a continued silent narrative, particularly for heterosexual men, where conversations about sexual difficulties can be difficult. Moreover, for men, living with sexual difficulties can also be seen as embarrassing and an erosion of masculinity. This chapter then makes an important contribution as it presents data from a representative sample of men and gives voice to their lived sexual and intimate partnered experiences.

References

Allen, K.R. and Roberto, K.A. (2009) 'From Sexism to Sexy: Challenging Young Adults' Ageism About Older Women's Sexuality'. *Sexuality Research and Social Policy Journal of NSRC*, 6(4): 13–24.

Anderson, E. and Fidler, C.O. (2018) 'Elderly British Men: Homohysteria and Orthodox Masculinities'. *Journal of Gender Studies*, 27(3): 248–59.

Bhasin, S., Cunningham, G.R., Hayes, F.J., Matsumoto, A.M., Snyder, P.J., Swerdloff, R.S., Montori, V.M. (2006) 'Testosterone Therapy in Adult Men with Androgen Deficiency Syndromes: An Endocrine Society Clinical Practice Guideline'. *Journal of Clinical Endocrinology & Metabolsim*, 91: 1995–2010.

Boloña, E.R., Uragam M.V., Haddad, R.M., Tracz, M.J., Sideras, K., Kennedy, C.C., Caples, S.M., Erwin, P.J. and Montori, V.M. (2007) 'Testosterone Use in Men with Sexual Dysfunction: A Systematic Review and Meta-analysis of Randomized Placebo-controlled Trials'. *Mayo Clinic Procedings*, 82: 20–8.

Bowling, A. and Dieppe, P. (2005) 'What Is Successful Ageing and Who Should Define It?' *British Medical Journal*, 331(7531): 1548–51.

Brooks, J. and King, N. (2012) 'Qualitative Psychology in the Real World: The Utility of Template Analysis'. British Psychological Society Annual Conference, 18–20 April, London.

Bytheway, B. (1994) *Ageism*. Buckingham and Philadelphia: Open University Press.

Bytheway, B. (2011) *Unmasking Age: The Significance of Age for Social Research*. Bristol: Policy Press.

Calasanti, T. and King, N. (2005) 'Firming the Floppy Penis: Age, Class, and Gender Relations in the Lives of Old Men'. *Men and Masculinities*, 8(1): 3–23.

Camacho, E.M., Huhtaniemi, I.T., O'Neill, T.W., Finn, J.D., Pye, S.R., Lee, D.M., Tajar, A., Bartfai, G., Boonen, S., Casanueva, F.F., Forti, G., Giwercman, A., Han, T.S., Kula, K., Keevil, B., Lean, M.E., Pendleton, N., Punab, M., Vanderschueren, D., Wu, F.C.W. and the EMAS Group (2013) 'Age-associated Changes in Hypothalamic-pituitary-testicular Function in Middle-aged and Older Men Are Modified by Weight Change and Lifestyle Factors: Longitudinal Results from the European Male Ageing Study'. *European Journal of Endocrinology*, 168: 445–55.

Cassell, C. (2008) 'Template Analysis'. In Thorpe, R. and Holt, R. (eds), *The SAGE Dictionary of Qualitative Management Research*. London: SAGE.

Clay, R.A. (2012) 'Later-life Sex. Psychologists are Working as Part of Health-care Teams to Help Older Adults Keep their Sex Lives Going Strong'. *American Psychological Association*, 43(11): 42, https://www.apa.org/monitor/2012/12/later-life-sex

Connell, R.W (2005) *Masculinités* (second edition). Cambridge, Polity.

Corona, G. and Maggi, M. (2010) 'The Role of Testosterone in Erectile Dysfunction'. *Nature Reviews Urology*, 7: 46–56.

Corona, G., Lee, D.M., Forti, G., O'Connor, D.B., Maggi, M., O'Neill, T.W., Pendleton, N., Bartfai, G., Boonen, S., Casanueva, F.F., Finn, J.D., Giwercman, A., Han, T.S., Huhtaniemi, I.T., Kula, K., Lean, M.E.J., Punab, M., Silman, A.J., Vanderschueren, D., Wu, F.C.W. and the EMAS Study Group (2010b) 'Age Related Changes in General and Sexual Health in Middle-aged and Older Men: Results from the European Male Ageing Study (EMAS)'. *Journal of Sexual Medicine*, 7: 1362–80.

Crabtree, B.F. and Miller, W.L. (1999) 'Using Codes and Code Manuals: A Template Organizing Style of Interpretation'. In Crabtree, B.F. and Miller, W.L. (eds), *Doing Qualitative Research* (2nd edition). Newbury Park, CA: Sage.

DeLamater, J. and Koepsel, E. (2015) 'Relationships and Sexual Expression in Later Life: A Biopsychosocial Perspective'. *Sexual and Relationship Therapy*, 30(1): 37–59.

Edwards, D. (2016) 'Sexual Health and Dysfunction in Men and Women with Diabetes'. *Diabetes and Primary Care*, 18: 288–96.

Field, N., Mercer, C.H., Sonnenberg, P., Tanton, C., Clifton, S., Mitchell, K.R., Erens, B., Macdowall, W., Wu, F., Datta, J., Jones, K.G., Stevens, A., Prah, P., Copas, A.J., Phelps, A., Wellings, K. and Johnson, A.M. (2013) 'Associations between Health and Sexual Lifestyles in Britain: Findings from the Third National Survey of Sexual Attitudes and Lifestyles (Natsal-3)'. *Lancet*, 382(9907): 1830–44.

Fileborn, B., Hinchliff, S., Lyons, A., Heywood, W., Minichiello, V., Brown, G., Malta, S., Barrett, C. and Crameri, P. (2017) 'The Importance of Sex and the Meaning of Sex and Sexual Pleasure for Men Aged 60 and Older Who Engage in Heterosexual Relationships: Findings from a Qualitative Interview Study'. *Archives of Sexual Behavior*, 46(7): 2097–110.

Francken, A.B., Van de Wiel, H.B.M., Van Driel, M.F. and Schultz, W.W. (2002) 'What Importance Do Women Attribute to the Size of the Penis?' *European Urology*, 42(5): 426–31.

Gledhill, S. and Schweitzer, R.D. (2014) 'Sexual Desire, Erectile Dysfunction and the Biomedicalization of Sex in Older Heterosexual Men'. *Journal of Advanced Nursing*, 70(4): 894–903.

Gonzales, A.M. and Rolison, G. (2005) 'Social Oppression and Attitudes Toward Sexual Practices'. *Journal of Black Studies*, 35(6): 715–29.

Griffith, D.M. (2012) 'An Intersectional Approach to Men's Health'. *Journal of Men's Health*, 9(2): 106–12.

Heywood, W., Minichiello, V., Lyons, A., Fileborn, B., Hussain, R., Hinchliff, S., Malta, S., Barrett, C. and Dow, B. (2017) 'The Impact of Experiences of Ageism on Sexual Activity and Interest in Later Life'. *Ageing & Society*, 39(4): 795–814.

Hinchliff, S., Tetley, J., Lee, D. and Nazroo, J. (2018) 'Older Adults' Experiences of Sexual Difficulties: Qualitative Findings from the English Longitudinal Study on Ageing (ELSA)'. *The Journal of Sex Research*, 55(2): 152–63.

Hughes, J. (2011) 'Are Older Men Taking Sexuality as Prescribed? The Implications of the Competing Influences on Ageing Male Heterosexuality'. *Australian Feminist Studies*, 26(67): 89–102.

Katz, S. and Calasanti, T. (2015) 'Critical Perspectives on Successful Aging: Does It "Appeal More Than It Illuminates"?' *The Gerontologist*, 55(1): 26–33.

Keenan, D.M., Takahashi, P.Y., Liu, P.Y., Roebuck, P.D., Nehra, A.X., Iranmanesh, A. and Veldhuis, J.D. (2006) 'An Ensemble Model of the Male Gonadal Axis: Illustrative Application in Aging Men'. *Endocrinology*, 14: 2817–28.

King, N. (2004) 'Using Templates in the Thematic Analysis of Text'. In *Essential Guide to Qualitative Methods in Organizational Research*. Sage, pp. 256–70.

King, N. (2012) 'Doing Template Analysis', in Symon, G. and Cassell, C. (eds), *Qualitative Organizational Research: Core Methods and Current Challenges*. London: Sage.

Kok, A.A., Aartsen, M.J., Deeg, D.J. and Huisman, M. (2016) 'Socioeconomic Inequalities in a 16-year Longitudinal Measurement of Successful Ageing'. *Journal of Epidemiology & Community Health*, 70(11): 1106–13.

Kontula, O. and Haavio-Mannila, E. (2009) 'The Impact of Aging on Human Sexual Activity and Sexual Desire'. *Journal of Sex Research*, 46(1): 46–56.

Laumann, E.O., Paik, A., Glasser, D.B., Kang, J.H., Wang, T., Levinson, B., Moreira, E.D., Nicolosi, A. and Gingwell, C. (2006) 'A Cross-national Study of Subjective Sexual Well-being Among Older Women and Men: Findings from the Global Study of Sexual Attitudes and Behaviors. *Archives of Sexual Behavior*, 35(2): 145–61.

Lee, D. and Tetley, J. (2017) *How Long Will I Love You? Sex and Intimacy in Later Life*. London: International Longevity Centre.

Lee, D.M. and Tetley, J. (2019) 'Sleep Quality, Sleep Duration and Sexual Health Among Older People: Findings from the English Longitudinal Study of Ageing. *Archives of Gerontology and Geriatrics*, 82: 147–54.

Lee, D.M., Tetley, J. and Pendleton, N. (2018) 'Urinary Incontinence and Sexual Health in a Population Sample of Older People', *BJUI International*, 122(2): 300–8.

Lee, D.M., Vanoutte, B., Nazroo, J., Pendleton, N. (2016b) 'Sexual Health and Positive Subjective Well-being in Partnered Older Men and Women. *The Journal of Gerontology: Series B*, 71(4): 698–710.

Lee, D.M., Nazroo, J., O'Connor, D.B., Blake, M. and Pendleton, N. (2016a) 'Sexual Health and Well-being Among Older Men and Women in England: Findings from the English Longitudinal Study of Ageing'. *Archives of Sexual Behavior*, 45: 133–44.

Lee, D.M., O'Neill, T.W., Pye, S.P., Silman, A.J., Finn, J.D., Pendleton, N., Tajar, A., Bartfai, G., Casanueva, F., Forti, G., Giwercman, A., Huhtaniemi, I., Kula, K., Punab, M., Boonen, S., Vanderschueren, D., Wu, F.C.W. and the EMAS study group (2009) 'The European Male Ageing Study (EMAS): Design, Methods and Recruitment'. *International Journal of Andrology*, 32(1): 11–24.

Lindau, S.T., Schumm, L.P., Laumann, E.O., Levinson, W., O'Muircheartaigh, C.A. and Waite, L.J. (2007) 'A Study of Sexuality and Health Among Older Adults in the United States'. *New England Journal of Medicine*, 357(8): 762–74.

Liu, H., Waite, L.J., Shen, S. and Wang, D.H. (2016) 'Is Sex Good for your Health? A National Study on Partnered Sexuality and Cardiovascular Risk Among Older Men and Women'. *Journal of health and Social Behavior*, 57(3): 276–96.

Mathers, C.D., Sadana, R., Salomon, J.A., Murray, C.J., Lopez, A.D. (2001) 'Healthy Life Expectancy in 191 Countries. 1999'. *Lancet*, 357: 1685–91.

McBride, K.R. and Fortenberry, J.D. (2010) 'Heterosexual Anal Sexuality and Anal Sex Behaviors: A Review'. *Journal of Sex Research*, 47(2): 123–36.

Milligan, C., Payne, S., Bingley, A. and Cockshott, Z. (2015) 'Place and Wellbeing: Shedding Light on Activity Interventions for Older Men'. *Ageing & Society*, 35(1): 124–49.

O'Connor, D.B., Lee, D.M., Corona, G., Forti, G., Tajar, A., O'Neill, T.W., Pendleton, N., Bartfai, G., Boonen, S., Casanueva, F.F., Finn, J.D., Giwercman, A., Han, T.S., Huhtaniemi, I.T., Kula, K., Labrie, F., Lean, M.E.J., Punab, M., Silman, A.J., Vanderschueren, D., Wu, F.C.W. and the European Male Ageing Study Group (2011) 'The Relationships between Sex Hormones and Sexual Function in Middle-Aged and Older European Men'. *Journal of Clinical Endocrinology & Metabolism*, 96: E1577–E1587.

Orwoll, E., Lambert, L.C., Marshall, L.M., Phipps, K., Blank, J., Barrett-Connor, E., Cauley, J., Ensrud, K. and Cummings, S, for the Osteoporotic Fractures in Men (MrOS) Study Group (2005) 'Testosterone and Estradiol Among Older Men'. *Journal of Clinical Endocrinoloby & Metabolism*, 91: 1223–5.

Potts, A. (2004) 'Deleuze on Viagra (or, What Can a "Viagra-body" Do?)'. *Body & Society*, 10(1): 17–36.

Public Health England (2016) *Promoting the Health and Wellbeing of Gay, Bisexual and Other Men who Have Sex with Men*. London. Public Health England.

Rowe, J.W. and Kahn, R.L. (1997) 'Successful Aging'. *The Gerontologist*, 37(4): 433–40.

Sandelowski, M. (2000) 'Combining Qualitative and Quantitative Sampling, Data Collection, and Analysis Techniques in Mixed-method Studies'. *Research in Nursing & Health*, 23(3): 246–55.

Sandberg, L. (2016) 'In Lust We Trust? Masculinity and Sexual Desire in Later Life'. *Men and Masculinities*, 19(2): 192–208.

Shamloul, R. and Ghanem, H. (2013) 'Erectile Dysfunction'. *Lancet*, 381: 153–65.

Simpson, P., Almack, K. and Walthery, P. (2018) '"We Treat Them All the Same": The Attitudes, Knowledge and Practices of Staff Concerning Old/er Lesbian, Gay, Bisexual and Trans Residents in Care Homes'. *Ageing & Society*, 38(5): 869–99.

Steptoe, A., Breeze, E., Banks, J. and Nazroo, J. (2013) 'Cohort Profile: the English Longitudinal Study of Ageing'. *International Journal of Epidemiology*, 42(6): 1640–48.

Steptoe, A., Jackson, S.E. and Wardle, J. (2016) 'Sexual Activity and Concerns in People with Coronary Heart Disease from a Population-based Study'. *Heart*, early online available at http://heart.bmj.com/content/early/2016/04/28/heartjnl-2015–308993.full [Accessed 30th May 2016]

Štulhofer, A., Hinchliff, S., Jurin, T., Hald, G.M. and Træen, B. (2018) 'Successful Aging and Changes in Sexual Interest and Enjoyment Among Older European Men and Women'. *Journal of Sexual Medicine*, 15(10): 1393–402.

Tajar, A., Forti, G., O'Neill, T.W., Lee, D.M., Silman, A.J., Finn, J.D., Bartfai, G., Boonen, S., Casanueva, F.F., Giwercman, A., Han, T.S., Kula, K., Labrie, F., Lean, M.E.J., Pendleton, N., Punab, M., Vanderschueren, D., Huhtaniemi, I.T. and Wu, F.C.W. (2010) 'Characteristics of Secondary, Primary, and Compensated Hypogonadism in Aging Men: Evidence from the European Male Ageing Study'. *Journal of Clinical Endocrinology & Metabolism*, 95: 1810–18.

Tetley, J., Lee, D.M., Nazroo, J. and Hinchliff, S. (2018) 'Let's Talk About Sex – What Do Older Men and Women Say About Their Sexual Relations and Sexual Activities? A qualitative analysis of ELSA Wave 6 data'. *Ageing & Society*, 38(3): 497–521.

Thompson Jr, E.H. and Whearty, P.M. (2004) 'Older Men's Social Participation: The Importance of Masculinity Ideology'. *The Journal of Men's Studies*, 13(1): 5–24.

Thompson, E.H. (2006) 'Images of Old Men's Masculinity: Still a Man?' *Sex Roles*, 55(9–10): 633–48.

Wade, K., Wu, F.C.W., O'Neill, T.W. and Lee, D.M. (2018) 'Association between Pain and Sexual Health in Older People: Results from the English Longitudinal Study of Ageing'. *Pain*, 159(3), 460–8.

Wang, C., Nieschlag, E., Swerdloff, R., Behre, H.M., Hellstrom, W.J., Gooren, L.J., Kaufman, J. M., Legros, J.-J., Lunenfeld, B., Morales, A., Morley, J.E., Schulman, C., Thompson, I.M., Weidner, W. and Wu, F.C.W. (2008) 'Investigation, Treatment and Monitoring of Late-onset Hypogonadism in Males: ISA, ISSAM, EAU, EAA and ASA Recommendations'. *European Journal of Endocrinology*, 159(5): 507–14.

Wright, H., Jenks, R.A. and Lee, D.M. (2019) 'Sexual Expression and Cognitive Function: Gender-Divergent Associations in Older Adults'. *Archives of Sexual Behavior*, 49: 941–51.

Wylie, K.R. and Eardley, I. (2006) 'Penile Size and the "Small Penis Syndrome"'. *BJU International*, 99: 1449–55.

Wu, F.C., Tajar, A., Pye, S.R., Silman, A.J., Finn, J.D., O'Neill, T.W., Bartfai, G., Casanueva, F., Forti, G., Giwercman, A., Huhtaniemi, I.T., Kula, K., Punab, M., Boonen, S., Vanderschueren, D. and the European Male Aging Study Group (2008) 'Hypothalamic-pituitary-testicular Axis Disruptions in Older Men Are Differentially Linked to Age and Modifiable Risk Factors: The European Male Aging Study'. *Journal of Clinical Endocrinology & Metabolism*, 93: 2737–45.

Weblinks

http://www.elsa-project.ac.uk

https://www.gov.uk/government/news/hpv-vaccine-to-be-given-to-boys-in-england

https://www.nhs.uk/live-well/sexual-health/sex-as-you-get-older/

https://www.relate.org.uk/relationship-help/help-older-people/common-problems-older-people

6

Sex and older gay men

Peter Robinson

Introduction

At the heart of this chapter are the stories of 11 gay men, aged 43–71, who spoke about adventurous sexual encounters with strangers. It would be an exaggeration to say that they structured their lives around casual sex but, as their stories show, they were willing and able to make time available to maximise opportunities for sexual adventures.

Analysis of the stories revealed two narratives. The first was the effect of age on their ability to satisfy their sexual desire, that is, whether or how an ageing body constrained their sexual activity. The second narrative related to age preference and whether they sought encounters with younger men or older men and their success in doing so. Both narratives included evidence of the effects of ageism and loss, how these are expressed, and, in line with the work of Simpson (2015), how they can be resisted.

This chapter rests on stories appearing across three books that the author has written on gay men's life stories and which focus on age and ageing. The first (Robinson, 2008) concerned three generations of Australian gay men, aged 22–79, and how changing social norms affected the ease with which they could be public about their sexuality. The second considered how age and ageing affected gay men's relationships (Robinson, 2013). Based on material from an international sample of men aged 20–87, it examined long-term relationships, fatherhood, various lived experiences of single men and generational differences regarding gay marriage. The third book (Robinson, 2017) looked at gay men's working lives from the perspective of three generations of gay men from the same international sample, as well as their views and experiences on retirement from paid work and on old age/later life.

The central argument in this chapter is that while ageing gay men do acquire and can call on 'resources of ageing' (Heaphy, 2007) to combat gay ageism, these are limited by the constraints imposed by their ageing bodies and how these are understood. In the case of those who continue to include in their lives episodes of sexual adventure, whose stories are examined in this chapter, there is evidence that the effects of physical ageing or illness can impinge on their making full use of resources of ageing.

Background literature

Two principal arguments influence the literature on gay ageing. The first one draws on scholarly work on ageing generally from the 1960s (Ariès, 1960; de Beauvoir, 1970; Elias, 1987), which examined the life course and why youth became the most valorised age. Adding to understandings of youth's appeal, which Ariès argued began at the time of World War One, were the advent in the 1950s of the 'teenager' as a new stage of life and market, and the youth culture of the 1950s and 1960s (Frank, 1998). For gay men, there was also an age-old narrative of intimate relations between adult males and adolescents, which underpinned citizenship rites and practices in Ancient Athens (Dover, 1978; Murray, 2000) and the youthful aesthetic that was associated with same-sex male desire there and in other ancient and contemporary cultures (Boswell, 1980; Hekma, 1999; Murray, 2000).

The second argument which has evolved since the late 1990s, when gay ageing began attracting more scholarly attention, is that ageing gay men have found ways to combat and resist ageist practices in the gay world, many of which have their origins in the long-standing valorisation of youthful bodies and youthfulness (Simpson, 2015; Westwood, 2016).

How changes to laws concerning marriage, adoption and access to IVF will affect the structure of gay relationships only the next 30 years or more will tell. Further, the extent to which gay men are domesticated by these also can be assessed only over time. The commercial scene of clubs and bars remains an important setting for gay socialising and coming out and, judging by the interview stories of the men examined in this chapter, bars and the like have been augmented but not superseded by online dating sites (Mowlabocus, 2010).

In addition to the public narrative of gay youthfulness that the gay and mainstream media favour, representations of gay men in advertisements and promotional material in online and traditional media are almost entirely of young men and young men's bodies, and personal value and desirability are construed in terms of youthfulness or youthful appearance. As a consequence, gay men's body-selves become commodified in much the same way as women's appearance.

Also, the pronounced youthful aesthetic in the gay world signals when those commodities are out of date and thus when their sexual and bodily worth has expired. This hierarchy persists today and is unlikely to disappear because it conforms to an established aesthetic in the West: 'Although the age with which maximum beauty is associated varies culturally, it is nearly always a young one' (Boswell, 1980, p 29).

Claims concerning gay men's decreased currency and visibility as they approach the age of 40 (Pollak, 1985; Green, 2011; Simpson, 2015) were corroborated by almost all interviewees featured in this chapter, all of whom were aged over 40. Among other things, they were asked to describe how they saw themselves in relation to other gay men. And most related how, because of their age, they felt like outsiders on 'the scene', the dominant narrative of which is one of youth and youthfulness.

The participants' sexual stories revealed another narrative, however, and one supporting arguments scholars such as Heaphy (2007) and Simpson (2015) have made, which is that middle-aged and older gay men have agency *because* of their age (Heaphy's 'resources of ageing') and how they have learned to navigate the gay scene and its practices. Such an aesthetic exists not only among 'Bear' communities (consisting of older, fatter, hairier and bearded men and their admirers) but also more generally and was present in the sexual stories of interviewees.

Evidence from their stories and from other research (Adam, 2007, p 123) suggests that the gay commercial scene of bars and so on might not be beneficial as a social setting for men in long-term relationships. Other research reported some in long-term relationships saying that they would return to the scene for a 'big night out' or to go dancing with their partner or friends. They were able, therefore, to move in and out of the scene with relative ease. Such men normally were in secure relationships and often employed in high-status occupations (Robinson, 2008, pp 72–94).

Methods

The men whose life stories were drawn on for this chapter were recruited in Auckland, London, Los Angeles, Melbourne and New York and interviewed 2009–11 as part of a larger project (Robinson, 2013). After formally consenting to an interview, all participants were asked open-ended questions about their working life, relationship story, view of their sexual attractiveness as they aged, and general views about old men in the gay milieu. In answering these questions, they provided information about their sexual practices and what effect they understood ageing to have on them.

Analysis of stories was undertaken on the understanding that human identity is narratively constituted, that is, in line with MacIntyre (1981) and Carr (2001), individuals are the sum total of the stories they tell about themselves. In the case of this relatively small international sample of 11 men aged 43–72, analysis of their interview transcripts proceeded on the grounds that these would reveal common narratives about sex, sexual practices, and ageing.

Transcripts were initially examined for common narratives. Once these were validated (on their own and in relation to the literature), they were used to sort the material provided in the transcripts. The sorted material was then examined for narratives that connected and made sense of the men's accounts of, for example, where they sought adventurous sexual encounters or how age differences affected their sense of their sexual worth or desirability and that of their sexual partner(s).

The largest decile from the sample comprised six men in their 50s, followed by three in their 40s, one in his 60s and one in his 70s. All but one of the 11 participants worked or had worked in white-collar jobs in fields such as business, education, health or media; the one who had not was employed by a care organisation as an administrative assistant. With the exception of two African American men, who lived in Los Angeles and New York, the sample comprised white, middle-class males.

Discussion

Interviewees drew on two principal narratives when explaining how age and ageing affected their sex lives. First, study participants spoke of how age affected their ability to satisfy their need for sex in terms of the change it had on (a) their self-regard or sex appeal and (b) their sex drive or performance. Second, they spoke of the part age preference played in their choice of sexual partners.

Effects of age/ageing

Changed self-regard, sex appeal

Five men, or slightly less than half the sample, reported some sort of change in their self-regard or their sex appeal as they got older. All but one were single at the time of interview. Their accounts suggested a high level of reflexivity, which can be common to gay men who socialise in the bars and clubs of the gay world, which Pollak (1985, p 44) described as markets where, 'in the last analysis one orgasm is bartered for another'. Either because of the transactional nature of social intercourse in these venues or because it is a feature of how masculinity is expressed and measured (Connell, 2000, p 217; Bourdieu, 2001, p 49), gay men appear to develop a very strong sense of their worth in relation to other men and do so in settings where sexual desire can be expressed (as a preliminary encounter) and/or in other settings where sexual exchange can occur.

There were mixed reports from the men as to the effect of ageing on their self-regard and sex appeal. Two reported increased self-regard or sex appeal as they aged and this was in the context of fairly regular sexual encounters, while, on the other hand, three reported that theirs had decreased.

The two who said their self-regard or sex appeal was better now were a 72-year-old from New York and a 53-year-old from London. Both were upper middle-class and still working. The older (Colin) worked in higher education and was eminent in the arts. The younger (Ryan) worked in media and spent half his year in Europe and the other half in the southern hemisphere.

Colin lived in Greenwich Village, New York and presented as an energetic man in his early 70s. He explained that he was a recovering alcoholic and an adherent of Body Electric – a support group for men positively to explore their masculinity which is open to men regardless of sexual identification – and sado-masochist (S&M). He reported that he regarded himself as more attractive now than when younger: "I thought I was uglier when I was cute and now that I am uglier, I think I am cute." This casual comment comparing how he remembers himself as a young man and sees himself now in his early 70s suggests that Colin has gained personal resources as he has aged but also that he grew up at a time when, or in a milieu where, young people were not expected to preen or boast of their good looks. He was cute "back then" but remembers thinking himself "ugly", while the reverse is now how he sees himself.

The S&M he referred to was in his view a means of subverting the power young men could exercise in the gay world of New York in the 2000s:

> 'It is more about what you do – the feeling of a master or slave – and age just becomes a little bit of an advantage. That is a nice thing for an older man to get involved in. It is a little hard to compete on the physical level, but … I like being a Daddy anyway.'

Apart from S&M, he also maintained a strong sense of self by taking part in activities organised by Body Electric. When interviewed, he was preparing to go to a camp in Pennsylvania where 800 naked gay men would spend ten days together:

> 'I am going to give a spanking seminar; I am going to play the piano; I am going to try out for Mr Leather, things that are unimaginable for me to have done in my youth. It would have been inappropriate then … but I am going to do it.'

Colin said that the camp would not be a sex-feast but an opportunity for older and old men to enjoy their nakedness and to relate in ways impossible in other settings:

> 'It is actually not a big orgy. It is fun to have a lot of workshops. They get a lot of people to do different things, put on shows. And they have different cabins and each one does a little something. I just discovered it last year … Because most of them are older, you do get a sense of a gay older community.'

This sort of development has potential for providing older men with connections not available elsewhere in the gay world. And from what Colin said, the connections seemed genuine and personally rewarding.

Ryan reported also an improved self-regard and sex appeal. A Londoner and in his early 50s, he travelled each year to South-East Asia for work and holidays, which he explained accounted for his improved social life: "I am making a lot of contacts and so my social life is getting slightly insane. I have got more and more friends." His friends included sexual partners: "I also meet people sexually and they become friends." And when he dedicated himself to improved body maintenance, his "sexual marketability" improved:

> 'I started going to the gym and … then I discovered that my body was changing even at my age … I was … meeting new people a lot of the time, so that was the currency that mattered. It did make a difference, so I continued doing it and my sex improved dramatically and got to the point where I was beginning to feel overwhelmed by it.'

Ryan's use of the word 'currency' suggests an understanding of the transactional nature of social/sexual relationships in the gay world and also of beauty practices, which, while originally understood as affecting women now have a more universal application.

One argument that explains Ryan's experience concerns a market for the exchange of beautiful bodies, which western consumer culture creates and supports and which operates as follows. First, the body is conceived of as a 'vehicle of pleasure'. Second, images supporting this idea appear in advertisements, the popular press, television, films and now social media. Third, as people 'work' on their body they are rewarded: 'the closer the actual body approximates to the idealised images of youth, health, fitness and beauty, the higher its exchange value' (Featherstone et al, 1991, p 177). This process is almost exactly as Ryan reported his experience of working on his body and the rewards that followed but with one exception: the increased currency he gained in the online gay sex market led to a feeling of being "overwhelmed". Ryan's admission that he felt overwhelmed suggests that resources of ageing can backfire when older gay men try to subvert ageism by building their body so as to appeal to younger gay men.

Three men said they believed their self-regard and sex appeal had decreased over time. They were from Melbourne and Los Angeles; two were in their 40s and one in his 50s. Theirs was a more typical ageing narrative, where the body is less a vehicle of pleasure and more a source of ailments and pain (Elias, 1987, p 69). The two Melbournians spoke of physical change. Calvin (aged 51) said that he was aware of being less attractive now, "as a single person who is also getting older and has grey hair as opposed to someone who has got thick, black hair". A connection he made between being single and growing old was not something other interviewees raised:

> 'I am a single person and ... that is a fact. If you are a couple, you would not necessarily go out to the bars so much looking for someone. Sometimes, they go out looking for sex or for someone to play with the two of them. If you are a couple, you tend to do things more with couples and more settled people.'

Calvin seemed to understand his pursuit of casual sexual partners as a consequence of being single and in relation to perhaps a fantasy notion of benefits available to gay couples. While he believed that his sex appeal had declined, he was adamant age had not diminished his capacity to engage in gay social activities:

> 'In terms of sex, when I was younger, I was able to pick up whenever I wanted. Nowadays, for social activities, I still go to the venues. I still go to dance parties. I still go to the

sauna if I want to. In terms of not going ... [out] ageing has not affected me. It may when I am in my 60s but at the moment it has not.'

Another Melbourne resident, Callum (early 40s), was also conscious of his body's physical change and the effects of this: "My body has changed. I am not as slim as I used to be and I have grey hair now. I like that but I also don't like it and I use humour to get through my anxiety about that." He also reported that he was now more sexually constrained. When he was in his 20s, HIV-AIDS was untreatable and he explained that its presence caused him to seek sexual encounters with a degree of urgency. Now, however, the HIV-AIDS panic had passed, he had less energy, and together these explained why he was "not wanton anymore".

Jude lived in Los Angeles and was 46 when interviewed. His perspective was different and concerned a theory on how other gay men aged: "I notice certain of these boys who are really pretty. They are 20 and because they have got the really soft features, it does not lend well to ageing ... I have been fortunate ... [in] that my strong jaw has enabled me to age with better grace." A fairly self-serving theory, to be sure, but one that was based on close examination of the young men who comprised the social/sexual marketplace in Los Angeles. Jude was a rich man who lived on income from a family trust. He was familiar with the bars and clubs of West Hollywood and while he rated himself as less attractive than he once was and in relation to soft-faced, young men, he refused to let age affect his currency:

'I also have been very diligent about staying in shape ... I was at the gym today so that I can make my dinner with my friend and not miss a workout ... I definitely sense that I am not as sexually attractive as I might once have been but I am still attractive. Some people like older guys.'

Changed sex drive

Gay men who came of age in the 1970s and 1980s – as did many from this sample – and who socialised in the bars and clubs of the gay scene can age differently from 'non-scene' gays and straights. On the scene, the normalisation of illicit drug use (Lewis and Ross, 1995), including drugs like amphetamines (speed) and MDMA (Ecstasy) (Australian Institute of Health and Welfare, 2017), can mean that older gay men have easy access to and can use them to stimulate their physical and sexual selves. And it could be argued that older gay men who use illicit drugs to achieve this are also masking the physical fact of old age as a time of marked slowing down – which Norbert Elias (1987) documented in his important work, *The Loneliness of the Dying*.

For young gay men, Viagra is used as an enhancer if their consumption of Ecstasy or alcohol causes short-term erectile difficulties. For older men, it is more often used as an enabler if the physical effects of ageing include difficulties getting and maintaining an erection. Three men from the sample who were in their 50s and 60s were determined to make sure that age or age-related illnesses would not constrain their pursuit of continuing sexual relations.

That stories of strategies used to overcome the physical effects of ageing were a feature of the life histories of men in their 50s and 60s should not come as a surprise. With age, men 'take longer to achieve an erection, the power of orgasm may decline, the volume and intensity of ejaculation decrease' (Seabrook, 2003, p 115). A decline in sex drive does not mean, however, an absence of sexual interest. As historical sociologist Laslett (1991, p 19) argued, people in their 60s and 70s should have every expectation of a continuing sex life: 'Sexual activity can continue both for men and women almost indefinitely into the Third Age [that period between retirement and loss of faculties or death] and does so in spite of the still persistent stereotype which would disavow it.'

The three interviewees who said that their sex drive had changed came from Los Angeles, Melbourne and New York. One was in his early 60s and the others in their 50s, and all three were in couple relationships. One theme connected their stories: all three had had illnesses of some sort which affected them physically and, in their view, their sex drive.

The only man from the sample who was HIV-positive was Parry, a 63-year-old New Yorker. He was vibrant and, in the interview, exhibited a positive, affirming view of his circumstances and future. In spite of being, in his own words, "a borderline diabetic" who had gout and experienced erectile dysfunction, he was determined to continue enjoying a meaningful sex life with occasional casual partners, his long-term partner being no longer interested in the same. According to Parry, age and ailments had changed his sex life but only in terms of how he engaged with the other: "ageing is only changing the method of sex and it is not changing my concept of my ability to have sex". He was aware, however, of how the drugs he took for his ailments could affect his perception of reality:

'The HIV meds always concern me because I never know how they are going to react. I am sometimes not fully present when I am under my meds and I am concerned what is going to happen, could happen, all that. As far as growing old in itself, I do not think getting older is a way not to have sex.'

Ageing was no obstacle in Parry's view to a continuing sex life, which made him an example of what Laslett argued was realistic for anyone in the Third Age.

Marvin was 59 when interviewed and lived in Los Angeles. He had been diagnosed with prostate cancer some years before and at about the same time he was withdrawing from an addiction for methamphetamine (colloquially known as Crystal Meth). According to Marvin, the drug he was given to treat his prostate cancer affected his testosterone level and this in turn reduced his sex drive, which together with his sexual appetite was considerable:

> 'Maybe if they take me off the drugs I'd be a horn–dog and be on the internet all the time. During my Crystal [Meth] period, I probably spent more time on the Internet than ever. I watched more porn than ever, went to more circuit parties. That was the norm for me, a manifestation of being fucked up and high as a kite, which I loved by the way … It was great. I do not look back at that with a whole lot of regret. I tend to romanticise it which actually gets me in trouble some times. I loved the circuit parties, including the one in Sydney. I have been to the Mardi Gras a couple of times. You guys know how to do it! Talk about substance abuse!'

When Marvin recalled his methamphetamine addiction and associated sex life, he observed that reminiscing about it gets him "in trouble sometimes". In the interview, which was on Skype, he was not asked to elaborate, but a possible inference is that his boyfriend does not like being told how much sex Marvin had then, especially as his sex drive had diminished:

> 'You know how you used to get an erection and hit the ceiling? That doesn't happen anymore. I'm not driven that way sexually because of the hormones or the ageing process, which makes me maybe sound shallow but I didn't realise how sexually driven I was before and how much I identified with being a sexually active person until all of a sudden it was removed from me. Is that ageing or illness? I don't know.'

This franker account occurred later in his interview when Marvin was relating the story of his intimate relationships. His great love was a man he met 20 years earlier and who died of an HIV-related illness during the epidemic's peak in the US. His current boyfriend was younger and devoted to him.

The third man with an account to relate of the effect of ageing on his sex drive was Isaac, a 56-year-old Melbournian. Like Marvin, his testosterone levels were affected also by treatment he was receiving for an illness. Diagnosed with Leukaemia two years before, the disease was in remission at the time of interview.

Isaac was certain that his chemotherapy treatment had reduced his sex drive: "during the chemo[therapy] my testosterone levels dropped below normal and my sex drive disappeared and it took a while to come back". The experience created in him a fatalistic response:

> 'What I learned was that [when] I didn't have a sex drive, I didn't care that I didn't have a sex drive … But [my] … memory told me this could be dealt with and I could have this life experience back. I could eat the apple again but since I wasn't hungry it didn't so much matter. It was fascinating.'

Aware of when his sex drive disappeared, Isaac rationalised that the effect of the chemotherapy would pass and it would return and that, while it was missing, lamenting its absence was pointless.

It could be argued that these accounts of changed sex drive were not associated with ageing but with illness. With the exception of Isaac's illness, which was not age specific (Cancer Council Victoria, 2013), the other men's illnesses were age related. The gout from which Parry suffered is generally accepted to be an illness of age as is the prostate cancer with which Marvin was diagnosed. His case was slightly complicated by his withdrawal from methamphetamine addiction at about the same time. It is worth noting that addiction to methamphetamine occurs across all age cohorts. The content in this section highlights the importance of sex to gay men aged 50 and older and what they were prepared to do to ensure its place in their intimate lives or how they rationalised its decline and still maintained meaningful intimate lives.

Age preference

The focus in this section is on the effects of gay ageism and how it operates. Its strongest expression was in the preference for younger men, evidence for which was found across all four deciles in the sample (40s, 50s, 60s and 70s). Ageism can also operate in an expressed preference for older men and within this sample there was one such individual who preferred older men and whose account is included in this section.

Some interviewees reported experiencing symbolically brutal ageism when seeking sex partners online, which is discussed later. These aside, many negotiated age preferences for others with a degree of awareness and provided similar accounts of doing so as did those Simpson interviewed (2015). Associated with the general preference for younger men was a parallel narrative of old gay men as unappealing because of their physical appearance: "It is a horrible prejudice in gay men. They do not want to touch someone who is not beautiful ... It is like [they are afraid] they would catch it" (Colin, 72, New York). And according to another interviewee (Marvin, 59, Los Angeles), older gay men were unattractive because so many men his age had "let themselves go":

> 'They have gained weight. This is not an attractive time for a lot of people my age ... And if you look at what our barometers are for beauty in the gay community, we are so outside the box on that one ... Maybe if we were a little nicer, less alcoholic, more joyous, it would not be that way but most of the older gays I have come across have some issues.'

Eight men related accounts of age preferences when seeking sexual partners: seven for younger and one for older ones. They were from all five cities, that is, Auckland, London, Los Angeles, Melbourne and New York; and were aged 46–72, the majority being in their 50s.

The only interviewee to express a preference for older men was Parry, a 63-year-old from New York, which had been the case since he was a young man: "In my 20s, I was dating people who were in their 50s, occasionally their 60s. They were a little too old for me at that time, but definitely 40s and 50s." As mentioned, Parry was in a long-term relationship where, because his partner was uninterested in sex, he could take casual sexual partners. And older men were still his preference: "I am still attracted to sugar daddies. There are some very hot-looking 70-year-old men."

The remaining six men related stories of sexual encounters with younger men and varying explanations for their success. Seventy-two-year-old Colin from New York, quoted earlier as saying he thought younger men feared touching the old in case they would catch it (old age), also said that a friend his age had developed a meaningful relationship with a hustler:

'If you are a young, beautiful man and you're paid by an older man, you can like them because the money makes it OK. I have a friend who does a lot of hustlers and has developed connections even relationships with them, which go well beyond the money. But the money makes it possible. They can relax. It takes it out of the bed. They can think, "I am only with him for the money". But it isn't that at all. It changes. It's interesting.'

Whether Colin's friend's experience could be generalised to all gay men who have sex with sex workers is moot. For occasional interactions it is unlikely, but what Colin seemed to be saying is that over time a relationship between an older man and a sex worker might develop into something more than a commercial transaction. This belief is the older man's perspective and it does not matter if the sex worker has a different understanding (who sees the relationship as a commercial exchange and that part of his expertise or skill is in getting the customer to believe it is 'for real') as it is what the older man wants to believe that sustains the relationship for him.

Another North American, Jude from Los Angeles (aged 46), preferred younger men but was also aware of problems associated with dating them:

'I met this young guy right after I turned 40. When we were together, he always wanted to have sex and would get mad at me when I didn't want to … But we would plan dates and he would cancel at the last minute because his friends planned to do something … A lot of twenty-somethings travel in packs. When I was dating [name], who was a sweet guy … you realise that for him his friends are his social anchor. I think you see a lot of that with young guys. It is flattering when you get hit on by a young guy – it happened last week – and you relax your standards until you realise that he wants to be with his friends. I think the older people get, the more they want the couple as the centre of the social life. Not all of us, but most of us. And young guys travel in packs.'

In this extract, Jude names some of the issues the older can face in a relationship where the age difference is 20 years or more, the most telling of which being that, while young people like to "travel in packs", the couple relationship is more central to the social-sexual life of many older people. If ageism is at work in Jude's relations with men in their 20s, it could be argued that it is in how he views the younger and not the other way around.

A common feature in the accounts of the others who spoke of a preference for younger men concerned the strategies they used to disguise their age. A 51-year-old from London admitted to lying about his age and then getting annoyed if the younger made a fuss when they discovered the truth. Another in his 50s from Melbourne observed a powerful ageism at work in Australian gay bars: "It is less evident in Europe and it is less evident in Asia in that I was pulling hot guys in their 20s in both places ... that I would probably not here" (Calvin, 51). And finally, a 49-year-old from Auckland said he would never approach a younger man:

> 'I do not approach younger men, even if I find them attractive. I have been approached by younger men on a number of times, which is very nice but I would never make the first move because I feel like ... I am buying into some sort of social model where it seems wrong for a man in his 40s to approach a man in his 20s and that has definitely affected how I operate sexually ... I put limits up because of how I perceive my age.'

The Aucklander's understanding of age differences in the gay world could suggest that what he experienced as a younger gay man is informing his behaviour as an older man. Awaiting a younger man's approach is in his mind appropriate while approaching a younger man is not. There is another interpretation, of course, which is that the older man is at greater risk of 'losing face' if the younger man rejects his approach.

Conclusion

Age and ageing no doubt affect gay men's sex lives. Almost all the men interviewed felt that their sex appeal declined as a result of growing older and this applied equally to those who never regarded themselves as attractive as it did to those who had unambiguous evidence of the high regard in which younger men held them. In other words, the participants associated youthfulness with sexual appeal and attraction, which might go a long way to explaining why people, gay and straight, associate ageing with loss of external appeal.

Evidence from the transcripts of this sample of older gay men would suggest, however, that ageing does not draw a curtain on sexual activity and that the resources of ageing can work in various ways. However, gay ageing forces those who wish to continue their sex life to adopt different ways and approaches to those which enabled them to find casual sexual partners when they were young. This could mean that older gay men are required to think strategically about how or if they approached younger men to whom they were attracted. The evidence here is that age preference was in the main for younger men, although there are men who prefer older men.

Where there was evidence of diminished sex drive or performance, it was in the context of drugs prescribed to help interviewees recover from illnesses, which reduced or affected their testosterone levels and the men accepted and advanced these medical stories to explain their reduced sex drive. The chief finding from this analysis of gay men's stories of continuing sexual adventure in middle age and older is that if they make it the central mandala of their life, as many baby-boomer men have done and still do, then they must accept limitations imposed by their ageing body or illness and approach the task differently from when they were young.

References

Adam, B.D. (2007) 'Relationship Innovation in Male Couples', in M. Kimmel (ed.) *The Sexual Self: the Construction of Sexual Scripts*, Nashville, TN: Vanderbilt University Press, pp 122–40.

Altman, D. (1982) *The Homosexualization of America, the Americanization of the Homosexual*, New York, NY: St Martin's Press.

Ariès, P. (1960) *Centuries of Childhood*, Harmondsworth: Penguin Books.

Australian Institute of Health and Welfare (2017) *National Drug Strategy Household Survey 2016: Detailed Findings. Drug Statistics series no. 31*. Cat. no. PHE 214, Canberra: AIHW.

Bourdieu, P. (2001) *Masculine Domination*, trans R. Nice, Cambridge: Polity.

Boswell, J. (1980) *Christianity, Social Tolerance, and Homosexuality: Gay People in Western Europe from the Beginning of the Christian Era to the Fourteenth Century*, Chicago, IL: University of Chicago Press.

Cancer Council Victoria (2013) 'What is Leukaemia?' (Melbourne: Cancer Council Victoria) https://www.cancervic.org.au/cancer-information/cancer-types/cancer_types/leukaemia.

Carr, D. (2001) 'Narrative and the Real World: An Argument for Continuity', in L.P. Hinchman and S.K. Hinchman (eds) *Memory, Identity, Community: The Idea of Narrative in the Human Sciences*, New York, NY: State University of New York, pp 7–25.

Connell, R.W. (2000) *The Men and the Boys*, Sydney: Allen & Unwin.

de Beauvoir, S. (1970) *Old Age*, trans. P. O'Brien, Harmondsworth: Penguin Books.

Dover, K.J. (1978) *Greek Homosexuality*, London: Gerald Duckworth & Co. Ltd.

Elias, N. (1987) *The Loneliness of the Dying*, trans. E. Jephcott, Oxford: Basil Blackwell.

Featherstone, M., Hepworth, M. and Turner, B.S. (eds) (1991) *The Body: Social Process and Cultural Theory*, London: Sage Publications.

Frank, T.C. (1998) *The Conquest of Cool: Business Culture, Counterculture, and the Rise of Hip Consumerism*, Chicago, IL and London: University of Chicago Press.

Green, A.I. (2011) 'Playing the (Sexual) Field: The Interactional Basis of Systems of Sexual Stratification', *Social Psychology Quarterly*, 74(3): 244–66.

Heaphy, B. (2007) 'Sexuality, Gender and Ageing: Resources and Social Change', *Current Sociology*, 55(2): 193–210.

Hekma, G. (1999) 'Same-sex Relations Among Men in Europe, 1700–1990', in F.X. Elder, L.A. Hall and G. Hekma (eds) *Sexual Cultures in Europe: Themes in Sexuality*, Manchester: Manchester University Press, pp 79–103.

Laslett, P. (1991) *A Fresh Map of Life: The Emergence of the Third Age* with a new preface by the author, Cambridge, MA: Harvard University Press.

Lewis, L.A. and Ross, M.W. (1995) *A Select Body: The Gay Dance Party Subculture and the HIV/AIDS Pandemic*, London: Cassell.

MacIntyre, A. (1981) *After Virtue*, 2nd ed., Notre Dame, IN: University of Indiana Press.

Mitternauer, M. (1992) *A History of Youth*, trans. G. Dunphy, Oxford: Blackwell Publishers.

Mowlabocas, S. (2010) 'Look at Me!: Images, Validation, and Cultural Currency on Gaydar', in C. Pullen and, M. Cooper (eds) *LGBT Identity and Online New Media*, London: Routledge, pp 201–14.

Murray, S.O. (2000) *Homosexualities*, Chicago: University of Chicago Press.

Pollak, M. (1985) 'Male Homosexuality– or Happiness in the Ghetto', in P. Ariès and A. Béjin (eds) *Western Sexuality: Practice and Precept in Past and Present Times*, trans. A. Forster, Oxford: Basil Blackwell, pp 40–61.

Robinson, P. (2008) *The Changing World of Gay Men*, Basingstoke and New York, NY: Palgrave Macmillan.

Robinson, P. (2013) *Gay Men's Relationships Across the Life Course*, Basingstoke and New York, NY: Palgrave Macmillan.

Robinson, P. (2017) *Gay Men's Working Lives, Retirement and Old Age*, Basingstoke and New York, NY: Palgrave Macmillan.

Seabrook, J. (2003) *A World Growing Old*, London: Pluto Press.

Simpson, P. (2013) 'Alienation, Ambivalence, Agency: Middle-aged Gay Men and Ageism in Manchester's Gay Village', *Sexualities*, 16: 283–99.

Simpson, P. (2015) *Middle-Aged Gay Men, Ageing and Ageism: Over the Rainbow?* Basingstoke and New York, NY: Palgrave Macmillan.

Simpson, P., Wilson, C., Brown, L., Dickinson, T. and Horne, M. (2017). '"We've Had Our Sex Life Way Back": Older Care Home Residents, Sexuality and Intimacy', *Ageing and Society*, 1–24. DOI: 10.1017/S0144686X17000101

Westwood, S. (2016) *Ageing, Gender and Sexuality: Equality in Later Life*, London: Routledge.

7

Thinking the unthinkable: older lesbians, sex and violence

Megan Todd

Introduction

The range of public stories which circulate about intimate relationships, including lesbian, gay, bisexual and trans (LGBT+) lives, as well as sexual abuse, has a profound impact on the ways in which individuals and couples make sense of their own experiences, behaviours and expectations in their relationships (Jackson, 1993; Jamieson, 1998). Current generations of older lesbians have experienced profound social changes over the course of their lives. Many were actively involved (Giddens, 1992), bearing witness to the transformation of understandings of ageing and sexuality. Despite such social shifts, ageism, heterosexism and sexism impact on their lives in various and complex ways, frequently rendering older lesbians invisible culturally and socially (Traies, 2012). Thus, older lesbians experience a tricky paradox, in that they live in an increasingly sexualised society, and a moment when in many ways it might be easier to be lesbian. Yet, they also live in a society that views their sexuality as unnatural, distasteful or a joke. In addition, as older members of the LGBT+ 'community' – arguably a commercialised, youth-orientated community – many older lesbians feel marginalised by the assumptions and privileging of heterosexual norms and values (Duggan's (2002) 'homonormativity'). What does this mean for women who experience sexual abuse within their relationships? What spaces are open to them to share and understand their experiences, to seek solace and support? This is a significantly under-researched area, with very little focusing specifically on the experiences of older lesbians. This chapter begins to fill in some of those gaps. Based on interviews from research into community responses to lesbian domestic violence, and data from a survey, and follow-up interviews, into LGBT+ lives in north-west England, I argue that cultural stereotypes of women, sexuality and age have a significant impact on who gets to tell their sexual story

(Plummer, 1995). Women's sense of inclusion/exclusion in relation to LGBT+ communities (if indeed it is salient to talk about communities) and wider society has a profound effect on their ability to both come out and 'come out' about sexual abuse. Thus, the violence and abuse older lesbians experience, I argue, is not sufficiently recognised and acknowledged either by professionals, or often the women themselves, as a direct result of hegemonic understandings of gender, sexuality, age and sexual violence.

This chapter begins by emphasising the continued importance of a feminist analysis of women's violence in the context of a heteronormative and patriarchal society. The chapter then explores why a focus on age in relation to sexual abuse is necessary. This is followed by a brief outline of my own research methods, before considering the ways in which the triple oppressions of ageism, sexism and homophobia shape understandings and experiences of, and responses to, sexual violence experienced by older lesbians in their intimate relationships.

Violent times? LGBT+ abuse

Sexual violence is clearly a significant 'everyday' social problem (Stanko, 2003). Amnesty International (2004, p 1) described global violence against women as 'the greatest human rights scandal of our times'. Feminist research into abuse in intimate relationships has asserted that it is imperative for us to explore and understand all forms of abuse, no matter how difficult they may be for us to acknowledge (Dominelli, 1989; Kelly, 1991; Ristock, 2003). Some of the research presented in this chapter was conducted in response to studies which attempted to assert either that there has been a collective feminist and lesbian refusal to acknowledge the issue of lesbian domestic violence, or that the existence of lesbian domestic violence renders previous feminist theorising and research into domestic abuse irrelevant. For example, Girshick claims that 'the feminist analysis views violence as inherently male ... and to admit woman-to-woman violence would discredit this analysis' (2002, p 55). Just because 'women do it too', a gendered analysis of violence, focusing on the wider socio-political and historical contexts, is still necessary. Lesbians do not live outside of patriarchal and heterosexist ideologies and institutions. Violence is still gendered; most violent crime, rape and abuse is perpetrated by men against women (Walby and Allen, 2004). Sexual abuse between women still requires a consideration of gender; if violence is understood as a masculine attribute, how does this impact on expectations of who is violent in a lesbian dynamic?

Are assumptions gendered, focusing on butch/femme dynamics for instance? While neither woman in a lesbian relationship enjoys male privilege and power, they occupy other identity/power positions in a society that promotes hierarchy, power differentials, inequality and violence, which are all pervasive features of patriarchy (Todd, 2013). Same-sex relationships are directly influenced by other societal power inequalities that impact all citizens, including sexism, and those based on class, age and ethnicity (Crenshaw, 1991; Bowleg, 2012). My own research has focused more specifically on the intersections of age and class with gender and sexuality. While not suggesting that all female violence is simply a result of social control, vulnerability or victimisation, these surely should be considered.

Boom(ers): an ageing time bomb?

That we live on a socially ageing globe has been well documented. Ageing populations have been common across Europe and beyond for some time. According to the Office for National Statistics (ONS, 2018), by 2066 a quarter of the UK population will be 65 and over, exceeding those aged 16 and under. However, this social ageing is often framed as a serious social 'problem', with concerns about how, with a declining working age population, society can afford adequately to care for its ageing population. Material deprivations structured by gender, class and ethnicity certainly continue and become exaggerated in later life. Austerity measures in the UK and countries like Greece, for instance, have impacted on older people, particularly women (see Papanastasiou and Papatheodorou, 2018). Yet, such 'moral panics' point to a key issue regarding ageing, that of ageism and stereotypes. These concerns stem from an underlying assumption that older people are financially unproductive burdens on society. Older people are culturally devalued, and old age is viewed as a state of decline and vulnerability, which has a direct impact on whether we can conceptualise older perpetrators of abuse.

Perhaps because of ageist and sexist stereotypes, until relatively recently, little effort had been made to explore the lives of older LGBT+ people, especially older lesbians (see Heaphy et al, 2003). The lack of a focus on age may, in part, be because older lesbians are a particularly hard-to-reach population. Heaphy et al (2003) also suggest the lack of recognition of age stems from a focus on sexuality as a key determining factor of LGBT+ experience, a factor which is assumed to be a prerogative of the young. This is of significance in relation to the sexual abuse of older lesbians.

While the twenty-first century has been a time of potentially progressive legislative and social change for LGBT+ people (the UK alone has seen the Civil Partnership Act (December 2004), Equality Act (Sexual Orientation) Regulations 2007 and the Same-Sex Marriage Act (which came into force in 2014)), many older lesbians have lived through less liberal times. They will have lived through both informal and formal discrimination. This might mean older lesbians find ageing less problematic than their heterosexual counterparts; negotiating non-heterosexual identities in adverse conditions can provide skills in 'crisis competence' (see Balsam and D'Augelli, 2006). However, it can both have a profound effect on their preparedness to 'come out' as LGBT+, and impact on their use, and experience, of a range of services, including health services (Fredriksen-Goldsen, 2011). In fact, older LGBT+ people are five time less likely to access services for older people than is the case in the wider older population because they fear discrimination and homophobia (Todd, 2011).

Older lesbians may have lived through times when making themselves invisible, 'passing' as heterosexuals, was a deliberate and necessary coping strategy; the alternative might have meant losing a job, friends or family (Barrett, 2008). This can lead to what is referred to as a fracturing of relationships (Barrett et al, 2016). Many will have experienced levels of discrimination to the point of violence in their earlier lives (DeLamater and Koepsel, 2017). Cronin and King (2014) have shown how fear of discrimination prevents many older LGBT+ people from making friends in the wider community. Such social isolation perhaps puts them at risk of abuse, in addition to preventing them from seeking support. Intimate relationships for older lesbians are often viewed as a safe space (Smalley, 1987), making it even more dangerous when things go wrong.

In recent years, Weeks (2007) argues, society has undergone a transformation, from being a place where same-sex desire is seen as an aberration, a sin or sickness, to becoming a culture where LGBT+ lives are 'respectable'. As Weeks has noted, the potential to age as an 'out' lesbian, in a comparatively tolerant society, is a relatively recent phenomenon and is itself a consequence of social change, a change many of the participants were involved with. Paradoxically, these women now often find themselves viewed as asexual – deemed physically unattractive in a youth-orientated society, uninterested in, incapable of, having sex (Heidari, 2016). Many of the women I spoke with in the study to be discussed later felt isolated within so-called lesbian communities almost as much as they did in society at large; for example: "Lesbian events are young events" (Barbara, 58, S1).

Gradually, the stereotype of the sexless older woman is shifting to a focus on life-long sexual relationships; 'successful' sex is seen as a key aspect of healthy ageing (Hinchliff and Gott, 2008). However, such a view is not without its own problems and perhaps places older lesbians under new pressures to comply to their partner's(') expectations. However, much of the violence against women literature ignores the experiences of older women – possibly because they were/ are positioned as asexual. Where violence is researched, it is often conceptualised as elder abuse (Todd, 2013).

These older women can experience new 'privileges' as fully recognised legal couples, through civil partnerships and marriage. The rewards which come with these – married couples' allowance, tax benefits and so on – potentially place people who are abused in a difficult position. This is a classed and gendered risk; working class women are more likely to be reliant on the state pension. Some have argued society is privileging particular relationship structures. Robson (2009, p 315) has called this 'compulsory matrimony'. It has the potential to create new social divisions in that some forms of relationship remain less visible, less socially recognised (Barker, 2012).

Methodology

In order to explore these matters, interview data from two separate studies has been used. The first, (S1), one of the earliest UK studies into lesbian domestic abuse, used in-depth interviews conducted in the north-east of England, to explore how communities responded to lesbian domestic violence over a period of 40 years. The research had a global reach; 25 self-identified lesbians were interviewed, aged 24–73, from across the UK, in addition to North Korea, Italy, Canada, Australia and the US. Interviews were conducted via telephone, email or in person. In addition to getting responses from diversely situated women in terms of age, culture and ethnicity, the research also considered the impact of social class on community membership. Though initially about whether LGBT+ communities had addressed the issue of same-sex abuse or ignored it, rather than personal experiences per se, it quickly became apparent that sexual violence was something which several women had experienced. In effect, the data from this research, which was carried out in 2005, has been 'recontextualised' (Moore, 2007, p 1).

The second piece of research, (S2), was conducted in collaboration with a charity providing advocacy and support services for LGBT+ people in north-west England. An online Smart Survey (conducted

October–December 2014) contained multiple-choice and open questions about a range of issues experienced by the wider LGBT+ population, including health and social care, social activities, crime, violence and abuse. Participants came from a range of rural and urban, prosperous and poor areas. This chapter uses data from six follow-up interviews with older lesbians who had experience of abuse in later life.

Sexual violence in older lesbians' relationships

A variety of themes emerged in relation to the sexual abuse of older women in lesbian relationships. This section will focus on a few, namely the problems of dominant and normalised narratives of abuse, how this effects our ability to conceptualise and articulate the sexual abuse of older lesbians, and a brief consideration of the impact of a sexualised lesbian culture.

Telling sexual stories: the impact of hegemonic discourse

A common theme is that victims often do not recognise themselves as victims of sexual violence and thus do not disclose it (Brossoie and Roberto, 2016). This impact of hegemonic narratives of abuse was echoed in my lesbian community study. None of the women discussed sexual violence without prompting when describing their own, or friends', experiences, although nearly all acknowledged that it was a possible aspect of domestic violence. When specifically prompted about sexual violence, many women recounted stories/memories of violence of a sexual nature:

> 'Another woman, she told me of a long term partner, she met her at university and they actually still live together now and throughout however many odd years they've known each other, which would be 30 years, there'd been various hiccups and problems in their relationship and her partner had done something similar to her and it had been unpleasant actually, this one was a really violent act. It's interesting as you start talking about this, all the things I'd forgotten about. I remember her describing that to me as quite vicious and nasty.' (Jo, 50, S1)

Sex and sexuality are notoriously difficult to talk about. Research on sexuality, sexual practice and relationships can cause unease and perhaps this is especially the case with sexual violence in lesbian relationships. The tentative nature of Jo's description reveals the difficulty facing many when discussing sexual violence. Although violence perpetrated by a woman is, for reasons discussed earlier, not expected, as Girshick (2002) states, 'the thought of a woman *rapist* is even more removed from our sensibility' (Girshick, 2002, p 3; emphasis in original). Is it simply that sex is still viewed, in a heterosexist world, as primarily vaginal penetration by a penis (Smart, 1989)? Sexism, ageism and heterosexism means that sexual violence and older women is hard to think about. The complexity of talking about such issues may be because of established, often legal, definitions of sexual violence, which are constructed around hegemonic understandings of male sexuality. A problem one of the participants considered: "I know of someone who was violated, raped by her partner with a glass bottle. Now I know legally it's not defined as rape but you can't tell me she didn't feel raped. The law just emphasises how ignored we are, it sort of minimises her experience"(Sarah, 56, S2).

The sexualisation of lesbians as a group may have also contributed to such views (Jeffreys, 2003). Lesbians, it has been argued, hold a contradictory position in society. On the one hand they have been feminised and sanitised to become the object of heterosexual male fantasy and, on the other, they can be read as 'morally dangerous' because of their perceived masculine sexuality (Wilton, 1995). It would be understandable, in this context, if many lesbians, especially older women who have lived through 'difficult' times, would not want to risk confirming society's suspicion that lesbians are sexual deviants, predatory and dangerous, by acknowledging sexual abuse in their relationships.

In the absence of the penis, conceptualisations of what has happened as rape or abuse were sometimes limited. In addition, the dominant reading of sexual violence as rape masked other forms of sexual abuse. Women have historically been constructed and read as sexually passive or receptive, therefore for a woman to conduct sexual abuse is virtually 'unthinkable', as Gina relates:

> 'Well, sexual violence I mentioned it earlier, you see and I feel that it would be easier for a man to commit sexual violence on a woman than two women because a man has a penis that he can poke in you which is attached and there, you know, I'm not saying that's the only form of sexual abuse but that's just my opinion.' (Gina, 59, S2)

Smart (1989) has written extensively of how, in a phallocentric culture, sexuality is always assumed to be heterosexuality and sex is always (only) penetrative. The law, of course, reinforces this by stating who can rape and who can be raped. In England and Wales, for instance, rape in marriage was not a crime until 1991 and men could not legally be victims of rape until 1994. Women still cannot legally be considered as rapists – only the penis is viewed as a weapon capable of rape. This clearly has repercussions for how sexual assault commissioned by women is viewed – hegemonic constructions of rape mean it is invisibilised by law and often not recognised by victims and the wider community.

Stereotypes of older lesbians as isolated, desperate and perhaps vulnerable may also render potential perpetrators (and victims) of domestic violence invisible, as Annette and Rebecca suggest:

> 'For lesbians, I think as we get older, it becomes easier for us to blend in with the rest of society. In a way all older women become more invisible, they are seen as sexless, they begin to look the same, and so lesbians generally and therefore abusers and victims aren't seen.' (Rebecca, 47, S1)

> 'I don't think we focus enough on age, whether in a heterosexual or same-sex situation. There's some stuff on elder abuse but I mean domestic violence. I think older people are seen as safe somehow and so we might not think that they can be violent but I know for a fact they are. A friend of mine was abused by her partner who was much older and I don't think people believed her partly because of the age of her partner.' (Annette, 24, S1)

It may be that we find it easier to conceptualise the possibility of an older victim of domestic violence. Again, however, perhaps as a direct result of the intersections of ageism and sexism, older lesbians may be viewed as asexual, and the potential is for that victim to be viewed more generally as a victim of elder abuse, rather than a victim of lesbian domestic violence (though of course there may well be important similarities in terms of experiences, as well as key distinctions) (O'Keefe et al, 2007).

Sexualised cultures and sexual abuse

Another divisive issue within lesbian and feminist communities since the 1980s, during the so-called 'sex wars', has been that of bondage and sadomasochism (BDSM) as a sexual practice (Jeffreys, 1994), a practice that became labelled by some as male-identified and/or heterosexual. For some of the younger women in the first study, BDSM was deemed to be something which allowed women to work through past abuses and issues of consent, and offered a counterpoint to recourse to the criminal justice system (Barker, 2013; Stryker and Dymock, 2014). For others, such practices encouraged or produced power inequality within lesbian relationships (Jeffreys, 2003). About a third of the women interviewed made a connection between domestic violence and BDSM, and three also believed lesbian porn and stripping encouraged violence. An important question, both for the women I interviewed and some academics, has been: do such sexual practices normalise sexual violence, and when do they become abusive (see Bindel, 1982)? As the following two quotes suggest, rather than just being a concern of the 1980s, this was still an issue for some women in the lesbian community:

> 'I think S/M clearly is linked to domestic violence. That particular relationship may not be abusive but it's making violence acceptable, desirable and normal. It works in the same way as stripping. An individual stripper may say she feels empowered but she's doing the wider community of women no favours because she's objectifying women and making it acceptable to see us as objects of men's pleasure.' (Julie, 54, S2)

> 'We need to combat all forms of violence – sexual violence, lesbian stripping, S/M, porn – which portray lesbians as appropriate objects of violence to other women. The lesbian sexual revolution in normalising sexual objectification between lesbians has had the effect of releasing lesbians from restraint. I regularly hear tales now of young lesbians having bad experiences in casual sex, pressurised into S/M – these were not problems so far as I was aware twenty years ago.' (Fiona, 57, S1)

For Fiona, the recent proliferation in ways to 'be a lesbian' and the rise of the 'lesbian sexual revolution' have resulted in behaviours which, for her, can be construed as violent. In a sense, she argues that lesbians are now subjecting women to an objectifying 'gaze', which enables abusive behaviours. Sheila Jeffreys (1994) echoes this view and has argued that (heterosexual) pornography justified sexual violence and that the 'selling' of the idea of pornography to women in the 1980s has done lasting damage. Many have challenged such notions, arguing that sex work needs to be framed in terms of consent and choice (Colosi, 2010; Grant, 2014).

A key strategy employed by the women to manage the impact of abuse was to compare their experience to others'. Often, participants minimised their own experiences, Jean (62, S2), for instance, constructed the abuse she experienced as "part of everyday life". Such 'normalisation' can be an effective coping mechanism but raises significant concerns about the longer-term, insidious harm of considering sexual abuse as 'normal'. The cumulative effect of routine, everyday abusive encounters, over a lifetime, can be considerable (Stanko, 1990).

Some participants, however, talked about the damaging effects of the abuse. For instance, one woman reported that the sexual abuse she experienced in her same-sex relationship triggered memories of past abuses: "I had forgotten, I think, or suppressed the memory but after she did that to me, I kept having flashbacks to something that happened with my uncle when I was young" (Lois, 53, S2). The way in which Lois articulates her past abuse also serves to minimise what had happened to her. As Lovett et al (2018) have argued, discourses of denial, deflection and disbelief are powerful, impacting on victims' awareness of the abuse they suffer and their ability to act on it at the time. This seemed particularly salient for the older women I spoke to. Many of the participants stated that they felt "stressed", "hopeless" or "anxious" as a result of the abuse.

For most of the older women, the sexual abuse meted out by their partners served to silence them. The majority had never disclosed what had happened to them to anyone before taking part in the research. Reasons put forward mirror reasons given in other studies, including embarrassment, shame and not wanting to 'dwell' on it (see Ristock, 2003; Donovan and Hester, 2011). Over half of the study participants stated that they did not believe anyone could do anything about it or would take it seriously. Only one woman had reported her sexual assault to the police and while this was ten years ago, worryingly, she said the experience was a poor one. For those women who have lived through less 'tolerant' times, this was a common expectation. Perhaps confirming Weeks et al's (2001) notion of the importance of 'families of choice' for the LGBT+ community, if any help or support was sought, women usually turned to their friends.

Civil partnerships and marriage: narratives of safety and danger

Given the ways in which many older lesbians feel isolated both within their wider communities but also within LGBT+ spaces, many, arguably, will seek solace in coupledom, indeed, it has been argued that neoliberalism has cemented the significance of the couple to LGBT+ lives (Williams, 2004). At the time of my earlier research, the Civil Partnership Act 2004, which came into operation on 5 December 2005, was a very new piece of legislation and the women I spoke to had very mixed feelings about it. Civil partnerships heralded a major shift, in that, for the first time in British history, lesbian relationships were now under state regulation. At the time, a significant area that was frequently overlooked in the debates surrounding citizenship and civil partnerships was how civil partnerships (and now marriage) relate to same-sex abuse. It could be argued that for the sexual abuse of older lesbians to be socially and culturally acknowledged, lesbian relationships must first be recognised. The introduction of civil partnerships meant that for the first time a certain type of lesbian relationship was publicly recognised. Civil partnerships (and now marriage) also offered legal protection from domestic violence. However, in the past, many feminists have critiqued the institution of marriage and identified how certain of its characteristics have provided a context in which abuses of power and violence can take place unchallenged (Kelly, 1988; Clark, 1995). Until very recently such critiques did not transpose to same-sex relationships given they have been denied access to this institution. It is important, therefore, to consider the possible impacts marriage and civil partnerships may have for domestic violence, including sexual abuse, in lesbian relationships.

Several participants were worried that civil partnerships could see the advent of new social divisions within the lesbian community, possibly leading to more sympathy for those who experience abuse in 'official' couples. A few were also concerned that marriage will effectively render same-sex couples as 'normal' or mainstream, further invisibilising lesbians (Ettlebrick, 1996). Many of the participants had, in the past, been committed, as feminists, to working outside of 'man-made' law, thus the increase in governmental scrutiny of lesbian relationships which comes with formalised relationships was a cause for caution. Some expressed a fear that civil partnerships or marriage may co-opt LGBT+ individuals, who will perhaps feel less inclined to forge relationships outside the system (Stychin, 2003), creating a move from compulsory heterosexuality (Rich, 1980), to compulsory coupledom.

One participant worried about the semantics of marriage: "I'm uncomfortable with the ownership implied with marriage, 'my' wife, seems less balanced than my partner" (Sally, 68, S1). She went on to consider whether this impacts on attitudes and behaviours in relationships. Her fear was civil partnerships may render more lesbians vulnerable to domestic abuse, ironically, at the same time as it becomes legally recognised. She believed civil partnerships may be to the detriment of lesbian communities, meaning that women who suffer abuse may not have access to community support. Such fears are supported by various academics. Claudia Card (1996), for example, expressed concern that same-sex marriage would make lesbian couples stay together for the wrong reasons. Christopher Carrington (1999) critiqued the push for legal same-sex marriage, arguing that marriage would trap more LGBT+ people in unhappy relationships and reinforce inequalities within those relationships, as well as between single and married LGBT+ people. Several women expressed a fear that investment in civil partnerships may lead some women to remain in abusive relationships; a few went so far as to suggest that civil partnerships may in themselves lead to abusive behaviour. Indeed, two of the women who were interviewed stated that the abuse started after they had moved in together and had a civil ceremony. This may of course be coincidental but it is something which needs to be considered in future research.

Conclusion

It seems we have much to celebrate in the UK, given that the international lesbian and gay association (ILGA, 2015) identified the UK as the most progressive country in Europe for LGBT+ rights. Sexual violence is rightly recognised as a problem of global proportions and in recent decades there has been much research to map the extent and nature of such abuse. There are serious gaps in our knowledge, however, particularly in relation to the sexual abuse of older lesbians in their intimate partnerships; older lesbians remain under-represented in literature on ageing, abuse and sexuality (Todd, 2013). Thus, we are left with many questions unanswered.

Richardson (2004) has highlighted the ways in which sexual citizenship rights, in many ways, are contingent on notions of responsibility and respectability. There are rewards, such as state tax breaks (Richardson, 2015), as well as cultural acceptance, for 'official' couples willing to stay in their relationships. But as down-payment for gains such as civil partnerships and marriage, perhaps has come 'compulsory coupledom' (Wilkinson, 2012). Riggs (2007) argues that liberalism, rather than understanding or valuing individuals' experiences, reduces a broad range of experience down to a particular dominant narrative. As a result, only certain groups of people are entitled to rights, often at the expense of others (Phelan, 2001). Richardson (2004) posits that recent attempts by some LGBT+ groups to gain equal rights are based upon claims of 'sameness'. If so, it is possible that we will lose sight of lesbian domestic violence, and the sexual of abuse of older women in particular, as a distinct phenomenon before we have had a chance to examine it sufficiently.

This potential disappearance of lesbian lives, particularly of older lesbians, needs to be examined more closely. Like Westwood and Lowe (2018, p 56), I see the invisibilising of older lesbians both as an outcome but also an 'ongoing process of social marginalisation and exclusion'. Rich's (1980) work on 'compulsory heterosexuality' shows how lesbian sexuality has not just been frowned upon or ignored, but has been constructed as unthinkable. The sexual lives of many older lesbians have been experienced within this context of social censorship (Waite, 2015). This chapter highlights the ways historic homophobia continues to shape the experiences of many older lesbians' sense of self and connectedness to the wider community. Many of the older women I spoke to no longer feel welcome within remaining LGBT+ spaces and/or were financially excluded from expensive bars and clubs (Chasin, 2000), the effects of ageism elevated by intersections with class. This means that there are fewer spaces in which older lesbians' opinions, experiences, histories and views can be heard (Todd, 2013; Westwood and Lowe, 2018). The loss of community support, I suggest, means some women may be driven into the arms of their abuser.

I argue that the myths which abound about rape, and sexual abuse more generally (Smart, 1989), impact on older lesbians too. The triple oppressions of sexism, ageism and heteronormativity place these women as unlikely victims (and perpetrators) of such violence. Hegemonic constructions of sex and dominant narratives which distinguish between 'real rape' – perpetrated by a male stranger against a younger, sexually attractive woman – and other forms of sexual assault, serve to render invisible the abuse many older lesbians experience. Such myths mean it is hard for us to comprehend of a female perpetrator and/or an older perpetrator; both are subject positions understood as passive and vulnerable.

I recognise that there is huge diversity within the category 'older', which often captures those aged between 45 and 100+, and exploring the breadth and depth of diversity relating to the topic is beyond the scope of this chapter. However, it is imperative that we begin thinking more seriously about the ways in which age impacts on the experiences and understandings of sexual assault. Elsewhere, I have written about how growing up through particular political moments, such as Section 28, impact on women's sense of identity (Todd, 2013). More consideration is needed in relation to the impact of the age at which a woman 'comes out' on her responses to abuse. What happens when older lesbians find themselves having to provide care for their abusive partners or conversely need to be cared for by their abusers? In what ways do the experiences of sexual assault and elder abuse relate and diverge? To what extent does the age of both victim and perpetrator – who may, for instance, have grown up in an age where rape in marriage was not a crime and may experience sex as something private and indeed taboo – impact on perceptions of abuse (Mann et al, 2014)? Perhaps the biggest gap in all the research is looking specifically at the experiences of older trans women who identify as lesbian. None of my participants identified as trans and there is a dearth of research into this. This is not to suggest that we should privilege the experiences of older lesbians but we need to begin opening up a space to recognise the violence experienced by older women and think through ways of addressing the problem.

References

Amnesty International (2004) *It's in Our Hands: Stop Violence Against Women*, Oxford: Alden Press.

Balsam, K. and D'Augelli, A. (2006) 'The Victimization of Older LGBT Adults: Patterns, Impact and Implications for Intervention', in D. Kimmel, T. Rose and S. David (eds) *Lesbian, Gay, Bisexual and Transgender Aging: Research and Clinical Perspectives*, New York, NY: Columbia University Press.

Barker, M. (2013) 'Consent Is a Grey Area? A Comparison of Understandings of Consent in Fifty Shades of Grey and on the BDSM Blogosphere', *Sexualities*, 16(8): 896–914.

Barker, N. (2012) *Not the Marrying Kind: A Feminist Critique of Same-Sex Marriage*, Basingstoke: Palgrave Macmillan.

Barrett, C. (2008) *My People: Exploring the Experiences of Gay, Lesbian, Bisexual, Transgender and Intersex Seniors in Aged Care Services*, Melbourne: Matrix Guild Victoria and Vintage Men.

Barrett, C., Whyte, C., Comfort, J., Lyons, A. and Crameri, P. (2016) 'Social Connection, Relationships and Older Lesbian and Gay People', in W. Bouman and P. Kleinplatz (eds) *Sexuality and Ageing*, London: Routledge.

Bindel, J. (1982) 'Coming to Power, Coming to Britain?', *Revolutionary and Radical Newsletter*, Autumn: 2.

Bowleg, L. (2012) 'The Problem with the Phrase Women and Minorities: Intersectionality – An Important Theoretical Framework for Public Health', *American Journal of Public Health*, 102: 1267–73.

Brossoie, N. and Roberto, K. (2016) 'Community Professionals' Response to Intimate Partner Violence Against Rural Older Women', *Journal of Elder Abuse and Neglect*, 27: 470–88.

Card, C. (1996) 'Against Marriage and Motherhood', *Hypatia*, 11: 1–23.

Carrington, C. (1999) *No Place Like Home: Relationships and Family Life Among Lesbians and Gay Men*, Chicago, IL: University of Chicago Press.

Chasin, A. (2000) *Selling Out: The Gay and Lesbian Movement Goes to Market*, Basingstoke: Palgrave.

Clark, A. (1995) *The Struggle for the Breeches: Gender and the Making of the British Working Class*. Berkeley, California: University of California Press.

Colosi, R. (2010) *Dirty Dancing: An Ethnography of Lap Dancing*, Abingdon: Routledge.

Crenshaw, K. (1991) 'Mapping the Margins: Intersectionality, Identity Politics and Violence Against Women of Color', *Stanford Law Review*, 43: 1241–99.

Cronin, A. and King, A. (2014) 'Only Connect? Older Lesbian, Gay and Bisexual (LGB) Adults and Social Capital', *Ageing and Society*, 34(2): 258–79.

D'Augelli, A. and Grossman, A. (2001) 'Disclosure of Sexual Orientation, Victimization, and Mental Health Among Lesbian, Gay, and Bisexual Older Adults', *Journal of Interpersonal Violence*, 16(10): 1008–27.

DeLamater, J. and Koepsel, K. (2017) 'Changes, Changes? Women's Experience of Sexuality in Later Life, *Sexual and Relationship Therapy*, 34(2): 211–27.

Dominelli, L. (1989) 'Betrayal of Trust: A Feminist Analysis of Power Relationships in Incest Abuse and Its Relevance for Social Work Practice', *The British Journal of Social Work*, 19(4): 291–307.

Donovan, C. and Hester, M. (2011) 'Seeking Help from the Enemy: Help-seeking Strategies of Those in Same-sex Relationships Who Have Experienced Domestic Abuse', *Child and Family Law Quarterly*, 23(1): 26–40.

Duggan, L. (2002) 'The new Homonormativity: The Sexual Politics of Neoliberalism', in R. Castronovo and D.N. Nelson (eds) *Materializing Democracy: Toward a Revitalized Cultural Politics*, Durham, NC: Duke University Press.

Ettlebrick, P. (1996) 'Wedlock Alert: A Comment on Lesbian and Gay Family Recognition', *Journal of Law and Policy*, 5(1): 107–64.

Fredriksen-Goldsen, K. (2011) 'Resilience and Disparities Among Lesbian, Gay, Bisexual, and Transgender Older Adults, *Public Policy and Aging Report*, 21(3): 3–7.

Giddens, A. (1992) *The Transformation of Intimacy: Sexuality, Love and Eroticism in Modern Society*, Cambridge: Polity.

Girshick, L. (2002) *Woman-To-Woman Sexual Violence: Does She Call It Rape?* Boston, MA: Northeastern University Press.

Grant, M.G. (2014) *Playing the Whore: The Work of Sex Work*, London: Verso Books.

Heaphy, B. (2009) 'Choice and Its Limits in Older Lesbian and Gay Narratives of Relational Life', *Journal of GLBT Family Studies*, 5:1–2: 119–38.

Heaphy, B., Yip, A. and Thompson, D. (2003) *Lesbian, Gay and Bisexual Lives Over 50: Report on the Project: 'The Social and Policy Implications of Non- heterosexual Ageing'*, Nottingham: York House Publications.

Heidari, S. (2016) 'Sexuality and Older People: A Neglected Issue', *Reproductive Health Matters*, 24(48): 1–5.

Hinchliff, S. and Gott, M. (2008) 'Challenging Social Myths and Stereotypes of Women and Aging: Heterosexual Women Talk About Sex', *Journal of Women and Aging*, 20(1–2): 65–81.

ILGA (2015) Annual Review of the Human Rights Situation of Lesbian, Gay, Bisexual, Trans and Intersex People in Europe, https://ilga-europe.org/sites/default/files/Attachments/01_full_annual_review_updated.pdf

Jackson, S. (1993) 'Even Sociologists Fall in Love: An Exploration in the Sociology of Emotions', *Sociology*, 23: 201–20.

Jamieson, L. (1998) *Intimacy: Personal Relationships in Modern Society*, Cambridge: Polity.

Jeffreys, S. (1994) *The Lesbian Heresy: A Feminist Perspective on the Lesbian Sexual Revolution*, London: Women's Press.

Jeffreys, S. (2003) *Unpacking Queer Politics*, Cambridge: Polity.

Kelly, L. (1988) *Surviving Sexual Violence*, Cambridge: Polity.

Kelly, L. (1991) 'Unspeakable Acts', *Trouble and Strife*, 21: 13–20.

Lovett, J., Coy, M. and Kelly, L. (2018) 'Deflection, Denial and Disbelief: Social and Political Discourses about Child Sexual Abuse and Their Influence on Institutional Responses: A Rapid Evidence Assessment', Child and Woman Abuse Studies Unit: London Metropolitan University.

Mann, R., Horsley, P., Barrett, C. and Tinney, J. (2014) *Norma's Project: A Research Study into the Sexual Assault of Older Women in Australia*, Melbourne: Australian Research Centre in Sex, Health and Society.

Moore, N. (2007) '(Re)Using Qualitative Data?', *Sociological Research Online*, 12(3), http://www.socresonline.org.uk/12/3/1.html doi:10.5153/sro.1496

O'Keeffe, M., Hills, A., Doyle, M., McCreadie, C., Scholes, S., Constantine, R., Tinker, A., Manthorpe, J., Biggs, S. and Erens, B. (2007) *UK Study of Abuse and Neglect of Older People: Prevalence Survey Report*, London: NatCen.

ONS (2018) 'Overview of the UK population: November 2018', Office for National Statistics, https://www.ons.gov.uk/peoplepopulationandcommunity/populationandmigration/populationestimates/articles/overviewoftheukpopulation/november2018

Papanastasiou, S. and Papatheodorou, C. (2018) 'Causal Pathways of Intergenerational Poverty Transmission in Selected EU Countries', *Social Cohesion and Development*, 12(1): 5–19.

Phelan, S. (2001) *Sexual Strangers: Gays, Lesbian, and Dilemmas of Citizenship*, Philadelphia, PA: Temple University Press.

Plummer, K. (1995) *Telling Sexual Stories: Power, Change and Social Worlds*, London: Routledge.

Rich, A. (1980) 'Compulsory Heterosexuality and Lesbian Existence', *Signs*, 5(4): 631–60.

Richardson, D. (2004) 'Locating Sexualities: From Here to Normality', *Sexualities*, 7: 391–411.

Richardson, D. (2015) 'Rethinking Sexual Citizenship', *Sociology*, 51: 208–24.

Riggs, D. (2007) 'Psychology, Liberalism and Activism: Challenging Discourses of "Equality With" in the Same-sex Marriage Debate', *Gay & Lesbian Issues and Psychology Review*, 3(3): 185–94.

Ristock, J. (2003) 'Exploring Dynamics of Abusive Lesbian Relationships: Preliminary Analysis of a Multisite, Qualitative Study', *American Journal of Psychology*, 31(3–4): 329–41.

Robson, R. (2009) 'Compulsory Matrimony', in M. Fineman, J. Jackson and A. Romero (eds) *Feminist and Queer Legal Theory: Intimate Encounters, Uncomfortable Conversations*, Aldershot: Ashgate.

Smalley, S. (1987) 'Dependency Issues in Lesbian Relationships', *Journal of Homosexuality*, 14(1–2): 125–35.

Smart, C. (1989) 'Rape: Law and the Disqualification of Women's Sexuality', in *Feminism and the Power of Law*, London: Routledge.

Stanko, E. (1990) *Everyday Violence*, London: Virago.

Stanko, E. (2003) 'Introduction: Conceptualizing the Meanings of Violence', in E. Stanko (ed) *The Meanings of Violence*, London: Routledge.

Stryker, K. and Dymock, A. (2014) 'Towards a Consent Culture', *Journal of the International Network of Sexual Ethics and Politics*, 2(1): 75–91.

Stychin, C. (2003) *Governing Sexuality: The Changing Politics of Citizenship and Law Reform*, Oxford: Hart.

Todd, M. (2011) 'Intimacies and Relationships', in C. Yuill and A. Gibson (eds) *Sociology for Social Work: An Introduction*, London: Sage.

Todd, M. (2013) 'Blue Rinse Blues? Older Lesbians' Experiences of Domestic Violence', in T. Sanger and Y. Taylor (eds) *Mapping Intimacies: Relations, Exchanges, Affects*, London: Palgrave Macmillan.

Traies, J. (2012) '"Women Like That": Older Lesbians in the UK', in R. Ward, I. Rivers and M. Sutherland (eds) *Lesbian, Gay, Bisexual and Transgender Ageing: Biographical Approaches for Inclusive Care and Support*, London: Jessica Kingsley Publishers.

Waite, H. (2015) 'Old Lesbians: Gendered Histories and Persistent Challenges', *Australian Journal on Ageing*, 34(2): 136–48.

Walby, S. and Allen, J. (2004) *Domestic Violence, Sexual Assault and Stalking: Findings from the British Crime Survey*, Home Office Research No. 276. London: Home Office.

Weeks, J. (2007) *The World We Have Won*, London: Routledge.

Weeks, J., Heaphy, B. and Donovan, C. (2001) *Families of Choice and Other Life Experiments*, London: Routledge.

Westwood, S. and Lowe, J. (2018) 'The Hidden Sexualities of Older Lesbians', in C. Barrett and S. Hinchliff (eds) *Addressing the Sexual Rights of Older People: Theory, Policy and Practice*, London: Routledge.

Wilkinson, E. (2012) 'The Romantic Imaginary: Compulsory Coupledom and Single Existence', in S. Hines and Y. Taylor (eds) *Sexualities: Past Reflections, Future Directions*, Basingstoke: Palgrave Macmillan.

Williams, F. (2004) *Rethinking Families: Moral Tales of Parenting and Step-Parenting*, London: Calouste Gulbenkian Foundation.

Wilton, T. (1995) *Lesbian Studies: Setting an Agenda*, London: Routledge.

8

Splitting hairs: Michel Foucault's 'heterotopia' and bisexuality in later life

Christopher Wells

This chapter reflects on both the sexual intimacies of the ageing bisexual and the limited research on such lived experiences of bisexuality in later life. Here I consider these two areas as an example of Michel Foucault's 'heterotopia'; as a space that is, paradoxically, both connected to, and disconnected from, the ageing gay and lesbian imaginary (Foucault, 1967, p 3). This chapter also demonstrates how the 'dynamic and fluid' complexities of lived bisexuality in later life, within mononormative care practices, ensure that older bisexual intimacies have historically existed (and continue to exist) as a 'bitopia' (Beemyn and Eliason, 1996, p 7). This 'bitopia' is defined here, within the conceptual framework of Foucault's 'heterotopia', as the simultaneous inclusion and exclusion of older bisexual intimacies and sexual practices from cultural, institutionalised and socio-historical discourses. I posit here that such practices and discourses are sustained by ideologies informed by long-established paradigms of what many bisexual scholars describe as 'mononormativity' and 'monosexual subjectivity', which describe assumptions that a person is exclusively hetero- or homosexual, indicated by the gender of their current partner (Garber, 1995, p 5; Monro, 2015, p 3). A central focus here is to utilise a literature review to identify how this lived 'bitopia' of older bisexuals in later life continues to be repressed, policed and sustained within a 'landscape of compulsory monosexuality' and how this repressive bi/heterotopia affects sexual practices and intimacies for older bisexuals (James, 1996, p 220). Furthermore, this chapter interrogates the reasons why older bisexual intimacies remain both part of, and excluded from, the sexual intimacies of the ageing lesbian and gay communities.

Foucault's 'heterotopia' and bisexual intimacies in later life

Bisexuality is often added as a footnote or at the end of a list of sexual minority groups. The B in LGBT is both an invisible and a silent letter, yet, paradoxically, also the largest letter. Consequently, it has long been contended that bisexual identities and sexual acts of intimacy exist, operate and are regulated as a silenced majority within an existing minority (Wolff, 1979; Klein, 1993; Garber, 1995; Ault, 1996; Hemmings, 1997; Angelides, 2001; Lingel, 2012; Barker and Langdridge, 2014; Monro, 2015). As of 2017 in the UK, 0.7 per cent of people identify as bisexual compared with 1.3 per cent of people who identify as *either* gay or lesbian (Guy, 2019). Similarly, in the US, 52 per cent of the LGBT community identify as bisexual (Gate, 2011). Problematically, however, it is difficult to extrapolate data from the ageing bisexual population as many older bisexuals do not readily identify with the label 'bisexual'. Reinish and Beasley (1990, p 45) noted that 'very little has been written about how sexuality is understood and expressed in later life among bisexual people' who 'remain invisible within mainstream practice, policy and research'. Within this 'landscape of compulsory monosexuality', many younger bisexuals are hesitant to disclose their bisexuality. The 2012 Stonewall report entitled *Bisexuality: A Stonewall Health Briefing* found that false assumptions about what bisexuality is means that bisexuals receive inappropriate healthcare information, and may not access relevant health services (Johnston, 2016, p 3). This 'uncertainty and doubt' around self-definition starts in younger life as 'six in ten bisexual men are not out to their GP or healthcare professional compared to three in ten gay men' (Ellis and Symonds, 1915, p 323; Guasp and Taylor, 2012, p 2). In 2015, within a sample of 1,050 heterosexual and 1,036 lesbian, gay and bisexual in later life, 25 per cent of bisexual men and one in six bisexual women claim to have experienced hostility or poor treatment from service staff due to their sexual orientation (Guasp, 2015, p 4).

Significantly, this self-erasure extends into later life. In the US, only 18 per cent of bisexuals over 45 claimed to be 'out to important people in their lives' compared with 77 per cent of gay men and 71 per cent of lesbians. Indeed, many older bisexuals continue to self-erase their bisexuality; a 61-year-old woman dismisses bisexuality as 'experimentation' and that such 'experimentation' was 'none of [her mother's] business' in the same way that 'it was none of her business how many men partners I had'. Another strikingly reoccurring justification for self-erasure was the idea that others did not need to know, or that disclosure of their bisexuality was something that was not necessary. Speaking of her partner, a 25-year-old bisexual woman attested that 'unless I decide to be with a girl long term, there is no reason for [her boyfriend] to know' (Dimock, 2013, pp 2, 3, 6).

However, such bi-erasure does affect older bisexuals' ability to participate in healthy sexuality, something felt by Kathleen, 61, who confided that '"when you get older, you find you become invisible – this is a great blow to one's self-esteem "'. This invisibility is compounded for older 'bisexual men and women [who] are more likely to have children'. As '73 per cent have children', it invites a response to their needs as a heterosexual person and thus erases their bisexuality. This means that older bisexuals are both included and often excluded from the collective fears and anxieties of older gay and lesbians, who collectively express concern about expecting the same quality of care such as 'independence, mobility, health' and 'housing' that they feel their heterosexual counterparts will receive unconditionally.[1] The older bisexual, if they have children, is differentiated from gay and lesbian fears around absolute exclusion from the lesser intense feelings of abandonment by family and friends (Guasp, 2011, pp 4, 12, 14).

This exclusion from the ageing gay and lesbian sexual imaginary is compounded further by the 'ageist erotophobia' of the 'post-sexual body' that assumes that 'sexuality is reserved for the young'. The systemic and insidious cultural assumptions that sexual needs 'stop at 55' mean that the sexual identity of older bisexuals are understood by many through the older bisexual's previous relationships or their current relationship. Such thinking limits the potential of older bisexuals to discover and experience agency as many healthcare professionals are arguably complicit in wider cultural attitudes that 'define older people as 'post-sexual'. Consequently, this can 'restrict an older bisexual's expression of sexuality and intimacy' because physiological healthcare needs supersede the importance of sexual agency. Bisexual residents in care homes are thus excluded from 'sexual/intimate citizenship' because physical and/or psychological autonomy overshadows concerns with sexuality (Simpson, 2018, p 1479). The objectives of service providers to extend autonomy in later life often 'prioritize physiological health needs above sexual needs', and thus they will treat bisexual acts and intimacies as a secondary need. Indeed, many service providers feel that 'information about sexuality is either irrelevant to their services or overly intrusive and embarrassing' (Johnston, 2016, p 5).

Consequently, the ageing 'post-sexual' bisexual body both 'represents' homo- and heterosexuality and romance while also 'contesting' and 'inverting' such mononormative alignment; the very few bisexuals who self-identify as 'bisexual' in later life will be enrolled into the heteronormative models of care afforded to 'those with children' or within the '[o]ther', the 'gay and lesbian' older communities (Foucault 1967, p 5). This auto-enrolment into either heterosexual or homosexual ageing care incites a scholarly focus on research that seeks to expose and recognise the institutional 'homophobia' that underpins 'homophobic prejudice' and the fear of 'possible harassment, prejudice and discrimination based on disclosures of being 'gay' or 'lesbian'. Such inclusion and exclusion, occupying an unfixed place, can have destructive consequences for bisexuals' sexuality (Simpson et al, 2018, pp 2, 3, 4). A key finding of the Movement Advancement Project was that 'bisexual older people are also more likely to exhibit more sexual risk behaviours than other older adults or younger bisexual people'. The report revealed that 'older bisexual men used condoms at lower rates than younger bisexual men' (MAP, 2016, p 5).

What Dworkin (2006, p 3) describes as 'the invisible of the invisible minority', or what Grant (2009, p 42) calls the 'double-edged sword' of bisexual ageing is best exemplified by the case of 78-year-old Muriel, who had both 'lesbian' and 'heterosexual' relations throughout her life but who, in identifying as bisexual later in life, presented problematic assimilation into the care provided at her residential home (Jones, 2011). The author attests here that Muriel is symptomatic of the wider community of ageing bisexuals that should be recognised as an example of Michel Foucault's heterotopia. In his March 1967 seminar paper *Des Espaces Autres* [Other Spaces], Foucault defines heterotopias as places that are:

> in every culture, in every civilization, real places – places that do exist and that are formed in the very founding of society – which are something like counter-sites, a kind of effectively enacted utopia in which the real sites, all the other real sites that can be found within the culture, are simultaneously represented, contested, and inverted. (Foucault, 1967, p 4)

While bisexuality has not existed as a specific spatial, temporal or geographical location, both the lived experiences and the 'scant empirical' research on the intimacies of the older bisexual subject 'simultaneously represent, contest and invert' stable and mononormative notions of sexuality and sexual intimacy (Almack et al, 2018, p 142). This occurs because bisexuality occupies a psychosexual space and a socio-sexological history of slippery notions and definitions, which, by its very nature, destabilises definitional stability within monosexual practices, intimacies and identities. Older bisexual intimacies and sexual practices exist within a 'place outside of all places', where heterosexual and homosexual intimacies are 'simultaneously represented, contested and inverted'. For it may be 'possible to indicate [the] location' of both heterosexual and homosexual desires 'in reality', it is a specifically bisexual identity and desire that operates as a 'counter-site' to the stability of monosexual identities and desires (Foucault, 1967, pp 3, 4).

The heterotopia, older bisexuality and the ongoing crisis of definition

Statistics on the numbers of older individuals who identify as bisexual are at best elusive because the definition of 'bisexual' is difficult to identify and can vary from study to study. Mosher et al (2005, p 23), for example, found that 1.8 per cent of men age 18 to 44 considered themselves bisexual yet 3.9 per cent identified, as before, as 'something else'.

While homosexuality signifies same-sex attraction and heterosexuality is defined by opposite-sex attraction, defining the essence of what constitutes bisexuality is comparatively more complex and ever changing. Christopher James defines bisexuality as 'the sexual or intensely emotional, although not necessarily concurrent or equal, attraction of an individual to members of more than one gender' (James, 1996, p 220). Similarly, Monro (2015, p 12) defines bisexuality as 'the coexistence of sexual desire and affection for both men and women'. The 'coexistence' of desires, as identified by Helt (2010, p 23), imbues bisexual intimacies and practices with the deconstructive potential to destabilise the binary of heterosexual desires that are set against homosexual desires, in a psychosexually 'rigid' and culturally 'permeable' binary (James, 1996, p 221; Monro, 2015, p 12). The various conceptualisations of bisexuality have frustrated the ability of sociologists and cultural theorists to categorically describe bisexuality as a 'stable and knowable state of being' (Garber,1995, p 34). The definitional instability of bisexuality was evidenced in research conducted by Fritz Klein in 1993. Klein explained that 'bi, as a linguistic prefix, means two, or dual', before elaborating that 'we call a person with a command of two languages bilingual' to which he reflects '… a simple definition'. Klein then contends that '[b]isexuality, however, is not so easily slotted. It is generally the most complex state of sexual relatedness with people. It exists to various degrees in everyone. Its dimensions are multiple' (Klein, 1993, p 12). In other words, the presence of both hetero- and homosexual desires, contained within one unified subject, ruptures the assumed 'dichotomous understandings of desire' (Barker and Langdridge, 2014, p 193). This demarcated duality of desire is destabilised by bisexuality because the bisexual, as a subject, can be romantically attracted to one gender and sexually attracted to another gender. This destabilises the dichotomy between two unified sexual drives that are defined by their '[o]ther'; homosexuality can (mostly) be defined as the '[o]ther' to non-heterosexuality; the lacking of opposite-sex desire correlates with the possessing of same-sex desire (Said, 1978, p 1). Bisexuality cannot be 'othered' within this mononormative logic that is sustained by the monosexual binaries of either heterosexual or homosexual. Biological, psychological, behavioural and cultural bisexuality contains both heterosexual and homosexual desire yet does not align wholly with either monosexual categories of homo- or heterosexuality. Bisexuality, as a unified model of composite sexuality, thus cannot assimilate within the channels of desire that compromise and constitute bisexuality's very existence. Bisexuality is dependent on both its inclusion and exclusion from monosexuality for its composition as a unified and whole bisexual self. This instability of assimilation within monosexual drivers leads the existence of bisexuality to continually deny and resist categorisation, a view espoused by Garber, who asserted that 'the erotic discovery of bisexuality reveals sexuality to be a process of growth, transformation, and surprise, not a stable and knowable state of being' (Garber, 1995, pp 33–4). James (1996, p 223) expanded this 'notion' as he attested that finding a singular bisexual definition was a 'slippery notion' because the nature of being attracted to two genders both contains a conflict between two sexual impulses and yet is also liminal, transient and resistant to the dialectical logic of binary opposition. Again, bisexuality is both, inclusive and exclusive, interdependent on the two poles of hetero- and homosexuality, yet is disconnected from both; a site of interior sexual subjectivity that 'simultaneously represents, contests and inverts' monosexuality. The older bisexual then occupies 'a place outside of all places' (a 'counter-site') that both reveals monosexual desire and identity as an 'unknowable state of being'. This was further exemplified by historian George Chauncey's claim that 'even the third category of "bisexuality" depends for its meaning on its intermediate position on the axis defined by these two poles' (Chauncey, 1994, p 34). Hence, for both the ageing bisexual and our contemporary sexual landscape of identity-politics, there circulate three meanings of 'bisexuality' according to Malcolm Bowie (1992, p 26): 'from Darwin, as an exclusively biological notion, synonymous with hermaphroditism; from early sexology, which concerns the co-presence of masculine and feminine psychological characteristics; and, finally, that which concerns the propensity of certain individuals to be sexually attracted to both men and women'.[2]

'Compulsory monosexuality' and the older bisexual subject

It has also been argued that the dominant ideologies of mononormativity sustain bi-erasure or bi-invisibility, two descriptors that are used interchangeably within queer theory to denote the denial of bisexual representation in both popular and medical discourses (Bailey et al, 2012). Mononormativity is a term used to describe both the wider cultural attitudes and assumptions that the gender of one's partner is a summative indication of a person's sexuality (Ault, 1996; Angelides, 2001; Hemmings, 2002). Mononormative assumptions systematically espouse the belief that there are *really* only two stable sexual identities: hetero- or homosexuality (Klein, 1993; Angelides, 2001). Therefore, bisexuals 'become the target of a politics of delegitimization' (Scroth and Mitchell, 2012: 106). Such mononormative assumptions were articulated rather crudely in a *New York Times* headline: 'Straight, Gay or Lying' (Carey, 2005).

Moreover, heteronormativity in later life restricts the representational tools and apparatus afforded to ageing homosexuals, mononormativity (or the assumptions around monosexuality) ensures that older bisexual intimacies and identities remain unseen and silent in both straight and gay communities and in legislative practice (Yoshimbo, 2000; Marcus, 2015). Paradoxically, however, bisexual intimacies remain at the heart of debates around the essence of human sexuality, as 'slippery definitions' of bisexuality destabilise and dismantle binarised logic around either/ or sexual object choices, confound summative definitions of sexual intimacy and compel academic trajectories around the postmodern sexual subject (Herdt and Boxer, 1995; Hemings, 2002; Callis, 2012). Yet, despite sustained contributions to our understanding of the complex sexual intimacies, bisexuality systematically repressed by its assimilation within mononormative identity categories such as hetero- and homosexuality wherein bisexuality is often perceived as a threateningly deconstructive agent of definitional stability (Alexander and Anderlni-D'Onofrio, 2012; Brennan-Ing et al, 2014). Indeed, it has been noted that bisexuality, the coexistence of both hetero- and homosexual desires, 'challenges the binary logic around which modern cultural notions of sexuality are organised, particularly the hetero/ homo divide that structures heteronormativity' (Alexander, 2012, p 34). The containment of bisexuality's definitional potential to rupture and transcend monosexual identities and behaviours has ensured that older bisexual practices and intimacies have largely been absent and 'curiously silent' (Callis, 2012, p 87) within the scholarship on older bisexual intimacies (Hemmings 1997; James, 1996). Consequently, older bisexual intimacies exist as a 'ghostly other' to non-heterosexual practices (Angelides, 2001, p 14).

This marginalisation of older bisexual intimacies has incited contemporary bisexual theorists to focus on the mechanisms of oppression enacted by the foregrounding of exclusively monosexual acts and intimacies. In only ever recognising older sexual intimacies as either homosexual or heterosexual, the possibility of bisexuality as an identity that can be accommodated within institutional settings is limited and therefore problematic. This affects a landscape of 'compulsory monosexuality' whereby the ageing bisexual subject recognises their sexual acts, intimacies and desires as either heterosexual or homosexual and often such older bisexuals will inevitable 'pick a side' and align with a falsely mononormative identity category (Bowes-Catton, 2007; Barker and Langdridge, 2014).

Further, Johnston's research has showed that it was not uncommon for staff to attest that '[b]isexuality is a phase'. Their reasons rest on the heterotopia wherein the 'ghostly other' of bisexuality is forever a liminal state of intermediary transition. One staff member in Johnston's study explained that 'we have one resident who used to be bisexual, but then he married a woman' (Johnston, 2016, p 4).

Another factor buttressing the 'bitopia' is that affirmation of non-existence, a product of both the aforementioned fear of coming out as bisexual in later life and on the assumptions that a resident's partner indicates their sexual orientation. The erasure of bisexuality is compounded by many staff supporting psychosexual development in later life, who dismiss the existence of even bisexuality by claiming that 'I know that we don't have any LGBT or bisexual constituents, so it's not a problem here' (Johnston, 2016). However, the landscape of 'compulsory monosexuality' that both incites and sustains such mononormative assumptions about ageing sexualities in 'gay and lesbian' communities is slowly dissipating as recent investigative research can reveal a disconnect between an institutional landscape of mononormative assumptions and the real existence of lived bisexual intimacies and practices (Johnston, 2016, p 2).

"I treat everyone the same and I don't discriminate. Why do I need to know if someone is bisexual?": exploring the bitopia

In *Looking Both Ways*, Almack et al (2018, p 146) conducted a very telling interview with Ian, a 51-year-old bisexual male, who describes being seen as 'utterly heterosexual' yet his whole life he had identified as bisexual as he describes how, 'I am still bisexual but not necessarily outwardly or vocally'. Ian elaborated that, 'I don't bother coming out unless there is a relevant discussion or whatever. I just can't be bothered ...'. This is highly symptomatic of Meyers' diagnosis of 'minority stress' in which invisibility can be internalised as a preventative coping mechanisms against hostility, exclusion and the threat of a lower quality of life, or in this case of service and care (Meyer, 2003, p 23). Ian's fears are not uncommon; 'fear of discrimination may keep individuals from disclosing their sexual orientation or gender identity, rendering them invisible to health care, long-term care, and social service providers' (Clark et al, 2001; Brotman, 2003; Fredriksen-Goldsen, 2016). Furthermore, LGB or transgender people, fearing discrimination, may wait too long to access care or avoid it altogether (Brotman, 2003; Grant, 2009). Ian's confessional shows one central feature of the 'bitopia' is the mononormative 'passing' of many older bisexuals. Within this 'bitopia', there exist many older bisexuals whose sexual acts and expressions of intimacy are categorised and rendered subject to care, based on the (assumed) gender identity of their current partner; an older bisexual male coupled with a heterosexual older female in community care will be perceived, cared for and supported solely as would be an older heterosexual. The socially negative stigmatisation of being both older and bisexual further guarantees suppressive subscription within this 'bitopia' (Sinnot, 2016). It is because of this mask of monosexuality that the bitopia embodies another characteristic of Foucault's heterotopia.

For Foucault, the heterotopia 'can make an existing heterotopia function in a very different fashion; for each heterotopia has a precise and determined function within a society and the same heterotopia can, according to the synchrony of the culture in which it occurs, have one function or another'. Foucault chooses to cite the 'graveyard' as such a heterotopia because 'it is a space that is connected with all the sites of the city, state or society or village, etc. since each individual, each family has relatives in the cemetery' yet adopts and signifies different meanings within different cultures. In the western world, the 'post-sexual' body of ageing bisexuals who reside in the institutionalised care home has taken on various forms: as an end of life sanctuary or as a means of psychiatric and medicinal clinical healthcare. Again, bisexual practices and intimacies within institutionalised care become problematic precisely because sexual practices and intimacies are superseded by physiological and biological needs (Simpson et al, 2017). Discursively, however, current scholarship shows that residents' continuous sexual desire and intimacy remains important up until the end of life and that age does not necessarily determine sexual desire, drive or the need for intimacy (Gott, 2005; Simpson et al, 2017).

Ian is symptomatic of the wider populace of bisexuals, including Whitney, who asks, '[w]hat speech, manners of dress or speech might I "put on" to prove myself bisexual?' (Whitney, 2002, in Callis, 2012, p 16). This notion of 'proof' and proving the authenticity of bisexual intimacies and sexual practices was a struggle in the 1970s/1980s, a time when many of those now in care were experiencing formative sexual experiences. To exemplify: a major 'exploratory study' of ageist erotophobia was Dorris Hammond's 1979 PhD research into 'Sexuality and Aging'. Hammond's workshops analysed the impact of bio-medical factors upon sexuality (heart disease, arthritis, hysterectomy, gynaecological problems, prostatectomy, impotence, cardiovascular conditions, strokes, Parkinson's disease, Organic Brain Syndrome). Hammond also explored cultural myths and misconceptions through religion, heritage and generational contexts. What is problematic in Hammond's research is that mononormative sexual orientations are assumed for all participants and no time is spent retrieving qualitative data around sexual orientation and sexual intimacies. The individual goals of participants reflect this as they include the goals of participants to 'cope and deal with problems', 'understand my own sexuality' and 'separate reality from myth'. There is, however, no anticipation of any other sexual orientations other than monosexuality, reflected, as Hammond indicates, in merely *one* 'question dealing with feelings towards a homosexual relationship for old people' (1979, pp 23–5).

While Hammond's research has done a lot to illuminate myths around sexuality and ageing, and psychiatric and provisional limitations imposed upon sexual development with older people, it has been quite damaging for bisexuality. Consequently, we can observe a fractured and decentred sexual subjectivity within many of those bisexuals who grew up during this time. It is precisely because of the lack of available language, psychological treatment, psychiatric resources, counselling or any other services throughout the 1970s that bisexuals suffer such dysphoria and conflict, which in turn fractures (bi)sexual intimacies as practices.

We can even observe how academics (Schiavi, 1999, p 34) can miscategorise bisexuality as homosexuality as they analyse case studies. To exemplify this point one can observe Schiavi's (1999) case study 6.1 of 'Mr G' who is cited in a chapter on 'Homosexuality and Aging'. Mr G is a '67-year old divorced man who sought treatment because of his inability to ejaculate anally with his 42-year old lover'. At 17, Mr G began a period of 'homosexual experimentation' before living through 'heterosexual experimentation' and marrying a woman at age 43, only to divorce due to 'a reactivation of his sexual attraction to men'. Mr G continued to conduct extra-marital affairs with both genders. Such an inability to identify with a concrete sexual label of bisexuality induced feelings of social isolation, commitment issues, lack of trust in other partners, a lack of self-esteem and the inability to engage in healthy bisexual intimacies. Coupled with this, Mr G has had no psychiatric support for managing his conflicting homo/heterosexual attractions (his bisexuality) and continues to be imprisoned by the bitopia of bisexual older age. As such, Mr G can only 'ejaculate following vigorous manual stimulation' but even so the 'pressure to reach orgasm triggered intense frontal headaches'. This conflict over his internalised biphobia and suppression of bisexual desires ensured he continued to suffer psychosomatically through paranoia that he may suffer stroke leading to 'essential hypertension'. Mr G's 'post-sexual' sexual intimacies are affected negatively by the trauma of not having any legitimate means of identification growing up. He is, like other bisexual-identified individuals, more likely to acquire sexually transmitted diseases, to be more 'promiscuous' and to be less capable of maintaining long-term romantic relationships (Casazza et al, 2015). Another instance where this fractured subjectivity has negatively impacted on bisexual intimacies and sexual experimentation and healthy psychosexual adjustment is that of 52-year-old Chryssy (Schiavi, 1999), whose entrapment within the bitopia of older age is compounded further by her indeterminate gender identity as one on the 'trans-feminine spectrum' and who self-consciously distances herself from mononormative binary categories of sexuality. In a similar way that Schiavi misidentifies Mr G as homosexual, 52-year-old Chryssy initially identified as homosexual and yet 'being part of the gay scene' of the late 1970s made her realise that monosexual categories were an insufficient means of expressing her intermediate sexual desires. After getting married and divorced due to sexual and intimacy issues, Chryssy admitted to 'searching for something that you don't know what it is, but you're searching in areas where you're likely to find these kinds of thing'. It is precisely this indeterminate and in-between 'non-space' of bisexual intimacies that induces psychosexual problems. Meyer's (2003) 'minority stress' within bisexual intimacies in these case studies exists as a block to healthy sexual practices, which in turn lead to divorce and inability to practise healthy sexuality. Perhaps Chryssy's self-reflexive and critical detachment from, and reluctance in attempting to identify with any monosexual categories is one transgressive escape from the bitopia of older age (Schiavi, 1999, p 96).

Foucault's (1967) '[t]hird principle' describes heterotopias as sites that are 'capable of juxtaposing in a single real place several spaces, several sites that are in themselves incompatible'. This juxtaposition manifests itself within older bisexuals whose institutionalised support in care homes aims to extend life through an enhancement of quality of life yet simultaneously restricts developmental opportunities for sexual practice and intimacies which are part of the ageing bisexual's psychosexual adjustment.

Like other older bisexuals, Chryssy's reluctant enrolment into monosexual identity categories sustains the 'fourth principle' of Foucault's 'heterotopia'. Here, Foucault expounds that 'heterotopias are most often linked to slices in time – which is to say that they open onto what might be termed, for the sake of symmetry, heterochronisms'. Foucault cites the 'cemetery' as a 'highly heterotopic place' as the cemetery signifies both a definitive and finitely quantifiable loss of life yet also symbolises immovability. In the same way that 'the cemetery' exists outside of time, the overly essentialist assignment of older bisexual intimacies to monosexual identity categories ensures that bisexual intimacies are lost in time as they are never explicitly recognised as bisexual acts, both as either expressions of homosexual or heterosexual desire. The older bisexual's need for intimacy is therefore rendered invisible within the 'heterochrony' of the care home. This is intensified within the bisexual community, in which private acts of sex and intimacies are progressively political routes towards bi-visibility, are made unobtainable, inaccessible and do not impact on the ageing sexuality of older bisexual subjects. The 'heterotopic' hegemony of older bisexual intimacies restricts access to literature that can offer both psychosexual growth and a more metaphysical awareness of one's own (bi)sexual subjectivity. For Foucault, sex is a socially constituted phenomenon, thoroughly cultural, contingent, and caught up in shifting forms of 'knowledge/power'. Hence older bisexuals' de-sexualised bodies exist outside of the culturally infused capitalistic modes of sexualised experiences and, as an expression of heterotopia, ageing bisexuals reflect the threat of the post-sexualised body that is also beyond agency and in a stasis that is neither liberated from nor restricted by the chains of commodified sexual capitalism that are allocated exclusively to younger people.

Indeed, younger people are allowed to be sexually active and money is made from this, but when people become older, their 'post-sexual' status, reinfantilises and positions them outside of the sexual imaginary. The sexual imaginary is propped up by a capitalist system that commodifies the sexualisation of younger bisexuals. Whereas the infant exists as pre-sexual in our culturally constitutive sexual culture, the elder is positioned within the marginal periphery of post-sexual; both are deemed as *non*-sexual within 'heterochrony'. An overarching impetus within contemporary scholarship on sexuality, ageing and intimacy is the concern that policies, staff training and care workers' attitudes towards elderly residents prioritise physiological needs over psychosexual enactment. Research suggests that older people are positioned outside of 'sexual/intimate citizenship' and are excluded from sexuality and intimacy as legitimate needs and as necessary practices for quality of later life (Plummer, 1995; Simpson, 2018). This displacement of older people from such 'citizenship' and the nullification of the older body as a sexual agent is buttressed by both cultural and institutional ideologies that renew dominant sexo-cultural ideologies that the ageing body is 'post-sexual'. What Simpson categorises as 'ageist erotophobia' encompasses the 'anxieties concerning older people as sexual beings', which are 'manifest in the widespread failure to imagine residents and older people generally as sexual beings' (Simpson et al, 2018, p 12). When the post-sexual body of the ageing bisexual is ignited through desire and intimacies, it is auto-enrolled into monosexual identity markers that inhibit and restrain specifically bisexual desires. In social practice and care this condition of the 'bitopia' has been shown to have destructive effects on the ageing bisexual. The mononormative frameworks that underpin any institutional or service response to the reactivation of the 'post-(bi) sexual body' commonly afford the older bisexual a response to their current sexual act, which is deemed as indicative of their presently existing sexual identity (Jones, 2011). The mononormative mechanisms of sexual reception and subsequent accommodation of sexual needs ensure that older bisexuals suffer poorer health and demonstrate lower levels of identity disclosure. Consequently, due to these sexual disadvantages that institutionalised mononormative care buttresses, older bisexuals disclose feelings of displacement and less of a sense of belonging to older LGBT communities.

In a 2016 study in the US conducted by Fredriksen-Goldsen, the researchers summarised, due to inadvertent assimilation into monosexual identity categories and mononormatively encoded disclosures of erotic desire, the ageing bisexual participants (who had a mean age of '66.7') suffered a 'sexual identity disadvantage'. Furthermore, it has bveen argued that ageing bisexuals have demonstrated 'lower levels of identity disclosure' and, as a conditioned response to their institutionalised assimilation into gay and lesbian sexualisation, all exhibited an 'elevated internalised stigma' about disclosing bisexual desires and/or self-identification as bisexual for fear of losing access to monosexual models of care and 'resources' (Almack et al, 2018, p 144).

Utopia?

There are many instances whereby the 'bitopia' of later life can serve as a liberating space because the idea of not being restricted by any mononormative sexual identity category can allow older people to activate a sexuality that is more aligned with social constructivists models of sexual subjectivity as 'flexible' and/or 'fluid and ambiguous' (Weeks, 2010, p 2). What should be a further limitation imposed upon sexual intimacies for older bisexuals (self-identification upon entry into community care services) can have the opposite effect. Many institutions ask older service users to indicate their sexual orientation, typically choosing between restrictive categories of heterosexuality and homosexuality. This should be problematic for those bisexuals who are not even out to their families and actively seek to remain invisible, however Margaret Rowntree's (2015) study of 67 'baby-boomers' (now in their 50s and 60s) shows interesting findings. For those who considered their sexual orientation not as 'exclusively' heterosexual or homosexual, Rowntree documented many narratives that evidence older bisexuals who utilise invisibility as a licence for sexual experimentation, as a sexual reawakening and as a rekindling of sexual excitement. A 50-year-old public servant explained how 'at 50 I feel more sexually desirable' and that 'my two children are older which means that I have more time to enjoy being with my husband'. Thus, the 'bitopic' exclusion from the sexual and intimate citizenship of middle age actually liberates this participant and enables her to fully engage with their bisexual intimacies. She goes on to explain that, 'as I've grown older I've become more aware of my sexuality. I feel more comfortable exploring it now than I did in my teens, and that's a revelation!' (Rowntree, 2015).

Liberation and freedom are thus experienced by many older bisexuals who exist within this 'bitopia'. Another public servant, a 54-year-old married bisexual man, announced that he 'intend[ed] to have sex with more men and younger women' and that he was 'particularly keen to live out fantasies, which [he] now regret[s] missing out on during a long-term relationship'. Similarly, a 64-year-old divorced bisexual man confessed that 'growing older has led me to discover/ recognize an aspect of my sexuality that I either didn't know existed or subconsciously ignored or denied'. The participation within the 'bitopia' has enabled and empowered this person to become 'more exploratory/adventurous aspect and a perceived need to experiment'. He explains that 'I feel that ageing brings with it a renewed need for excitement and experimentation for people like me' (Rowntree, 2015). This bisexual male continues to elaborate that by participating within this bitopia he has been able to renegotiate his bisexuality as he elaborates:

> For some, that may not be a sexually oriented revolution but for me, it has been. Changes in my sexual orientation may be a product of living on my own since my divorce 13 years ago and having the freedom and inquisitiveness to pursue alternatives to socially accepted heterosexuality, albeit that the changes have only really manifested themselves in the last four years or so. (Almack et al, 2018, p 145)

Paradoxically, in acknowledging contemporary cultural developments within definitions of non-mononormative sexual identity categories this participant has been empowered by his ability to reject cultural heteronormativity and pursue non-normative, non-heterosexual erotic modalities. It is only through the exclusion from the sexual imaginary and a simultaneous inclusion within the bitopia of older life that this participant has been able to experiment and engage with bisexual intimacies that satiate and satisfy his sexual impulses. Overall, many of the participants in this study utilise sexual identity markers which are themselves products of a post-structuralist and postmodern worldview whereby sexualised subjectivity is not inherently biological or of any essentialised essence (Butler, 1990) but is a product of social systems of power and oppression; or, in the case of bisexuality, invisibility and self-regulation and policing of this invisible sexual intermediary.

However, this qualitative data set shows that many elderly bisexuals who have been marginalised within the periphery of gay and lesbian liberation movements have adapted a coping mechanism, be it conscious or unconscious, of self-sustaining invisibility by not acknowledging their ambivalent indeterminate and intermediary sexual preferences. Such socially scripted behaviour is a product of the cultural conditioning felt by older bisexuals through formative years whereby sexual intimacies were felt not to conform to mononormative modes of sexual expression and thus delegitimised as stable sexual identity (Gagnon and Simon, 1973, p 198). However, analysing the participants' descriptions of their sexual intimacies shows that some people are liberated within older age; in a sense not belonging / displacement from mononormativity has created opportunities for greatly enhanced and honest sexual practices. Outside of the public discourses that sustain bi-visibility older people can live out fantasies and sexual expression more freely. The older people described earlier are liberated from the bitopia of sexual identity precisely because sex is a socially constructed concept that is heavily institutionalised and regulated by capitalistic systems of power and control, which themselves are driven by mononormative ideologies that seek to stabilise heterosexuality as the 'mainstream' and homosexuality as the alternative with little room in between.

Conclusion

As a final note, it is useful to consider Foucault's 'repressive hypothesis' within the context of older bisexual intimacies. Within Victorian social paradigms of sexuality, Foucault asserts that the parents' bedroom was the proto-capitalist site of sexual reproduction for two heterosexual citizens who perform sexual acts out of nationalistic duty of care. Foucault described this as a 'the single locus of sexuality' which was heavily policed by the 'Victorian bourgeoisie' (Foucault, 1967/ 1991). If we reconsider Foucault's notion of 'Victorian bourgeoisie' as the youth-centred sexual culture, and youthful heterosexuality as the 'single locus of sexuality', we can begin to mark out the zones of culturally constituted sexual landscape as one of the various sites of power that exclude older people from 'sexual citizenship' whereby 'silence bec[omes] the rule'. The 'post-sexual body' of bisexuals in later life is treated in the same way as sex was by the 'Victorian bourgeoisie' as Foucault (1967/1991) described it. Of sex, Foucault argued that it would be 'driven out, denied and reduced to silence' and 'would be made to disappear upon its least manifestation-whether in acts or words'. For those older bisexual subjects, 'a general silence *is* imposed' as why a 'studied silence *continues to be* imposed (emphasis mine)' because the needs of the ageing bisexual sexual, under the institutional imaginary of the 'post-sexual' gay and lesbian body are assigned 'an injunction to silence, an affirmation of nonexistence' and, by implication, an admission that there is 'nothing to say about such things, nothing to see, and nothing to know' (Foucault, 1978 in Rabinow, 1991, p 292).

As the post-sexual bisexual body operates outside of the dominant ideology of commodified sexual capitalism reserved primarily for the youthful, the 'injunction to silence' is sustained through mononormative institutions (care homes) and cultural spaces and artefacts (bars, media, erotic literature) that sustain such 'affirmation of non-existence' (Foucault 1978 in Rabinow 1991). There is not a clear cut and 'known sequence' of progression from bisexual lived experiences of intimacies and sexual practices that can continue into old age because of such an invisibilised sexual identity (Ochs, 2011).

Notes

[1] The specific statistics are very revealing and should be read in full within Stonewall's report on 'LBG experiences in later life'. The report demonstrates that older gay, lesbian and bisexual men and women collectively express concern around 'hostility, harassment and prejudice'.

[2] It is also significant that the history of westernised bisexual subjectivity has developed within such a 'heteroptopic' space where both hetero- and homosexuality, within early sexological theorisations of bisexuality, were 'simultaneously represented, contested and inverted'. Both the inclusion and exclusion of bisexuality in the emerging institution of sexual science at the turn of the twentieth century existed in part because of the 'uncertainty and doubt' that the existence of bisexuality incited within purportedly immutable and immovably 'stable and knowable' states of monosexual categories. Such contingency frustrated both Havelock Ellis and Sigmund Freud, who attested that 'bisexuality embarrasses' their theoretical lines of enquiry into 'inversion' (non-heterosexuality) (Freud, 1905, p 294; Ellis, 1915, p 323; Foucault, 1967, p 3). Historically, the term 'bisexuality' was used interchangeably as both signifier of physical hermaphroditism in early scientific research (the term was first coined by a Russian embryologist named Aleksandr Kovalevsky to describe a hermaphroditic ascidian (or sea squirt)) in Charles Darwin's *The Origin of Species* in 1859 as 'the missing link' in evolution of invertebrate to vertebrate, as a 'psychic hermaphroditism' (Erikson and Mitchell, 2012, p 111). The indeterminacy between gender identity, sexual practice and sexual subjectivity continued as early sexologists struggled to pin down and define exactly what bisexuality was. Yet paradoxically, there emerged convictions that bisexuality was a foundational aspect of everyone's sexual identity yet was also a sexuality that morphed, altered and adjusted to a monosexuality (eventually the subject will align to either homo/hetero). Examples of such paradoxical discourses include the fact that bisexuality was both innate yet alterable. Wilhelm Stekel claimed in 1922 that 'all persons are originally bisexual in their predisposition. There is no exception to this rule' and Havelock Ellis claimed that 'the basis of sexual life is bisexual' (Wollf, 1979, p 32). However, admissions were made about the progressive power of bisexuality in thwarting any attempt to apply binarised medicinal categories to sexuality. Freud's admission in 1937 that bisexuality 'embarrasses all our enquiries into the subject and makes [sexuality] harder to describe' (Freud, 1937, in Angelides, 2001, p 56) coupled with Ellis's conclusion that as a sexual

identity category, bisexuality 'introduces uncertainty and doubt' (Ellis, 1915, p 323). Indeed, Rapoport (2012, p 88) identifies bisexuality to be 'construed as the deeper truth of human sexuality' in 'most' of Freud's writings. However, Rapoport acknowledges that Freud assumed bisexuality as lived sexual experience/identity as 'impossible in practice' as 'primordial bisexuality always lurks in the background, yet fundamentally, one is always physically identified as a man or a woman, and one's object choice is always complementary to this identification'. In other words, the 'polymorphous perversity' (or multiplicity of desire) of a child's subjectivity inexorably aligns with either hetero/homosexual subjectivity.

References

Alexander, J. and Anderlini-D'Oofrio, S. (2012) 'Bisexuality and Queer Theory: An Introduction', in Alexander, J. and Anderlini-D'Oofrio, S. (eds) *Bisexuality and Queer Theory Intersections, Connections and Challenges*, London: Routledge, pp 1–19.

Almack, K., Jones, R. and Scicluna, R. (2018) 'Bisexuality and Ageing: Why It Matters for Social Work Practice', in Hafford-Letchfield, T. and Dunk-West, P. (eds) *Sexuality, Sexual and Gender Identities and Intimacy Research in Social Work and Social Care: A Lifecourse Epistemology*, London: Routledge, 2018, pp 142–54.

Angelides, S. (2001) *A History of Bisexuality*, Chicago, IL: University of Chicago Press.

Ault, A. (1996) 'Hegemonic Discourse in an Oppositional Community: Lesbian Feminist Stigmatization of Bisexual Women', in Beemyn, B. and Eliason, M. (eds) *Queer Studies; A Lesbian, Gay, Bisexual, and Transgender Anthology*, New York, NY: New York University Press, pp 204–16.

Ault, A. (1999) 'Ambiguous Identity in an Unambiguous Sex/Gender Structure: The Case of Bisexual Women', in Storr, M. (ed) *Bisexuality: A Critical Reader*, London: Routledge, pp 167–85.

Bailey, H., Bower, J. and Gurevich, M. (2012) 'Querying Theory and Politics: The Epistemic (Dis)Location of Bisexuality within Queer Theory', in Alexander, J. and Anderlini-D'Onofrio, S. (eds) *Bisexuality and Queer Theory Intersections, Connections and Challenges*, London: Routledge, pp 43–66.

Barker, M. and Langdridge, D. (2014) 'Bisexuality: Working Within a Silenced Sexuality', in Burr, V. (ed) *Gender and Psychology Critical Concepts in Psychology*, London: Routledge, pp 191–6.

Barker, M., Richards, C. and Bowes-Catton, H. (2005) 'All the World Is Queer Save Thee and Me ...': Defining Queer and Bi at a Critical Sexology Seminar', *Journal of Bisexuality*, 9(3/4): 363–79.

Barrett, C. and Latham, J.R. (2015) 'Trans Ageing and Aged Care – An Evidence-Based Guide to Inclusive Services' (from the 'Trans Ageing' projects), Melbourne: Australian Research Centre in Sex, Health and Society, La Trobe University.

Bauer, M., Fetherstonhaugh, D., Tarzia, L., Nay, R. and Beattie, E. (2014) 'Supporting Residents' Expression of Sexuality: The Initial Construction of a Sexuality Assessment Tool for Residential Aged Care Facilities', *Bio-Medical Geriatrics*, 14(1): 82–8.

Beemyn, B. and Eliason, M. (eds) (1996) *Queer Studies; A Lesbian, Gay, Bisexual, and Transgender Anthology*, New York, NY: New York University Press.

Bowes-Catton, H. (2007) 'Resisting the Binary: Discourses of Identity and Diversity in Bisexual Politics 1988–1996', *Lesbian & Gay Psychology Review*, 8(1): 58–70.

Bowie, M. (1992) 'Bisexuality', in Wright, E. (ed) *Feminism and Psychoanalysis: A Critical Dictionary*, Oxford: Blackwell Publishers.

Boxer, A. and Herdt, G. (2013) 'Bisexuality: Toward a Comparative Theory of Identities and Culture', in Gagnon, J. and Parker, R. (eds) *Conceiving Sexuality: Approaches to Sex Research in a Postmodern World*, New York, NY: Routledge, pp 70–84.

Brennan-Ing, M., Seidel, L., Larson, B. and Karpiak, S.E. (2014) 'Is There a Greater Risk of Depression Among Sexual Minority Elders Who Identify as Bisexual?' *American Society on Aging*, http://www.asaging.org/blog/there-greater-risk-depression-among-sexual-minority-elders-who-identify-bisexual [accessed 12 December 2019].

Brotman, S. (2003) 'The Limits of Multiculturalism in Elder Care Services', *Journal of Aging Studies*, 17(2): 209–29.

Butler, J. (1990) *Gender Trouble: Feminism and the Subversion of Identity*, London: Routledge.

Butler, J. (1993) *Bodies that Matter: On the Discursive Limits of Sex*, London: Routledge.

Butler, S.S. (2008) 'Gay, Lesbian, Bisexual, and Transgender (GLBT) Elders: The Challenges and Resilience of This Marginalized Group', *Journal of Human Behavior in the Social Environment*, 9(4): 25–44.

Callis, A. (2012) 'Playing with Butler and Foucalt: Bisexuality and Queer Theory', in Alexander, J. and Anderlini-D'Onofrio, S. (eds) *Bisexuality and Queer Theory Intersections, Connections and Challenges*, London: Routledge, pp 21–41.

Carey, B. (2005) 'Straight, Gay or Lying', *The New York Times* [online] https://www.nytimes.com/2005/07/05/health/straight-gay-or-lying-bisexuality-revisited.html [Accessed 12 December 2019].

Casazza, S.P., Ludwig, E. and Cohn, T.J. (2015) 'Heterosexual Attitudes and Behavioral Intentions Toward Bisexual Individuals: Does Geographic Area Make a Difference?', *Journal of Bisexuality*, 3(3): 532–53.

Center for Disease Control and Prevention (2013) *The State of Aging and Health in America 2013*, Atlanta, GA: Centres for Disease Control and Prevention, https://www.cdc.gov/aging/pdf/state-aging- health-in- america-2013.pdf [Accessed 12 December 2019].

Chauncey, G. (1994) *Gay New York: Gender, Urban Culture, and the Making of the Gay Male World 1890–1940*, New York, NY: New York University Press.

Clark, M.E., Landers, S., Linde, R. and Sperber, J. (2001) 'The GLBT Health Access Project: A State-funded Effort to Improve Access to Care', *American Journal of Public Health*, 91(6): 895–6.

Cramere, P., Barret, C. and Whyte, C.L. (2015) 'It's More Than Sex and Clothes: Culturally Safe Services for Older Lesbian, Gay, Bisexual, Transgender and Intersex People', *The Australasian Journal on Ageing*, 34(2): 21–5.

Cronin, A. and King, A. (2010) 'Power, Inequality and Identification: Exploring Diversity and Intersectionality Amongst Older LGB Adults', *Sociology*, 44: 876–92.

Dhingral, I., De Sousa, A. and Sonavane, S. (2016) 'Sexuality in Older Adults: Clinical and Psychosocial Dilemmas', *Mental Health*, 1(3): 131–9.

Dimock, M. (2013) 'A Survey of LGBT Americans, Chapter 3: The Coming Out Experience', *Pew Research Center*, http://www.pewsocialtrends.org/2013/06/13/chapter-3-the-coming-out-experience

Doll, G.A. (2012) *Sexuality and Long-term Care: Understanding and Supporting the Needs of Older Adults*, Baltimore, MD: Health Professions Press.

Dworkin, S.H. (2006) 'The Aging Bisexual: The Invisible of the Invisible Minority', in Kimmel, D., Rose, T. and David, S. (eds) *Lesbian, Gay, Bisexual and Transgender Aging: Research and Clinical Perspectives*, New York, NY: Columbia University Press, pp 332–45.

Dyar, C., Feinstein, B.A. and London, B. (2014) 'Dimensions of Sexual Identity and Minority Stress Among Bisexual Women: The Role of Partner Gender, *Psychology of Sexual Orientation and Gender Diversity*, 1: 441–51.

Ellis, H. (1915) 'Studies in the Psychology of Sex: Volume Two', in Bland, L. and Doan, L. (eds) (1998) *Sexology Uncensored: The Documents of Sexual Science* Cambridge: Polity, pp 52–7.

Ellis, H. and Symonds, J.A. (1915) *Studies in the Psychology of Sex, Volume II: Sexual Inversion*, reprint, Philadelphia: F.A. Davis (1994).

Erikson, S. and Mitchell, J. (2012) 'Queering Queer Theory, or Why Bisexuality Matters', in Alexander, J. and Anderlini-D'Onofrio, A. (eds) *Bisexuality and Queer Theory Intersections, Connections and Challenges*, London: Routledge, pp 105–23.

Fabbre, V. (2016) 'Queer Aging: Implications for Social Work Practice with Lesbian, Gay, Bisexual, Transgender, and Queer Older Adults', https://academic.oup.com/sw/article-abstract/62/1/73/2527536?redirectedFrom=fulltext

Foucault, M. (1967) 'Of Other Spaces: Utopias and Heterotopias', *Architecture/Mouvement/Continuété*, http://web.mit.edu/allanmc/www/foucault1.pdf

Foucault, M. (1967) 'We Other Victorians', in Rabinow, P. (ed) (1991) *The Foucault Reader*, London: Penguin Books, pp 292–329.

Fredriksen-Goldsen, K. (2016) 'The Future of LGBT+ Aging: A Blueprint for Action in Services, Policies and Research', *Generations*, 40(2): 6–15.

Freud, S. (1905) 'Three Essays on Human Sexuality', in (2005) *The Essentials of Psychoanalysis*, London: Vintage, pp 123–88.

Gagnon, J.H. and William, S. (1973) *Sexual Conduct: The Social Sources of Human Sexuality*, Chicago: Aldine.

Garber, M. (1995) *Vice Versa: Bisexuality and the Eroticism of Everyday Life*, London: Routledge.

Gates, G.J. (2011) How Many People Are Lesbian, Gay, Bisexual and Transgender?, *The Williams Institute*, https://williamsinstitute.law.ucla.edu/publications/how-many-people-lgbt/

Gott, M. (2005) *Sexuality, Sexual Health and Ageing*, Maidenhead: Open University Press.

Grant, J.M. (2009) 'Outing Age 2010: Public Policy Issues Affecting Lesbian, Gay, Bisexual and Transgender (LGBT) Elders', *National Gay and Lesbian Task Force Policy Institute*, http://www.thetaskforce.org/outing-age-2010/

Guasp, A. (2011) 'LGB People in Later Life', *Stonewall*, available from: www.stonewall.org.uk/publications [Accessed 12 February 2019].

Guasp, A. (2015) 'Stonewall, Lesbian Gay and Bisexual People in Later Life', *Stonewall*, available from: https://www.stonewall.org.uk/resources/lesbian-gay-and-bisexual-people-later-life-2011 [Accessed 5 January 2020].

Guasp, A. and Taylor, J. (2012) 'Bisexuality Stonewall Health Briefing', *Stonewall*, available from: www.stonewall.org.uk/publications [Accessed 2 January 2020].

Guy, A., Legate, N., DuBois, S. and Kendell, A. (2019) 'Partnership-Health Associations Among Bisexual Individuals in a U.S Population-Level Sample', *Journal of Bisexuality*, 19(3): 361–85.

Hafford-Letchfield, P. (2008) 'What's Love Got to Do With It? Developing Supportive Practices for the Expression of Sexuality, Sexual Identity and the Intimacy Needs of Older People', *Journal of Care Services Management*, 2(4): 389–405.

Hammond, D.I. (1979) *An Exploratory Study of a Workshop on Sexuality and Aging* (Unpublished Ph.D Thesis), University of Georgia, Athens, Georgia (GA).

Helt, B. (2010) 'Passionate Debates on "Odious Subjects": Bisexuality and Woolf's Opposition to Theories of Androgyny and Sexual Identity', *Twentieth-Century Literature*, 56(2): 131–67.

Hemmings, C. (1997) 'Bisexual Theoretical Perspectives: Emergent and Contingent Relationships', in Davidson, P., Eadie, J., Hemmings, C., Kaloski, A. and Storr, M. (eds) *The Bisexual Imaginary*, London: Cassell, pp 14–37.

Hemmings, C. (2002) *Bisexual Spaces: A Geography of Sexuality and Gender*, New York, NY/London: Routledge.

Herdt, G. and Boxer, A. (1995) 'Bisexuality: Towards a Comparative Theory of Identities and Culture', in *Conceiving Sexualities: Approaches to Sex in a Postmodern World*, London: Routledge, pp 69–84.

James, C. (1996) 'Denying Complexity: The Dismissal and Appropriation of Bisexuality', in Beemyn, B. and Eliason, M. (eds) *Queer Studies; A Lesbian, Gay, Bisexual, and Transgender Anthology*, New York, NY: New York University Press, pp 217–41.

Johnston T. (2016) 'Bisexual Aging and Cultural Competency Training: Responses to Five Common Misconceptions', *Journal of Bisexuality*, 16(1): 99–111.

Jones, R.I. (2011) 'Bisexuality Through the Lifespan – Imagining Bisexual Futures: Positive, Nonnormative Later Life', *Journal of Bisexuality*, 11(2): 245–70.

Klein, F. (1993) *The Bisexual Option* (2nd edn), New York, NY: The Haworth Press.

Kuyper, L. and Fokkema, T. (2010) 'Loneliness Among Older Lesbian, Gay, and Bisexual Adults: The Role of Minority Stress', *Archives of Sexual Behaviour*, (39): 1171–80.

Lingel, J. (2012) 'Adjusting the Borders: Bisexual Passing and Queer Theory', in Alexander, J. and Anderlini-D'Onofrio, S. (eds) *Bisexuality and Queer Theory Intersections, Connections and Challenges*, London: Routledge, pp 189–213.

Marcus, N.C. (2015) 'Bridging Bisexual Erasure in LGBT-Rights: Discourse and Litigation', *Michigan Journal of Gender and Law*, 22(2): 343–55.

Meyer, I.H. (2003) 'Prejudice, Social Stress, and Mental Health in Lesbian, Gay, and Bisexual Populations: Conceptual Issues and Research Evidence', *Psychological Bulletin*, 129(5): 674–97.

Mitchell, J. and Erickson-Schroth, L. (2012) 'Queering Queer Theory, Or Why Bisexuality Matters', in Alexander, J. and Anderlini-D'Onofrio, S. (eds) *Bisexuality and Queer Theory Intersections, Connections and Challenges*, London: Routledge, pp 105–23.

Monro, S. (2015) *Bisexuality: Identities, Politics, and Theories*, London: Palgrave Macmillan.

Mosher, W.D., Chandra, A. and Jones, J. (2005) 'Sexual Behaviour and Selected Health Measures: Men and Women 15–44 Years of Age, United States, 2002', *Advance Data from Vital and Health Statistics*, 362(4). Baltimore, MD: National Centre for Health Statistics, Available from: https://pubmed.ncbi.nlm.nih.gov/16250464/

Movement Advancement Project (2016), 'Invisible Majority: The Disparities Facing Bisexual People and How to Remedy Them', *Movement Advance Project*, http://lgbtmap.org/policy-and-issue-analysis/ invisible-majority [Accessed 11 January 2020].

Novak, D., Schnarrs, P. and Rosenberger, J. (2016) 'Differences in Sexual Health, Sexual Behaviors, and Evaluation of the Last Sexual Event Between Older and Younger Bisexual Men', *Journal of Bisexuality*, 16(1): 212–33.

Ochs, R. (2011) 'Why We Need to "Get Bi"', *Journal of Bisexuality*, 11(2): 171–5.

Plummer, K. (1995) *Telling Sexual Stories: Power Intimacy and Social Worlds*, London: Routledge.

Rapoport, E. (2012) 'Bisexuality in Psychoanalytical Theory: Interpreting the Resistance', in Alexander, J. and Anderlini-D'Onofrio, S. (eds) *Bisexuality and Queer Theory Intersections, Connections and Challenges*, London: Routledge, pp 87–104.

Reinish, J. and Beasley, R. (1990) *The Kinsey Institute New Report on Sex: What You Must Know to Be Sexually Literate*, London: Penguin.

Rowntree, M. (2015) 'The Influence on Ageing on Baby Boomers not so Straight Sexualities', *Sexualities*, 18(3): 12–45.

Rust, P. (2012) 'Aging in the Bisexual Community', in Witten, T.M. and Eyler, A.E. (eds) *Gay, Lesbian, Bisexual and Transgender Aging: Challenges in Research Practice and Policy*, Baltimore, MD: Johns Hopkins University Press, pp 343–77.

Said, E.W. (1978) *Orientalism: Western Conceptions of the Orient*, London: Harmondsworth.

Schiavi, R.C. (1999). *Aging and Male Sexuality*, Cambridge: Cambridge University Press.

Simpson, P., Wilson, C., Brown, L., Dickinson, T. and Horne, M. (2018) 'We've Had Sex Life Way Back', *Aging and Society*, 38(7): 1478–501.

Sinnott, J. (2016) 'Introduction to the Special Issue on Aging and Bisexuality: Can These Complex Life Patterns Be an Impetus for Identity Flexibility and Growth? *The Journal of Bisexuality*, (16)1: 545–56.

Weeks, J. (2010). *Sexuality* (Fourth Edition), London: Routledge.

Wolff, C. (1979) *Bisexuality: A Case Study*, London: Quartet Books Limited.

Yoshino, K. (2000) 'The Epistemic Contract of Bisexual Erasure', *Stanford Law Review*, http://www.kenjiyoshino.com/articles/epistemiccontract.pdf

9

The age of rediscovery: what is it like to gender transition when you are 50 plus?

Laura Scarrone Bonhomme

Introduction

Just a short time ago, we started to witness a slow but steady progression supporting the protection, inclusiveness and increased visibility of gender and sexual minorities. Almost half a century has passed since homosexuality was finally removed from the second edition of the Diagnostic and Statistical Manual of Mental Disorders (American Psychiatric Association, 1973), and now it is time for gender-diverse individuals to follow the very same steps. Only in 2019 did the World Health Organization recognise Gender Incongruence (HA60) to be a condition related to sexual health, rather than a mental health issue (WHO, 2020). Having excised the stigmatising stamp of 'insanity', we have been granted a golden opportunity to bring a compassionate understanding to the experiences of those who struggle with gender dysphoria; this is the central aim of this chapter.

There is a dearth of information surrounding the experiences of gender-diverse individuals that come to transition during their midlife, not only because the media has predominantly focused on voicing concerns around young transgender people, but also because there tends to be a general neglect of issues relating to older age. Individuals undergoing transition will often require support from multidisciplinary specialist teams composed of doctors, surgeons, psychologists, speech and language therapists, and many others. This reflects the bio-psycho-social nature of gender and the need for establishing a holistic approach when attempting to understand what it is like to transition when on the other side of 50.

To describe the process of transition, the chapter will first focus on the psychological processes involved in gender exploration. It is worth noting that not everyone proceeds with a physical transition and, when doing so, this comes at a later stage. Therefore, emulating the order in which most people experience these changes, the effects of physical interventions will be discussed in the final sections. Foremost, a common understanding of gender diversity and transition will be established. The section 'Transition During Midlife, Why Now?' shares an examination of likely life trajectories and the questioning involved in 'coming out'. This will be followed by 'Transition in Later Life, the Other Adolescence', where the reader will consider the re-enactment of experiences often associated with teenage years during the individual's midlife. In 'Characteristics of the 50-plus Population', the demographics of this group will be reviewed. The chapter ends with a description of the 'Impact of Physical Interventions in Love, Sex and Intimacy' and the 'Social Aspects of Physical Transition'.

The author is cisgender and hence the discussion does not derive from an expert-by-experience viewpoint but from listening to the narratives of trans community members and their loved ones. The selection of topics has been guided by the author's clinical experience of how frequently gender-diverse people of this age group have wished to reflect about the earlier-mentioned issues, particularly while engaging with psychological therapy. Queer theory and other gender-related academic discourses are an implicit part of this work. This chapter has a psychological focus that should be helpful to therapists and clinicians, therefore practical rather than theoretical perspectives have been prioritised. Finally, the chapter uses affirmative and inclusive language in relation to trans and non-binary individuals, and as the vast majority of people of this age group identify as trans women, special attention will be given to them.

Gender diversity and transition

Across cultures and within days of their arrival in this world, every newborn's genitals are examined and, as a consequence, the baby is pronounced either 'male' or 'female'. In reality, this is not a mere anatomical judgement but it is a label that comes with its own set of expectations involving the presentation, psychological makeup, place in society, and even presumed future sexual interests of an individual. Most people come to accept this given label and feel largely comfortable being associated with the social constructs of masculinity and femininity – a group commonly referred to as 'cisgender'. However, a recent systematic review found that between 0.5 and 4.5 per cent of adults (Zang et al, 2020) experience a sense of incongruence with their birth-assigned sex and therefore identify as 'transgender', or simply 'trans'. The latter denomination is largely used by community members who consider that it removes pathologising historical undertones.

Gender incongruence is manifested in a wide array of forms. The current understanding of this issue is that trans people describe their gender identity as either 'binary' and entirely identify with being a man or a woman; or as 'non-binary', expressing a partial or full rejection of a binary identity and often using sub-labels such as agender, genderfluid, genderqueer and other emerging terms that describe their nuanced sense of self. It was reported by Koehler et al (2018) that approximately 80 per cent of trans people have a binary gender, whereas 20 per cent are non-binary.

Gender-diverse people experience varying degrees of *gender dysphoria* (Coleman et al, 2012), defined as the distress caused by the incongruence between an individual's internal sense of self, body phenotype, and social gender role. Transitioning allows individuals to reduce dysphoria and to increase their sense of gender congruence, which is understood as the sense of connection that is achieved once the person is able to live authentically in a gender-congruent body and social role. Hence, people of all ages may decide to pursue a social role transition and/or a physical transition, which may include interventions like hormone therapy, surgery, psychological therapy, speech and language therapy, and so on.

It is important to clarify that although gender diversity and sexual identification have traditionally been conflated in LGBTQI+ groups, human rights movements, and medical models, these are not necessarily linked. Therefore, it is possible to find a rich variety of sexual and/ or romantic attractions in cisgender, trans, and non-binary people. In simple terms, this concerns less 'who you are' (this is to say trans man, woman, agender, genderfluid, and so on) and more 'who or what you like' (this is to say men, trans women, androgynous people, anal sex, kink, group sex, and so on).

Gender transition during midlife, why now?

The age at which a person decides to transition can be crucial in terms of differentiating their experience from someone younger. People above the age of 50 will likely be faced with a number of issues corresponding to these developmental stages, such as: experiencing changes to their physical health and appearance; bearing economic and emotional responsibility for their families; confronting the death or illness of their parents; and undergoing secondary psychological shifts in the way they perceive, value and plan life. All these elements are likely to be affected by transition; therefore, when considering the implications of 'coming out' halfway through life, one may ask, why now?

Applying the concept of intersectional identity (Crenshaw, 1991), it is argued that those belonging to the post-World War Two 'Baby Boom' and 'X' generations (born between 1946 and 1980) were exposed to specific societal norms, political views and familial values that will have influenced the timing of their decision. While growing up, the only accessible images of gender-diverse individuals (if any) were those of 'transvestites' or 'cross-dressers', who were painted in a manner that portrayed the queer world as obscure and deviant. The majority of people of these generations were never exposed to positive trans role models, or to information that would indicate that transitioning was even an option. Society has clearly evolved and now in their midlife, they have been granted greater opportunities to live authentically and in a dignified manner. It may also be that once reaching this age, many individuals acquire greater psychological resilience to assert their identity, and economic resources to fund their transition. However, it seems that accessibility to transition can be mediated by ethnicity; gender-diverse people belonging to Black and Minority Ethnic (BAME) groups report greater obstacles in accessing healthcare, describing higher rates of discrimination than white gender-diverse and BAME cisgender people (Chávez, 2011; Kattari et al, 2015), potentially hindering the speed of transition.

It has been reported extensively in clinical encounters that most people considering transitioning start to consciously question their gender identity during adolescence. This self-exploration is commonly triggered by physical maturational changes, many of which are unwelcome. Like the idea of being held hostage by one's body, individuals struggling with dysphoria may describe this period as one of helplessness and uncertainty. This transformation pushes the person to occupy an adult male or female identity, relinquishing the (social and physical) gender neutrality that childhood once granted, and accentuating social divisions. Many relate feelings of inadequacy, having no place to call home, neither one's body nor one's environment, and it is in this realisation that the individual embarks upon the pursuit of belonging. This quest persuades some to portray behaviours that are seen as 'acceptable' and to repress those leading to social opprobrium – most likely because humans have evolved to be part of a group, a structure which facilitated survival. Rejected individuals were separated from the group, becoming vulnerable to worldly threats. For this reason, avoiding shame and seeking connection has a vital role in human existence (Gilbert, 2009, 2017).

Most people that come to transition after the age of 50 describe a lifelong history of personal questioning and hesitation, a back-and-forth decision, purchasing and purging gender-affirming clothes, hiding from oneself and from others, and against one's desires, complying with societal expectations of how to dress, how to behave or whom to marry. Some of these constraints are not foreign to cisgender people, nonetheless trans and non-binary folk may particularly challenge heteronormative and cisnormative assumptions of acceptability. This struggle places gender-diverse individuals at higher risk of developing anxiety and depression, which are largely caused by the impact of minority stress and discrimination (Mustanki and Liu, 2013). In addition to this, Ellis et al (2016) described how trans people's perceived levels of risk exceeded actual experiences of victimisation. Hence, trans individuals who live in their authentic gender role are likely to experience stigma and those who do not may live in fear of this.

Many trans or non-binary individuals delay 'coming out' for 10, 20, 30 years and establish deadlines which may be linked to significant life events, for instance retirement from work, or which may be dependent on the well-being and stability of others, for example transitioning once a child finishes university studies. Such reasoning provides the individual with an external locus of control over their distress, which may defer the development of confidence and agency required to resolve this conflict and 'internal' debate. So, although the public may be persuaded by the idea that transitioning primarily concerns appearance, this process will involve an existential questioning, a period during which trans and non-binary people have to reckon and live with the worry that their life, as they know it, would end.

Many trans individuals talk of having arrived at a juncture where transitioning was not perceived as a choice, but as a matter of life or death, feeling that they can no longer repress who they are and often experiencing an emotional breakdown in anticipation of rejection by their loved ones. Bailey et al (2014) suggested that, compared to the global average, trans people could be up to seven times more likely to attempt suicide. This is very much linked with the fact that one of the most significant contributors to the well-being of trans people (and indeed, most people) is having a social support network and stable relationships (Davey et al, 2014) providing protection against ignorance and hostility.

Transition in later life, the other adolescence

Individuals embarking on gender transition undergo great change, commonly involving the transformation of their body and appearance, the shift of social relationships, and the psychological expression of manifold aspects of their identity, some of which, until that point, were unexplored. For these reasons, many will describe their transition as a 'second adolescence', one that will undeniably revive some of the old physical, social and psychological battles that were first encountered during teenage years. This concept is related in the sections to come and used as a frame to understand the experiences that arise from transition. To encourage empathy here, we need only recall our own puberty and adolescence and imagine what it would be like to relive it at this point in life.

Considering this non-normative life trajectory by which one may be able to re-experience adolescence midway through life, the concept of *queer time* becomes relevant. Halberstam (2005, p 1) defined 'queerness as an outcome of strange temporalities [and] imaginative life schedules'. In reality, many transgender and cisgender people have surrendered to societal pressures that would lead them to establish predictable and *chrononormative* lifestyles assuming a cisgender and heteronormative pattern, linearly marked by adolescence, marriage, parenthood, retirement and death. Nonetheless, individuals that hold queer and, particularly, trans identities, may follow different journeys or temporalities as they relive some of these stages during their midlife. Transition would therefore facilitate reshaping one's appearance, relearning one's body, reframing one's sexual desires, and other re-enactments that will certainly challenge what is broadly considered to be the 'natural order of things'.

In what contexts do gender-diverse people first question whether they belong in a cisnormative frame? Most people acquire their earliest sense of self as a member of a given family, a child of ..., a sibling of .... Undoubtedly, the start of life is dominated by our survival needs, which drive us to attach to our caregivers, and part of this both physical and psychological bond is the tendency to idolise our parents. During childhood, we take their guidance unquestioningly and integrate within our identity the intersectional elements that we have inherited from them: their ethnicity, religion, social status and, inadvertently, the expectation of being cisgender and heterosexual. However, having passed puberty and as we reach adulthood, we start to assert ourselves as equals. Caregivers no longer hold all the answers about who we are or what is best for us, and more disputes tend to emerge as a result of this realisation. This process of assertion is an essential part of adolescence and in psychology it is defined as the *separation-individuation* process. This mechanism allows us to explore our unique identities by redrawing the boundaries that separate us from others. Furthermore, this process often precedes the gender questioning of trans and non-binary people, when separating from their birth-assigned gender to develop a personally congruent gender identity. Alongside this process, individuals may also begin to question their sexual orientation. In contrast with their first adolescence, those who transition in later life would have experienced a developmental separation from their family of origin, placing greater emphasis on the need for support and validation from the family/social network they have created. In accepting their identity to be other than cisgender, a second separation-individuation process begins – this time around, from partners, offspring or friends.

In adolescence, the differences just described are not only marked through conflict, but also through the start of puberty, triggering a concrete transformation of the young person's appearance and, in many cases, a resemblance of their biological mother or father. Equally, adults pursuing a physical transition through hormone replacement therapy (HRT) may also undergo physical changes that would prompt the resemblance of their biological parents or siblings. In the case of trans people who have lost these family members, this transformation can bring alive their image, invoking emotional memories. As Pines (1993, p 162) explains: '… it was as if her own body still belonged to her mother and was unconsciously her well-tended memorial, since she had no concrete inheritance from her and no tombstone to visit'. This might elicit questions about what deceased loved ones would have said about their transition. Trans people who were adopted or in care may perceive these changes as a further reinforcement of their individuation, by which they feel and look different from their carers.

Parents of adolescents grieve the loss of the child they once had, just as the family of gender-diverse people may too grieve the loss of their brother, wife or father, as their appearance, identity and even the language around them changes. In letting go of culturally established concepts of femininity and masculinity, families challenge this human-made concept, creating the space to rethink and reconfigure their daily lives. For example, while considering previous relationship dynamics, a son of a trans person may come to understand that although his 'father' will transition to a female role, this does not necessarily mean that they are no longer able to watch rugby together. Secondly, particularly for the partner, there would be an examination of their sexual identity in relation to the trans or non-binary person. For instance, if for 20 years we have been in a lesbian relationship and my 'wife' transitions to a male role, does this make me heterosexual? Thirdly, there would be a questioning of the familial identity: what will other people say about us and will we still be accepted in church?

People change in every interaction and so not only the individual going through adolescence or gender transition changes, but those around them do so too, as they re-examine their own identity as partner or child of a person who is trans. Small resistances to change (often born of deep habit) may be apparent in the misgendering and 'dead-naming' of gender-diverse individuals, the latter referring to the use of a person's birth name after having requested to be addressed differently. Adolescents and people going through transition separate and individuate from their past identity and in the process they too may mourn the elements within it. For example, adolescents may miss the times in which they had fewer responsibilities and when life may have seemed easier. Similarly, older adults going through transition may mourn the advantages of having blended in society without the felt pressure to try and pass within their new gender role.

Trans people and their loved ones frequently express concerns about the impact that gender transition may have on children. This evidently stems from a wish to protect the youngest members of the family from change and stigma associated with gender diversity. Remarkably, young children show greater acceptance and flexibility to these changes than adults; while in contrast, adolescents tend to take their parents' transition personally. However, it is worth noting that this reaction predominantly relates to their own developmental needs (Motmans et al, 2018). Parental collaboration on how to disclose the intention to transition has a positive effect on the well-being of all parties and research has shown the important role that the parent who is not transitioning holds, as their attitudes can act as a mediator and moderator of transition related-change, therefore having the potential to influence the relationship between the trans parent and the child (Freedman et al, 2002; Hines, 2006; White and Ettner, 2004, 2007; Haines et al, 2014).

Characteristics of the 50-plus population

Interestingly, the majority of people who transition during midlife (and beyond) are trans women, as reported by Bouman et al (2016), who studied the sex ratio of gender-diverse people above the age of 50 attending a gender identity clinic in the United Kingdom. They found that in this age group, the ratio of trans women was 23.7 times higher than trans males. In terms of the common characteristics of the trans feminine population, most of them were of white ethnicity, either employed or retired, had divorced, and had children. An earlier study established that 70 per cent of trans women who had transitioned around their midlife had children (White and Ettner, 2004). Based on this information, it would be possible to formulate that, prior to transition, trans feminine people of this age (who were assigned male at birth) were more likely to live heteronormative lifestyles, forming partnerships with females, and having children.

Furthermore, White and Ettner (2004) suggested that trans masculine individuals were less likely to marry males and to have children. Based on the aforementioned research, it seems that a larger proportion of people (who were assigned female at birth) with a trans masculine or non-binary identity may have entered seemingly lesbian relationships, perhaps allowing for greater flexibility to present in a masculine 'butch' role that felt more congruent to them.

At this stage, research around non-binary gender is lacking, particularly in respect of the age group we are describing. It is worth noting that this form of gender identification has only been academically described and researched since around 2010. Given its newness, it would not be surprising to think that a small proportion of individuals above the age of 50 would either understand their gender in non-binary terms or use this label to describe it. For this reason, it has not been possible to address in greater detail experiences that would relate specifically to this population.

The impact of physical interventions in love, sex and intimacy

Individuals going through a physical gender transition may access a variety of hormonal and surgical treatments, which have the potential to elicit changes to the person's experience of their body, relationships and sexuality. The accessibility of these treatments is often mediated by country of residence, denoting either private or public healthcare, and further, the quality of healthcare. It is expected that people of higher socio-economic status would benefit from faster access to a larger variety of available treatments, including those that could be considered cosmetic but that would equally alleviate dysphoria. Additionally, individuals older than 50 years of age commonly experience health difficulties and chronic conditions which might prevent them from accessing some desired interventions.

As a point of reference that would allow us to understand the changes gender-diverse people may go through, here is a description of some of the most prevalent secondary changes facilitated by testosterone and oestrogen therapy. These will be similar to those undergone during male and female puberty. It should be borne in mind that this is not a complete list and that there are health risks associated with these treatments, and so, for detailed information, see Seal (2017).

People who were assigned female at birth (AFAB) with a trans masculine or non-binary identity may wish to masculinise/neutralise their body through testosterone therapy, which would facilitate some of the following changes: increased facial and body hair growth, voice deepening, clitoral enlargement, increased energy and sexual drive, and cessation of menstruation (if this has not already happened due to menopause or other health issues). Anecdotally, some patients have reported changes to their emotional life and to their bodily smell. When working with non-binary or trans masculine people above the age of 50, it is important to consider the drastic shift that HRT may trigger, particularly if they are already experiencing symptoms related to the menopause, some of which may include reduced energy and libido. In most cases, testosterone therapy will not only cease menopause-associated symptoms, but will spark an opposite reaction, placing the individual in a physical and psychological pubertal state which is likely to increase their energy levels and sexual drive. Just as any adolescent going through male puberty would, the trans person in their midlife would have to learn to adapt and control these possibly unfamiliar bodily responses, integrating them within their understanding of their gender and general identity. Meier et al (2013) established that 51 per cent of trans masculine people who were in a relationship remained together after transition.

Moreover, individuals who were assigned male at birth (AMAB) with a trans feminine or non-binary identity wishing to feminise/neutralise their body may access (among many others) oestrogen therapy. These are some of the changes elicited by this treatment: reduced body and facial hair growth; breast development; erectile dysfunction; reduction of libido; and skin softening. Additionally, some patients have reported emotional changes, such as a greater ability to connect to their feelings and a sense of calmness.

The emotional changes described by gender-diverse individuals may be attributed not only to hormone therapy, but also to the psychosocial elements associated with transitioning into a gender-affirming role. Considering the physical and psychological differences that exist in the perception of female and male sexuality (understood from the standpoint of their phenotype), when undergoing HRT the sexual experiences of trans people, as well as their partners', tend to noticeably change. Erectile dysfunction in trans feminine individuals can play a crucial role; they are often accustomed to owning visual evidence of their arousal, whereas in oestrogen therapy, this tends to disappear, not only affecting the person's own understanding of their desire but that of their partner's. Many trans women perceive this as a positive effect that supports the reduction of genital dysphoria, but this can be a source of conflict with the partner who may wish to have penetrative sex; therefore, negotiations play an important part in a person's transition. These unfolding events prompt trans feminine people and their partners to form a different sort of intimacy, based not only on penetration, but also on emotional connectedness (Sanger, 2010; Arambura Alegria and Ballard-Reisch, 2013; Davidman, 2014).

HRT will help materialise visual and non-visual changes to the body and while not frequently considered, other senses like smell, hearing or touch will also shift to accommodate the person's embodied sense of their gender (Scarrone, 2019). These changes will stir questions about erotic preferences, opening a window of experimentation to redefine one's desire. An individual's sexuality can comprise broad elements like sensation, body, partner, power dynamics, love, vulnerability, consent, pleasure, risk, intelligence and spirituality (Bornstein, 2013).

Also, as previously described, trans people's partners may be prompted to question the solidity of their sexual identification to redefine this and its associated relational boundaries. Apart from denoting attraction, sexual orientation also relates to political ideology, struggles and community memberships (Twist, 2017). Given the dissimilar effects of oestrogen and testosterone therapy, there are differential themes in the experience of trans feminine and trans masculine people's partners. The latter reported that following their partner's transition, their sexual satisfaction improved (Joslin-Roher and Wheeler, 2009). This is unsurprising, since gender dysphoria can act as a barrier to emotional and sexual intimacy, often preventing explorations involving some body parts or gender roles that may trigger distress. Hence, dysphoria has the potential to act as precursor for low sexual desire and celibacy. Finally, it should be considered that trans people belonging to the 50-plus population may be in relationships with cisgender female partners of a similar age, many of whom would be going through the menopause. Consequently, the couple would be placed in a dynamic of sexual and energy disparity, by which the trans partner is in a pubertal state (elicited by HRT) and opposite to them, the cisgender female partner would be in a menopausal state.

In addition to hormonal treatments, gender-diverse people can access a variety of surgical interventions to masculinise, feminise or neutralise their body appearance. In the following section, some of the most commonly requested surgeries and their particular implications for people in their midlife will be briefly addressed. To start with, breasts tend to be one of the most prevalent visual clues that would support the gendering of a person as female. Often this area is the source of great dysphoria and is subject to surgical interventions. People AFAB with a trans masculine or non-binary identity access chest surgery to masculinise or neutralise the appearance of this body part. To a lesser degree, trans feminine people may also wish to access breast augmentation surgery, although many of the changes tend to be satisfactorily facilitated by HRT.

In terms of genital reconstructive surgery (GRS), non-binary and trans masculine people AFAB are generally provided with an option between metoidioplasty (formation of a phallus, mostly without capacity for penetration) or phalloplasty (formation of a phallus with capacity for penetration). Further, trans feminine and non-binary people AMAB commonly choose between vulvoplasty (formation of a cosmetic vulva without capacity for penetration) or vaginoplasty (formation of a vulva and vagina with capacity for penetration). For more information about these and other surgeries, see Ralph et al (2017) and Bellringer (2017).

When trying to decide whether to undergo GRS, gender-diverse people often face similar dilemmas, particularly in light of the developmental issues and health decline that tends to accompany an individual's midlife. Broadly, trans people measure against the degree of dysphoria, the risks of the surgeries, recovery time, and the potential for needing additional surgeries. So, although many trans feminine people aim to have a neo-vagina with capacity for penetration and trans masculine people may wish to have a phallus with the ability to hold erections, the complexities of these surgeries may prevent them from having the genitals that would fully match their gender identity. It is imperative to clarify that some might not be interested in using their genitalia sexually, only wishing to resolve the felt incongruence with this body part. However, gender-diverse people often relate the worry that at this stage in their lives they might not be able to find anyone who would accept their trans identity and body configuration and that perhaps, it is too late to experience sex, love and intimacy.

Social aspects of physical transition

The start of pubertal changes is experienced individually and on a broader social level. We need only recall the ambivalent mix of excitement and anxiety in relation to this phase within the life course. A common experience among cisgender and trans women undergoing feminising hormonal changes is to anticipate the development of their breasts, perceived by some as a tangible affirmation of their womanhood and sexuality. Similarly, cisgender and trans men may particularly look forward to their voice deepening or to growing facial hair. In adolescence, we observed and compared the metamorphosis of our bodies with those around us, placing different expectations on what these changes would do for us. Adults undergoing physical transition often wait for years to receive treatment and during this time they are likely to get in contact with others going through the same process. Trans and non-binary people commonly allude to what is like sitting in the waiting room of a gender identity clinic and how this, sometimes inevitably, makes them wonder, 'am I part of this community?', 'do I have anything in common with them?' Often, the emotions triggered during these moments may be indicative of the degree of self-acceptance or, opposed to it, internalised transphobia. Some may feel alienated and others as though they finally belong, but almost invariably there would be a comparison of oneself with those around them.

Such considerations around identity now abound on social media. It is therefore pertinent to ask how social media might shape the experiences of people above the age of 50 who are undergoing transition. First, social media can enable a crucial sense of community for trans individuals, especially for those who are living in isolated areas. Social media has propelled the development of specific language around gender-diverse identities that has facilitated the expression and understanding of trans people's unique experiences, though the risk of feeling understood only by people behind a screen is that it can create further isolation. Younger trans and non-binary people actively use these platforms to document their physical transition, increasing the visibility of specific standards of beauty. This potentially propagates ideas around the importance of having an invisible trans identity, commonly referred as 'passing'. Trans youth who have undergone HRT early in their lives will be perceived as more 'passable', retaining fewer features associated to their phenotype, often carrying a lesser stigma, and in the eyes of some, being more successful. What does this leave for the older generation of trans folk? Therefore, when being confronted with these ideals, some may feel discouraged from the idea of transitioning, others may experience increased gender dysphoria wishing to resort to surgery, and a few may be able to dismiss external pressures. A similar dilemma is faced during adolescence, as while observing the transformation of their bodies, young people are exposed to beauty canons that will potentially increase body dissatisfaction, making them feel different from the norm. Society places higher expectations on women's appearance and pro-social behaviour. Learning how to apply makeup, what clothes match one's style, and how others perceive us based on our presentation is something that most cisgender girls absorb through play during childhood and adolescence. A significant proportion of middle-aged trans women historically lacked a space in which to develop these skills; only once they come out are they are allowed to catch up with this learning, and many use so-called 'transformation services' to, for the first time, explore the expression of their female identity.

To conclude, gender diversity, and particularly its intersections with older age, remain mostly under-explored. When coming out, gender-diverse people frequently feel unsupported by professionals, many of whom seem prejudiced or misinformed. This forces trans people to educate on the very same matters they are seeking support with. It is healthcare providers' responsibility to become aware of issues relating to gender and sexual diversity; it is time to challenge cisnormative and heteronormative models of care to allow for human diversity to be explored and expressed. This chapter provides a foundation level of information addressing the bio-psycho-social impact of transition. Transition during midlife is a quest with an uncertain destination, but for many, it is the only route to happiness and congruency. Gender-diverse individuals remind us of the pursuit for authenticity through the life course and that it is never too late to 'be oneself'. Being aged 50 or over does not represent the tail-end of life and, indeed, as evidenced in the idea of a 'second adolescence', for some, 50 plus has become the age of rediscovery.

References

American Psychiatric Association (1973) *Homosexuality and sexual orientation disturbance: Proposed change in DSM-II*, 6th printing, p 44 (APA Document Reference No. 730008), Washington, DC.

Aramburu Alegría, C. and Ballard-Reisch, D. (2013) 'Gender Expression as a Reflection of Identity Reformation in Couple Partners Following Disclosure of Male-to-female Transsexualism', *International Journal of Transgenderism*, 14(2): 49–65.

Bailey, L., Ellis, S. and McNeil, J. (2014) 'Suicide Risk in the UK Trans Population and the Role of Gender Transition in Decreasing Suicidal Ideation and Suicide Attempt', *Mental Health Review Journal*, 19(4): 209–20.

Bellringer, J. (2017) 'Surgery for Bodies Commonly Gendered as Male', in Richards, C., Bounman, W.P and Barker, M.-J. (eds) *Genderqueer and Non-Binary Genders*, London: Palgrave Macmillan, pp 247–63.

Bornstein, K. (2013) *My New Gender Workbook: A Step-By-Step Guide to Achieving World Peace through Gender Anarchy and Sex Positivity* (2nd edn), London: Routledge.

Bouman, W.P., Claes, L., Marshall, E., Pinner, G.T., Longworth, J., Maddox, V., Witcomb, G., Jimenez-Murcia, S., Fernandez-Aranda, F. and Arcelus, J. (2016) 'Sociodemographic Variables, Clinical Features, and the Role of Pre-assessment Cross-sex Hormones in Older Trans People', *The Journal of Sexual Medicine*, 13(4): 711–19.

Chávez, K.R. (2011) 'Identifying the Needs of LGBTQ Immigrants and Refugees in Southern Arizona', *Journal of Homosexuality*, 58: 189–218.

Coleman, E., Bockting, W., Botzer, M., Cohen-Kettenis, P., DeCuypere, G., Feldman, F.L., Green, J., Knudson, G., Meyer, W.J. and Monstrey, S. (2012) 'Standards of Care for the Health of Transsexual, Transgender, and Gender-nonconforming People, Version 7', *International Journal of Transgenderism*, 13(4): 165–232.

Crenshaw, K. (1991) 'Mapping the Margins: Intersectionality, Identity Politics, and Violence Against Women of Color', *Stanford Law Review*, 43: 1241–99.

Davey, A., Bouman, W.P., Arcelus, J. and Meyer, C. (2014) 'Social Support and Psychological Wellbeing: A Comparison of Patients with Gender Dysphoria and Matched Controls', *Journal of Sexual Medicine*, 11(12): 2976–85.

Davidman, S. (2014) 'Imag(in)ing trans partnerships: Collaborative photography and intimacy', *Journal of Homosexuality*, 61(5): 636–53.

Ellis, S.J., Bailey, L. and McNeil, J. (2016) 'Transphobic Victimisation and Perceptions of Future Risk: A Large-scale Study of the Experiences of Trans People in the UK', *Psychology and Sexuality*, 7(3): 211–24.

Freedman, D., Tasker, F. and di Ceglie, D. (2002) 'Children and Adolescents with Transsexual Parents Referred to a Specialist Gender Identity Development Service: A Brief Report of Key Developmental Features', *Clinical Child Psychology and Psychiatry*, 7(3): 423–32.

Gilbert, P. (2009) *The Compassionate Mind*, London: Constable & Robinson.

Gilbert, P. (2017) *Compassion: Concepts, Research and Applications*, London: Taylor & Francis.

Haines, B.A., Ajayi, A.A. and Boyd, H. (2014) 'Making Trans Parents Visible: Intersectionality of Trans and Parenting Identities', *Feminism and Psychology*, 24(2): 238–47.

Halberstam, J. (2005) *In a Queer Time and Place: Transgender Bodies*, New York: New York University Press.

Hines, S. (2006) 'Intimate Transitions: Transgender Practices of Partnering and Parenting', *Sociology*, 40(2): 353–71.

Joslin-Roher, E. and Wheeler, D.P. (2009) 'Partners in Transition: The Transition Experience of Lesbian, Bisexual, and Queer Identified Partners of Transgender Men', *Journal of Gay and Lesbian Social Services*, 21(1): 30–48.

Kattari, S.K., Walls, N.E., Whitfield, D.L., and Langenderfer-Magruder, L. (2015) 'Racial and Ethnic Differences in Experiences of Discrimination in Accessing Health Services Among Transgender People in the United States', *International Journal of Transgenderism*, 16(2): 68–79.

Koehler, A., Eyssel, J. and Nieder, T.O. (2018) 'Gender and Individual Treatment Progress in (Non-) Binary Trans Individuals', *The Journal of Sexual Medicine*, 15(1): 102–13.

Meier, S.C., Sharp, C., Michonski, J., Babcock, J.C. and Fitzgerald, K. (2013) 'Romantic Relationships of Female-to-male Trans Men: A Descriptive Study', *International Journal of Transgenderism*, 14(2): 75–85.

Motmans, J., Dierckx, M. and Mortelmans, D. (2018) 'Transgender Families', in Bounman, W. and Arcelus, J. (eds) *The Transgender Handbook: A Guide for Transgender People, Their Families and Professionals*, New York, NY: Nova Science Publishers.

Mustanski, B. and Liu, R.T. (2013) 'A Longitudinal Study of Predictors of Suicide Attempts Among Lesbian, Gay, Bisexual, and Transgender Youth', *Archives of Sexual Behavior*, 42(3): 437–48.

Pines, D. (1993) *A Woman's Unconscious Use of Her Body*, London: Virago.

Ralph, D., Christopher, N. and Garaffa, G. (2017) 'Genital Surgery for Bodies Commonly Gendered as Female', in Richards, C., Bounman, W.P. and Barker, M.-J. (eds) *Genderqueer and Non-Binary Genders*, London: Palgrave Macmillan, pp 265–82.

Sanger, T. (2010) *Trans People's Partnerships: Towards an Ethics of Intimacy*, London: Springer.

Scarrone, B.L. (2019) 'Gender Dysphoria and the Mirror: A Mediator between the First Person and Third Person Perspective', *Counselling Psychology Review*, 34(1): 51–9.

Seal, L. (2017) 'Adult Endocrinology', in Richards, C., Bounman, W.P. and Barker, M.-J. (eds) *Genderqueer and Non-Binary Genders*, London: Palgrave Macmillan, pp 183–213.

Twist, J. (2017) 'Transitioning Together: Narratives of Sexuality and Intimacy' *Psychology of Sexualities Review*, 8(2): 77–92.

White, T. and Ettner, R. (2004) 'Disclosure, Risks and Protective Factors for Children Whose Parents Are Undergoing a Gender Transition', *Journal of Gay and Lesbian Psychotherapy*, 8(1–2): 129–45.

White, T. and Ettner, R. (2007) 'Adaptation and Adjustment in Children of Transsexual Parents', *European Child and Adolescent Psychiatry*, 16(4): 215–21.

World Health Organization (2020) *International statistical classification of diseases and related health problems* (11th edition) https://icd.who.int/

Zhang, Q., Goodman, M., Adams, N., Corneil, T., Hashemi, L., Kreukels, B., Motmans, J., Snyder, R. and Coleman, E. (2020) 'Epidemiological Considerations in Transgender Health: A Systematic Review with Focus on Higher Quality Data', *International Journal of Transgender Health*, 21(2): 125–37.

10

Ageing asexually: exploring desexualisation and ageing intimacies

Ela Przybylo

> ... *now she becomes a different being, asexual but complete: an elderly woman.*
>
> (Simone de Beauvoir, 1949, p 626)

> *what you got against old people talking about sex? You think we are not sexy anymore? You think I didn't have my share of husbands and lovers? You think sexy expires?*
>
> (Leanne Simpson, 2013, pp 106–7)

Deep-seated ageist beliefs would have us take for granted that 'sexy expires', in the words of poet Leanne Simpson. According to this logic, as bodies age they become less attractive, less desirable, and less desiring of sex. This logic of 'sexy expiring' is deeply grounded in gendered and ageist colonial ideals of beauty and sexuality. The idea that with age 'sexy expires' is also, though less obviously, tied up in compulsory sexuality (Przybylo, 2011; Emens, 2014; Gupta, 2015) – or the idea that a person *needs* to be sexy and have sex in order to attain optimal health, vitality, and a 'successful' ageing process.

In this chapter, I unpack how compulsory sexuality operates alongside desexualisation for ageing adults in western countries at the end of the twentieth and beginning of the twenty-first centuries, where the pressure to have sex and remain vigorous into late life looms strong. Following asexuality studies and critical disability studies scholar Eunjung Kim (2010), I mark a difference between asexuality and desexualisation. Asexuality, or low-to-no sexual attraction to others, I take for granted as a real sexual identity and orientation that can exist at any age as well as emerging later in life (Przybylo, 2016). Further, I mark desexualisation as a harmful process of barring or preventing access to sex, sexual fulfilment, and sexual identity. Understood in this way, asexuality and desexualisation are not one and the same, since asexuality is affirmatively embraced as a component of identity, and desexualisation is a process by which equitable access to sex and sexual expression is prevented.

Desexualisation is at work in a complex way in contemporary western contexts in relation to older adults. On the one hand, through being encouraged not to have sex – through being desexualised – older adults are left out of the fold of full social and intimate participation. In this sense, the desexualisation of ageing adulthood is a form of harm. On the other hand, new discourses have surfaced that encourage ageing adults – especially when wealthy or upper middle class, white, heterosexual, and able-bodied – to be sexual and 'sexy' for as long as possible and by any means possible, as a way to preserve youth and ability. In the words of Stephen Katz, there is a '[broad] cultural background of contradictory images that marginalize, denigrate, and desexualize older people' even while older adults are enjoined to 'resist their own ageing through active and independent lifestyles' (2011, p 187). Exploring these two twin sets of discourses for ageing adulthood, this chapter holds on to the possibility of imagining ageing bodies as affirmatively asexual, emphasising asexual identities and experiences as valid and life-making. The chapter concludes with a brief exploration of a piece by Sandra Lee Bartky (2000), which offers a window into a mode of ageing that is neither desexualised nor hostile to ideas of asexuality.

Ageing and desexualiaation

Ageing, ageism, and racism

Ageing refers to any number of vastly dissimilar experiences structured by variegated social and geographical conditions. For instance, older adults or the elderly span an age difference of over 40 years, from 65 to upward of 100 years – age groups shaped by differing eras, politics, values, and life experiences (Brock and Jennings, 2007, p 244). Older adults are groupable under one category only in the sense that they are discriminated against through a broad 'social antipathy towards the elderly' that takes on toxic and life-undermining forms (Segal, 2014, p 2). This 'antipathy', commonly termed ageism, comprises the institutionally sanctioned removal of the right to govern one's body, the loss of social and political status, and the sometimes forced removal from one's home. It is characterised by systemic physical, financial, psychological, and sexual exploitation that includes verbal denigration;

ageist hate speech; threats; interception of one's decision-making powers; financial theft and misuse of resources; abuse of financial guardianship; bodily neglect; hitting and physical abuse; not providing proper nutrition, clothing, and shelter; isolation; lack of necessary medical care and attention; sexual assault; and public humiliation (Muehlbauer and Crane, 2006; Phillips et al, 2013). More than being 'vulnerable' to 'elder abuse', older adults are produced – discursively, spatially, institutionally – as discardable, 'disposable' (Khanna, 2009). One way in which ageing adults are produced as disposable is through desexualisation.

Desexualisation entails the spatial, institutional, and discursive repositioning of some bodies, such as the elderly, as not in need of sex because they are, after all, already approaching death, and 'old age is taken as synonymous with death – social and actual' (Simpson et al, 2016, p 10). Paul Simpson et al name this 'ageist erotophobia,' which 'defines older people as post-sexual, [and] restricts opportunities for the expression of sexuality and intimacy' (Simpson et al, 2016, p 1). Because contemporary western colonial contexts are invested in compulsory sexuality, sexual activity, and sexual expression as pivotal to one's identity and belonging, to be desexualised amounts to being barred from social participation.

At the same time, being able to reach old age is in itself an accomplishment for many whose life is under state erosion from childhood, such as indigenous people, racialised people, and people with disabilities. Evelyn Reynolds has written that ' "aging while black" is an act of survival' because far too often age does not in itself determine when a Black person dies due to systemic and institutionalised racism (2017, n.p.). While stereotypes suggest that 'Black don't crack' or that Black women do not show signs of ageing as a means to celebrate Black beauty and ageing, the reality is that in addition to state-sanctioned violence, the stress of racism increases the chance of life-threatening conditions and premature death (Mondé, 2018). Indeed, Ruth Wilson Gilmore points out pithily that racism is the state-sanctioned production of 'group-differentiated vulnerability to premature death', suggesting that it is the design of institutional racism to *not* permit people of colour, and specifically black people, to reach old age in the first place (2007, p 28).

By extension, discourses around the desexualisation of ageing, while harmful to all bodies and communities as an imposed framework for discarding the value of maturity and ageing, are fundamentally about whiteness. While ageing adults are revered in many communities, including in Black, indigenous, and immigrant communities, white colonial society has been invested in diminishing the value of even white ageing because of attachments to productivity, reproductivity, and the conflation of youthful beauty with (white) morality. Extending Ianna Hawkins Owen's work on the racialisation of 'asexual' discourses, ideas around ageing mobilise asexuality as a resource of pristine whiteness, as an accomplishment (2018). In regard to ageing, the accomplishment of 'asexuality' is the accomplishment not of sexual restraint but of sexual conclusion, of wrapping up one's life project of reproduction and production (and sex) for the nation state and being able to rest after a job completed. It is within this context of a maturity narrative grounded in whiteness that the desexualisation of ageing takes effect.

Desexualisation as disgust

Desexualisation functions to dispose of ageing adults in at least two ways. First, it does so through rendering older adults as sexually undesirable. To be rendered sexually undesirable relies on an intricate and multisensory ableism that picks up on the scents, textures, and appearances of ageing and elicits a mode of disgust in a culture fixated on youth, beauty, health, and ability. As one 64-year-old lesbian participant in a study that looked at older women's views on sex comments: 'I think it's partially because aging is seen as disgusting in this youth culture. And so sex among disgusting beings is even more disgusting' (Bradway and Beard, 2015, p 512). Or as another study that examines college students' attitudes towards ageing adults puts forward, the affect of disgust is attached in particular to the sexuality of ageing bodies (Waterman, 2012).

Disgust functions as validation for disposability, producing ageing bodies as disgusting and banning them from sex (Ehrenfeld at al, 1997). It is thus not that the ageing body is naturally disgusting, but that it is structured, through the operation of ageism, as disgusting so as to keep it in its place. If the 'young' are ill-disposed to the ageing, it is because a habitual disgust is cultivated that serves a non-intergenerational project of compulsory sex and sexuality, rendering some bodies sexy and others 'unfuckable'. Since 'disgust is an affect that forces us to confront our bodily existence', the displacement of disgust onto the bodies of the elderly through a banning of sex and 'sexiness' permits a deferral of anxieties around ageing, bodily change, and senescence (Meagher, 2003, p 24). Expressions of disgust are a common device for enforcing social norms and punishing those who do not adhere to them. Importantly, disability and ageing are often tightly linked, as Susan Wendell explores, and while 'aging is not always and never *just* being sick or dying ... it is also these. Ageing is also disabling, and especially disabling in societies where inadequate provision is made for the participation of people with nonideal, limited, or suffering bodies' (2000, p 135). In this sense, expressions of disgust aimed at ageing bodies can also be considered ableist in that they enforce strict norms of bodily comportment, function, and appearance.

Notably, the attribution of non-sexiness is especially harmful to women, who are commonly habituated to assessing their value in terms of youth, beauty, and sexiness. The effect of this is the process by which, through a devaluing of their appearance – that is, the loss of their sexiness – a ban against sexual enjoyment is implemented, since 'if elderly women can't be beautiful, they obviously can't have sex, either' (Lindemann Nelson, 2000, p 89). Also, cisgender women are understood to be disposable in a particular way after they cease to be reproductively useful and capable of procreation. If disgust is a visceral response that points to a desire to maintain bodily boundaries and one's psychic sense of self, then a disgust-based response to ageing keeps the segregation of the young and ageing in place, facilitating the enactment of compulsory sexuality for the young and young-approximating, and the desexualisation of the elderly.

Desexualisation and the spatialisation of disposability

In addition to disgust-based responses to ageing that render an ageing adult 'not sexy', desexualisation also takes effect through a spatialisation of disposability. Sociologist Erving Goffman discussed the 'total institution' as 'an enclosed, formally administered round of life ... prison-like ... whose members [may] have broken no laws' (Goffman, 1961, p xiii). These spaces are tightly scheduled, populated by 'a batch of similar others', under ongoing surveillance, where staff and inmates form distinct social groups and the 'social mobility between the two strata is grossly restricted' (Goffman, 1961, pp 6, 7). For example, the staff within nursing homes, often overworked and underpaid, prioritise 'bed-and-body' work, striving to execute tasks efficiently and abet 'the efficient running of the nursing home as a whole' (Persson and Wästerfors, 2009, p 8). The result of this is the handling of ageing adults as a 'batch' and the diminishing of opportunities for personalised routines, life habits, and self-expression (Goffman, 1961, p 11). Even such aspects as deciding when to eat, whether to shower, when to get out of bed or go outdoors, or what to wear are impossibilised in the 'batch living' of a nursing home because individuals are processed as groups rather than as independent beings (Goffman, 1961, p 11).

Interestingly, while sex could be conceived of as part and parcel of 'bed-and-body' work such that it is configured as part of the care of the body, in the current system it is often not (Simpson et al, 2016, p 9). The elderly, when requesting a personalisation of the schedule, are instead conceived of by staff as 'difficult' or uncooperative, standing in the way of the efficient execution of work tasks in pursuit of 'trivialities' (Persson and Wästerfors, 2009, p 6). The time of the long-term facility or nursing home is in this way 'organised around a non-negotiable daily schedule' in which daily routines are rigidly fixed (Sellerberg, 1991, p 69). The desexualised adult in the long-term facility, prevented from exercising basic agency over their body, is rendered passive in a way suitable to the conditions of the total institution. There 'are few opportunities for socially dignifying relationships within the nursing home' since elderly adults are plucked out of their home environments and inserted into fabricated communities founded on age segregation – or, as one participant from a recent study commented, they are 'warehoused' (Pleschberger, 2007; Bradway and Beard, 2015, p 511). Care and ethics theorist Joan Tronto argues that 'everyone's life … is diminished by living in age-segregated circumstances', since it homogenises the nursing home environment as well as the community outside the home (2000, p 262).

The space of the long-term facility and nursing home functions to desexualise older adults through the implementation of spatial means that make intimacy and sex nearly inconceivable. The presence of staff, the batch living, the tightly scheduled days, and the constant presence of 'similar others' make for displays of intimacy, including but not limited to sex, difficult and near impossible even for able-bodied elders (Goffman, 1961, p 6). Access to sex is prevented through institutional policy, the spatialised absence of privacy, surveillance by similar others and staff, as well as through an absence of personnel who would facilitate access to sex for elders with disabilities or mobility constraints (Hinchliff and Gott, 2008).

For example, a study of the implications on older age sexuality for health care providers depicts an account of two nursing home residents who formed an intimate bond in the form of hand-holding and smiling. Because one of the residents was married, 'the nurses perceived these interactions as inappropriate and dangerous to Pedro's marriage [and] the decision was made to not place the wheelchairs side-by-side and limit the interaction. They were no longer able to share a touch or smile; shortly after Sue died' (Watters and Boyd, 2009, p 307). In this case, access to intimate interactions was directly intercepted and banned by the staff, demonstrating the extent to which bodily agency is limited and intimacy censored in the desexualisation of older adults. Under the guise of 'safety', nursing homes are designed to limit privacy with such measures as open-door and no-locked-door requirements and a paucity of single-inhabitant rooms (Deacon et al, 1995, p 497; Cornelison and Doll, 2012; Simpson et al, 2016, p 16). Also, resident rooms and the space of the nursing home in general compose a space part-private, part-public, where the very idea of whose 'home' it is remains unclear, since staff feel inclined to move through the space freely, compromising the residents' autonomy and privacy (Rebec et al, 2015). Residents can also be expressly punished for exhibiting whatever is deemed 'improper' sexual conduct (Cornelison and Doll, 2012).

If ageing adults are permitted to engage in sex, it is often in consultation with their families, undermining an ageing adult's agency over their own body (Holmes et al, 1997). Family, staff, and managers are thus in the structural position to decide whether one is allowed to engage in sexual activity, effectively dispensing or banning sex at their own whim, as influenced by their own sense of sexual morality and potential ageist attitudes toward older adult sexuality (Cornelison and Doll, 2012). This position of needing to negotiate sex in a context of widespread desexualisation can likewise lead to the practising of unprotected sex (Scherrer, 2009; Breland, 2014). Queer and transgender people face the additional nullifying of their gender and sexual identities if removed from their homes and placed into long-term care facilities where they may be met with the heterosexual presumption as well as with homophobic and transphobic peers and staff who may refuse to recognise their gender and sexual identities (Siverskog, 2015). In this sense, the desexualisation of LGBTQ2+ older adults is combined with harmful homophobic and transphobic intent. Indeed, LGBTQ2+ older adults experience entry into the space of the nursing home as particularly alienating, and they experience ongoing non-conscious bias (Phillips and Marks, 2008; Foglia and Fredriksen-Goldsen, 2014). Through the process of desexualisation, older adults are maintained as residents within a facility, without bodily autonomy, and as bodies to be preserved and protected rather than as sites of rich subjectivity entitled to gender and sexual identities.

Widowhood and other modes of singlehood are likewise acutely prone to old-age disposability. Unprotected by the structure of couple privilege, single older adults have fewer social structures to prevent their social and sexual diminishment. This affects women disproportionately, since older women are over twice more likely to live alone than older men (Segal, 2014, p 227). Facing widowhood in older age, for instance, involves the loss not only of a close other, but also of the accompanying social networks and sense of belonging (Watters and Boyd, 2009, p 310). Singlehood in old age also becomes a contributing factor to structural disposability, since one has to resourcefully seek out sex with others in ways that are made difficult due to the rendering of older adults as 'unsexy' (Huyck, 2001). Ageing widows are also desexualised in specific ways, since as 'unsexy,' they are understood and perhaps understand themselves as lacking the tools necessary to recruit sexual accomplices (Deacon et al, 1995, p 499; Sears-Roberts Alterovits and Mendelsohn, 2009). As studies show, widowhood is a central deciding factor for whether older adults are sexually active (Deacon et al, 1995; Minichiello et al, 1996; DeLamater and Sill, 2005; Antoniassi Baldissera et al, 2012; Antoniassi Baldissera et al, 2012).

Also, adults who are not deemed able-minded may not be legally permitted to offer their own consent, further functioning to ban them from intimate and sexual activities. For instance, residents with dementia in many US states cannot legally partake in sex since they are not viewed as having the 'capacity to consent' (Wilkins, 2015). Sexual activity with a person with dementia or another mental 'impairment' may be criminalised, functioning to deprive many adults of autonomy over their bodily lives. Persons with dementia are also held to a higher standard in terms of consent than the general public (Wilkins, 2015, p 719). A third party or guardian might have decision-making authority over whether an older adult with dementia can partake in sexual activity (Breland, 2014, p 184). In concord with ableism, ageism here functions to ban individuals from sexual intimacy and expression in a context of limited personal freedom. Significantly, the spaces of ageing and disability are overlapping, since the US census suggests that in 2000, 54.7 per cent of people over 65 had a disability, a number that includes both life-long and acquired disabilities (Lightfoot, 2007, p 202). This suggests that many older adults experience both ageism and ableism in their lives and that the two become intertwined and inseparable in their experiences.

While the spatiality of the nursing home is conducive to desexualisation, it need not be this way. The nursing home could be a space of community, communal living, alternate intimacies, and life-sustaining relationships. In the following section, I explore how anti-ageist approaches seek to recuperate sexuality for ageing adults, even while doing so through a dismissal of asexual possibilities.

Challenging desexualisation

Desexualisation and asexuality

When sexuality is researched in relation to ageing, too often sexological paradigms are drawn on to decide whether ageing adults are having 'enough' sex, 'reduc[ing] sexuality to a book-keeping approach that concerns who is still having sex ... and how often' (Simpson et al, 2016, pp 4, 9). An approach focused on 'how much' considers sex as necessarily contributing to health and well-being. Such an approach tends to quantify sexual activity rather than thinking about the emotions, relationships, or contexts behind it.

In parallel to debates within critical disability studies, which until recently have sought sex-positive affirmations of disability through the distancing of disability from asexuality, literature on critical ageing presents asexuality as overwhelmingly undesirable and harmful to older adults without engaging affirmatively asexual perspectives that recognise asexuality as a sexual orientation that can add meaning and happiness to one's life (Kim, 2010; Lund and Johnson, 2015). Desexualisation often gets misnamed as asexuality in relation to older adult sexuality. Understandably, this distancing of older adult sexuality from asexuality takes place as a means to combat the institutional and discursive desexualisation of older adulthood. Yet this misnaming does damage to the sexual identity of asexuality while ineffectually portraying the structures of desexualisation. Misnaming desexualisation as asexuality denies the possibility for positive asexual identification, making asexual identity improbable and undesirable, inadvertently situating asexuality as inherently damaging to older adult health and well-being.

Also, the misnaming of desexualisation as asexuality provides a cover for the oppressive banning of sex. When older adults' desexualisation is framed as 'asexuality' it is rendered incidental, an effect of changing bodies, erasing the active process that makes ageing sexuality impossible. As long as ageing is understood in terms of asexuality and not in terms of desexualisation, we are incapable of grasping the ongoing harm many encounter upon ageing, of which a denial of sexuality is just one component.

Some research, for example, tends to assert that sex and sexuality are necessarily healthy, discounting both the iterations of sex that may be deleterious, including sex without consent, as well as possibilities for asexual ageing. For instance, as Emily Waterman writes in her study of college students' reactions to the sexuality of older people, 'research shows that a healthy sex life in old age greatly contributes to happiness and quality of life [... and that] premature loss of sexual functioning can contribute to emotional and physical deterioration in people; hanging onto sexuality can lessen feelings of loss in old age and increase self-esteem' (Waterman, 2012, p 46). Such a conclusive statement, that sexuality and sex are necessarily healthful and that they can fight the harmful effects of ageing, draws on compulsory sexuality to advocate for an extension of able-bodied healthiness into older age. Not only are possibilities for asexual ageing edited out, but sex is encouraged at any cost and mostly on heterosexual terms. Such an approach to ageing, which announces that if you have sex, you will stave off the effects of ageing, disregards the social conditions of ageism.

'Successful ageing' and compulsory sexuality

The late twentieth and early twenty-first centuries are characterised by narratives of 'successful ageing' which include the expansion of an ethics of optimism, bodily optimisation, attractiveness, sexiness, health, vitality, and an active sex life to older segments of the population. On the one hand, the successful ageing paradigm invites ageing adults to engage in fitness, beauty practices, and relationship building as a way to lead dynamic and self-sustaining lives. On the other hand, successful ageing presents very narrow ideas of success that rely on ableist and ageist modes of seeking meaning in life. While encouraging ageing adults to remain active and to ward off isolation, an emphasis on successful ageing tends to individualise ageing, neglecting to account for the systemic ageism that ageing bodies experience. It also does not conceive of survival as in itself a 'success', ignoring the realities of racism, which makes survival into old age an accomplishment for those faced with racism in its many guises.

Within a successful ageing paradigm, it is active, quantifiable sex and sexual desire that become signals of 'successful' and 'healthy' ageing (Katz and Marshall, 2003, pp 13, 4). For example, Viagra, Flibanserin, hormone replacement, and other modes of sexual optimisation have transformed what it means to have sex while ageing, while binding sex to expert knowledge, access to pharmaceuticals, and upper-middle-class whiteness (Katz and Marshall, 2002; Potts et al, 2003; Loe, 2004). Treatments for sexual dysfunctions are meant to 'reanimate [the] bodies and lives' of ageing adults even while they consistently overlook queer and trans bodies and entrench penetrative coital sex as the benchmark of success (McGlotten and Moore, 2013, p 261).

In this sense, more and more older adults – of certain health, resources, ability, and vitality levels – are encouraged to engage in sex, seemingly undermining the desexualisation of older adults. Yet, as Stephen Katz and Barbara Marshall suggest, such techniques of successful ageing produce new norms for what it means to age, norms that are tightly tied to able-bodiedness and health as the new morality, as well as to wealth, couple privilege, and compulsory sexuality (Katz and Marshall, 2003; Metzl and Kirkland, 2010). So, while sex and sexuality are encouraged for some ageing adults, this process is actually productive of a more stringent set of criteria for sexual citizenship, under which failure is imminent and self-monitoring is encouraged (Edmonds, 2014, p 249). 'Successful ageing' thus emerges on particular terms that are not only compulsorily sexual, but also set against an imagined 'bad ageing' that is characterised by disability and ill health, or the 'relentless hostility to physical decline and its tendency to regard health as a form of secular salvation' (Cole, 1992, p 239; Rowe and Kahn, 1997). Even the fit ageing body is in need of self-surveillance so that it does not slip into symptoms of hated ageing, which include slowness, inactivity, isolation, illness, and disability. Sexual activeness is part of this refusal to slow down, understood as functioning to ward away isolation, social decline, and overall bodily deterioration.

Notably, sexual fitness is also aestheticised, requiring particular gendered enactments of attractiveness, or 'sexiness' throughout the life course that are difficult, expensive, and hazardous to maintain (Edmonds, 2014, p 254). Practices such as plastic surgery in the service of maintaining a youthful and wrinkle-minimised face, for example, are in part directed at maintaining the sexiness of a body and upholding narrow ageist ideals of beauty (Przybylo and Rodrigues, 2018, p 9). With the reconceptualisation of 'healthy' ageing as a time of compulsory sexuality, desire disorders and physiological problems that are understood to get in the way of sex, including ' "erectile dysfunction" [are framed] as a threat to both the physical and psychological well-being of an ageing population, and hence as a matter for public concern' (Katz and Marshall, 2002, p 55). Critics of 'successful ageing' have thus argued that 'the stereotype of the asexual old age' has 'the potential to create a new myth about ageing sexuality, which is just as oppressive to older people as the stereotype it seeks to deconstruct' – entrenching sex as mandatory at all costs (Gott and Hinchliff, 2003, p 1618; Hinchliff and Gott, 2008, p 67). In refuting the 'asexuality' of older adults, sex, sexiness, and sexual desire are produced as compulsory components of successful – that is, healthy, able-bodied, and responsible – ageing, which is imbued with the potential to 'stave off old age' (Gott, 2005;

Gupta, 2011). As compulsory sexuality is extended into older age, not only is the possibility for affirmative asexuality diminished, but the effects of desexualisation – that is, of exclusion from the sexual fold – become more and more detrimental. Sex in older adult life thus becomes also a marker of a certain non-disposability among those lucky enough to retain access to it.

It is thus not that ageing adults are not sexual, but rather that ageing adults are produced as not sexual by ageist social structures. This production of desexualisation is grounded in ideas that continue to inform white maturity as a site of an asexual ideal – that is, as a white supremacist moral position of sexual distancing that characterises the supreme evolutionary achievement of whiteness. The maturity narrative of asexuality – as both an evolutionary narrative of refined whiteness as sexually restrained as well as the narrative life arc as one ending in sexual disinterest – is used in turn to justify the enforcement of desexualisation. The shift of focus that is needed is from understanding sexual decline as attributable to bodily senescence and deterioration to understanding sexual decline as a product of social fabrication stemming from an unjust corporeal politics. When research upholds asexual identification as undesirable for older adults, it tends to reinforce ideas that sex (especially for able-bodied ageing adults) is either healthful or youth maintaining. Upholding compulsory sexuality for ageing adults also assumes that to be without sex is to be less fulfilled, less of a person, and less of a 'successful' ager. In the following section, I turn to an asexually affirmative analysis of older adulthood through exploring possibilities for rethinking intimacy in older age.

Rethinking intimacy

> I shall close with a fantasy I have about these women, my neighbors in a huge and faceless 1950s high-rise ... Here is my fantasy: these elderly widows abandon their deeply entrenched homophobia ... and, just as they have learned to meet each other's needs for visibility and admiration, they go one step further and begin to meet each other's needs for physical intimacy. This intimacy need not be sexual, but if it is sexual, so much the better. Perhaps there are women whose needs extend farther than hugging and embracing, frequent nuzzling kisses, the comfort of a warm body touching one's own body in bed on a winter night. For the women who need sex and have not had it for decades,

I fantasize wild sexual excitement and fulfillment and the special kind of confidence that comes with the knowledge that one has the capacity to arouse sexual desire in another. Their condo would come alive with couplings and rumors of couplings, dalliance, flirting, gossip, matchmaking, lovers' quarrels, *liaisons innocentes ou dangereuses*. Now these suddenly energetic sisters will have more to talk about than the ingratitude of their children, the day's ration of soap operas, or the thoroughly exhausted topic of the cuteness of their grandchildren. (Bartky, 2000, pp 72–3)

Michael Warner writes evocatively of all the relational forms that emerge from queer cultures: 'each relation is an adventure in nearly uncharted territory ... There are almost as many types of relationships as there are people in combination ... Most have no labels. Most receive no public recognition ... Who among us would give them up?' (Warner, 1999, pp 115–16, 139). Widely read feminist theorist, Sandra Lee Bartky, in an essay titled 'Unplanned Obsolescence: Some Reflections on Aging' (2000) offers us such a queerly potent, asexually resonant relational model of ageing (Bartky, 2000). Speaking against the deadening and flattening landscape of 'a huge and faceless 1950s high-rise', she envisions a utopian lesbian community of ageing women who fight the structural oppression of ageism by coming together to cultivate new forms of intimacy (Bartky, 2000, p 72). Maintaining their independence, the ageing women of this fantasy turn to each other for pleasure, solace, love, friendship, and what Bartky speaks of as 'dalliance' (Bartky, 2000, p 73).

There is much I am drawn to in this fantasy: ageing women coming together to discover the world anew through a lesbian utopia that confronts the structures of ageism, misogyny, couple privilege, and age-based segregation. Most of all, I am drawn to this fantasy for its capacity to speak affirmatively of ageing adult sexuality even while de-emphasising sex on specific terms, and envisioning opportunities for asexual intimacy. As Bartky writes, 'this intimacy need not be sexual' and includes 'hugging and embracing, frequent nuzzling kisses, the comfort of a warm body touching one's own body in bed on a winter night', even while it also articulates 'wild sexual excitement' (Bartky, 2000, p 73). In short, Bartky's fantasy successfully frames an old age sex positivity that does not rely on compulsory sexuality or shut the door on asexuality.

Bartky's fantasy refuses an attachment to heteronormative life cycles, time orders, and compulsory sexuality. Some scholars discuss the ways in which ageing sexuality provides insight on 'the warmth and tenderness of emotional intimacy' or 'the creation of a profound connection with another human while being acutely aware of one's own sense of wholeness as a separate person' (Deacon et al, 1995, p 498; Brock and Jennings, 2007, p 251). Affirming sexuality among older adults, as Bartky's fantasy explores, can thus also mean broadening notions of intimacy so that they include both touch- and non-touch-based connection, 'the need for someone to be available to talk with and be close to; the need to be touched and appreciated, the need to smile, and the need to know someone else cares' (Deacon et al, 1995, p 498; Watters and Boyd, 2009, p 312). Celebrating ageing adult sexuality in this way shifts strict understandings of sex as health-providing to other forms of romantic touching, including cuddling, kissing, embracing, holding hands, and grooming, as well as solitary acts such as masturbation (Deacon et al, 1995; Brock and Jennings, 2007, pp 244, 251; Watters and Boyd, 2009, p 312; Wilkins, 2015, p 716). In this sense, ageing in itself might present asexually attuned opportunities to question what constitutes desire and intimacy.

As I have discussed in this chapter, while the body changes with ageing, it is indeed ageism that has the effect of desexualising older adulthood. Respecting the sex positive approach of scholars and practitioners who argue for the value of sex as one ages, this chapter has sought to imagine what an ageing sexuality might look like if it is both critical of desexualisation and of compulsory sexuality, pushing against ideas that one must have sex to age successfully. Remaining critical of systems of desexualisation that deny sexual identity and pleasure to ageing adults, it is just as important to recognise that intimacy can come in many forms.

Acknowledgements
A version of this chapter appears as Chapter 4 in my monograph *Asexual Erotics: Intimate Readings of Compulsory Sexuality* (Ohio State University Press, 2019). Thank you to Ohio State University Press and my editor Tara Cyphers for permission to include it in this important collection.

References
Baldissera, A., Denardi, V., Bueno, S.M.V. and Hoga, L.A.K. (2012) 'Improvement of Older Women's Sexuality through Emancipatory Education', *Health Care for Women International* 33(10): 956–72.

Bartky, S.L. (2000) 'Unplanned Obsolescence: Some Reflections on Aging' in Margaret Urban Walker (ed) *Mother Time: Women, Aging, Ethics*. New York, NY: Rowman and Littlefield, 61–74.

Beauvoir, S. de (2012 [1949]) *The Second Sex*. New York, NY: Vintage Books.

Bradway, K.E. and Beard, R.L. (2015) ' "Don't Be Trying to Box Folks In": Older Women's Sexuality', *Affilia: Journal of Women and Social Work* 20(4): 504–18.

Breland, L. (2014) 'Lost Libido, or Just Forgotten? The Legal and Social Influences on Sexual Activity in Long-Term Care', *Law and Psychology Review* 38: 177–92.

Brock, L.J. and Jennings, G. (2007) 'Sexuality and Intimacy' in Blackburn, J.A. and Dulmus, C.N. (eds) *Handbook of Gerontology: Evidence-Based Approaches to Theory, Practice, and Policy*, Hoboken, NJ: John Wiley and Sons, 244–68.

Cole, T. (1992) *The Journey of Life: A Cultural History of Aging in America*. Cambridge: Cambridge University Press.

Cornelison, L.J. and Doll, G.M. (1995) 'Management of Sexual Expression in Long-Term Care: Ombudsmen's Perspectives', *The Gerontologist* 53(5): 780–9.

Deacon, S., Minichiello, V. and Plummer, D. (1995) 'Sexuality and Older People: Revisiting the Assumptions', *Educational Gerontology* 21(5): 497–513.

DeLamater, J. and Sill, M. (2005) 'Sexual Desire in Later Life', *The Journal of Sex Research* 42(2): 138–49.

Edmonds, A. (2014) 'Surgery-for-Life: Aging, Sexual Fitness and Self Management in Brazil', *Anthropology and Aging Quarterly* 34(4): 246–59.

Ehrenfeld, M., Tabak, N., Bronner, G. and Bergman, R. (1997) 'Ethical Dilemmas Concerning the Sexuality of Elderly Patients Suffering from Dementia', *International Journal of Nursing Practice* 3(4): 255–9.

Emens, E.F. (2014) 'Compulsory Sexuality', *Stanford Law Review* 66(2): 303–86.

Foglia, M.B. and Fredriksen-Goldsen, K.I. (2014) 'Health Disparities among LGBT Older Adults and the Role of Nonconscious Bias', *LGBT Bioethics: Visibility, Disparities, and Dialogue*, special report, *Hastings Center Report* 44(5): S40–S44.

Gilmore, R.W. (2007) *Golden Gulag: Prisons, Surplus, Crisis, and Opposition in Globalizing California*. Berkeley, CA: University of California Press.

Goffman, E. (1961) *Asylums: Essays on the Social Situation of Mental Patients and Other Inmates*. Garden City, NY: Anchor Books.

Gott, M. (2005) *Sexuality, Sexual Health and Ageing*. Berkshire: Open University Press.

Gott, M. and Hinchliff, S. (2003) 'How Important Is Sex in Later Life? The Views of Older People', *Social Science and Medicine* 56(8): 1617–28.

Gupta, K. (2011) ' "Screw Health": Representations of Sex as a Health-Promoting Activity in Medical and Popular Literature', *Journal of Medical Humanities* 32(2): 127–40.

Gupta, K. (2015) 'Compulsory Sexuality: Evaluating an Emerging Concept', *Signs: Journal of Women in Culture and Society* 41(1): 131–54.

Hinchliff, S. and Gott, M. (2008) 'Challenging Social Myths and Stereotypes of Women and Aging: Heterosexual Women Talk about Sex', *Journal of Women and Aging* 20(1/2): 65–81.

Holmes, D., Reingold, J. and Teresi, J. (1997) 'Sexual Expression and Dementia. Views of Caregivers: A Pilot Study', *International Journal of Geriatric Psychiatry* 12(7): 696–701.

Huyck, M.H. (2001) 'Romantic Relationship in Later Life', *Generations* 25(2): 9–17.

Katz, S. (2011) 'Hold On! Falling, Embodiment, and the Materiality of Old Age' in Casper, M.J. and Currah, P. (eds) *Corpus*. New York, NY: Palgrave Macmillan, 187–205.

Katz, S. and Marshall, B. (2002) 'Forever Functional: Sexual Fitness and the Ageing Male Body', *Body & Society* 8(4): 43–70.

Katz, S. and Marshall, B. (2003) 'New Sex for Old: Lifestyle, Consumerism, and the Ethics of Aging Well', *Journal of Aging Studies* 17(1): 3–16.

Khanna, R. (2009) 'Disposability', *differences: A Journal of Feminist Cultural Studies* 20(1): 181–98.

Kim, E. (2010) 'How Much Sex Is Healthy? The Pleasures of Asexuality' in Metzl, J.M. and Kirkland, A. (eds) *Against Health: How Health Became the New Morality*. New York, NY: New York University Press, 157–69.

Lightfoot, E. (2007) 'Disability' in Blackburn, J.A. and Dulmus, C.N. (eds) *Handbook of Gerontology: Evidence-Based Approaches to Theory, Practice, and Policy*. Hoboken, NJ: John Wiley and Sons, 201–29.

Lindemann Nelson, H. (2000) 'Stories of My Old Age' in Walker, M.U. (ed) *Mother Time: Women, Aging, Ethics*. New York, NY: Rowman and Littlefield, 75–95.

Loe, M. (2004) 'Sex and the Senior Woman: Pleasure and Danger in the Viagra Era', *Sexualities* 7(3): 303–26.

Lund, E. and Johnson, B. (2015) 'Asexuality and Disability: Strange but Compatible Bedfellows', *Sexuality and Disability* 33(1): 123–32.

McGlotten, S. and Moore, L.J. (2013) 'The Geriatric Clinic: Dry and Limp: Aging Queers, Zombies, and Sexual Reanimation', *Journal of Medical Humanities* 34(2): 261–8.

Meagher, M. (2003) 'Jenny Saville and a Feminist Aesthetics of Disgust', *Hypatia* 18(4): 23–41.

Metzl, JM. and Kirkland, A. (eds) (2010) *Against Health: How Health Became the New Morality.* New York, NY: New York University Press.

Minichiello, V., Plummer, D. and Seal, A. (1996) 'The "Asexual" Older Person? Australian Evidence', *Venereology* 9(3): 180–8.

Mondé, G.C. (2018) '#BlackDontCrack: A Content Analysis of the Aging Black Woman in Social Media', *Feminist Media Studies* 18(1): 47–60.

Muehlbauer, M. and Crane, P. (2006) 'Elder Abuse and Neglect', *Journal of Psychosocial Nursing and Mental Health Services* 44(11): 43–8.

Owen, Ianna Hawkins (2018) 'Still, Nothing: Mammy and Black Asexual Possibility', *Feminist Review* 120(1): 70–84.

Persson, T. and Wästerfors, D. (2009) ' "Such Trivial Matters": How Staff Account for Restrictions of Residents' Influence in Nursing Homes', *Journal of Aging Studies* 23(1): 1–11.

Phillips, J. and Marks, G. (2008) 'Ageing Lesbians: Marginalizing Discourses and Social Exclusion in the Aged Care Industry', *Journal of Lesbian and Gay Social Services* 20(1/2): 187–202.

Phillips, L.R., Guo, G. and Kim, K. (2013) 'Elder Mistreatment in U. S. Residential Care Facilities: The Scope of the Problem', *Journal of Elder Abuse & Neglect* 25(1): 19–39.

Pleschberger, S. (2007) 'Dignity and the Challenge of Dying in Nursing Homes: The Residents' View', *Age and Ageing* 36(2): 197–202.

Potts, A., Gavey, N., Grace, V.M. and Vares, T. (2003) 'The Downside of Viagra: Women's Experiences and Concerns', *Sociology of Health & Illness* 25(1): 697–719.

Przybylo, E. (2011) 'Crisis and Safety: The Asexual in Sexusociety', *Sexualities* 14(4): 444–61.

Przybylo, E. (2016) 'Introducing Asexuality and Asexuality Studies' in Seidman, S. and Fischer, N. (eds) *Introducing the New Sexuality Studies* (third edition). New York, NY: Routledge, 181–91.

Przybylo, E. and Rodrigues, S. (eds) (2018) *On the Politics of Ugliness.* New York: Palgrave Macmillan.

Rebec, D., Karnjuš, K., Ličen, S. and Babnik, K. (2015) 'Breaking Down Taboos Concerning Sexuality among the Elderly' in Mivsek, A.P. (ed) *Sexology in Midwifery.* Rijeka: InTech Open, 189–207.

Reynolds, E. (2017) 'In America, Aging while Black Takes Solidarity, Activism and Magic', *Huffpost*, https://www.huffingtonpost.com/entry/aging-while-black-activism_us _58a477efe4b094a129f106eb

Rowe, J. and Kahn, R. (1997) 'Successful Aging', *The Gerontologist* 37(4): 433–40.

Scherrer, K. (2009) 'Images of Sexuality and Aging in Gerontological Literature', *Sexuality Research and Social Policy* 6(4): 5–12.

Sears-Roberts Alterovits, S. and Mendelsohn, G.A. (2009) 'Partner Preferences across the Life Span: Online Dating by Older Adults', *Psychology and Aging* 24(2): 513–17.

Segal, L. (2014) *Out of Time: The Pleasures and Perils of Aging.* London: Verso.

Sellerberg, A.-M. (1991) 'Expressivity within a Time Schedule: Subordinated Interaction on Geriatric Wards', *Sociology of Health and Illness* 13(1): 68–82.

Simpson, L. (2013) 'Gezhizhwazh' in *Islands of Decolonial Love.* Winnipeg: Arp Books, 105–12.

Simpson, P., Horne, M., Brown, L.J.E., Wilson, C.B., Dickinson, T. and Torkington, K. (2016) 'Old(er) Care Home Residents and Sexual/Intimate Citizenship', *Ageing and Society* 37(2): 1–23.

Siverskog, A. (2015) 'Ageing Bodies That Matter: Age, Gender and Embodiment in Older Transgender People's Life Stories', *NORA: Nordic Journal of Feminist and Gender Research* 23(1): 4–19.

Tronto, J.C. (2000) 'Age-Segregated Housing as a Moral Problem: An Exercise in Rethinking Ethics' in Walker, M.U. (ed) *Mother Time: Women, Aging, Ethics.* New York, NY: Rowman and Littlefield, 261–77.

Warner, M. (1999) *The Trouble with Normal: Sex, Politics, and the Ethics of Queer Life.* Cambridge, MA: Harvard University Press.

Waterman, E. (2012) 'Reactions of College Students to the Sexuality of Older People', *Journal of Student Research* 1(1): 46–50.

Watters, Y. and Boyd, T.V. (2009) 'Sexuality in Later Life: Opportunity for Reflections for Healthcare Providers', *Sexual and Relationship Therapy* 24(3–4): 307–15.

Wendell, S. (2000) 'Old Women Out of Control: Some Thoughts on Aging, Ethics, and Psychosomatic Medicine' in Walker, M.U. (ed) *Mother Time: Women, Aging, Ethics.* New York, NY: Rowman and Littlefield, 133–50.

Wilkins, J. (2015) 'More Than Capacity: Alternatives for Sexual Decision Making for Individuals with Dementia', *The Gerontologist* 55(5): 716–23.

11

Older people, sex and social class: unusual bedfellows?

Paul Simpson

If youth is associated with sexual vitality, older people are thought to represent the death of sexuality (Mahieu et al, 2014). There are few media images that validate older people as sexual beings, and the physical, aesthetic and status-related losses associated with age contribute to thinking of them as unattractive and thus uninterested in sex (Garrett, 2014). It is unsurprising then that older people come to internalise beliefs concerning their non-sexual or post-sexual status (Garret, 2014; Simpson et al, 2018).

The ageism just described appears thoroughly normalised. Indeed, what I term 'ageist erotophobia' (Simpson et al, 2018) that is disgust at, refusal or more often failure to imagine or acknowledge older people as sexual beings, finds resonance in the observation that sex and intimacy have largely been 'designed out' of social policy, care practice and academic research concerning later life (Hafford-Letchfield, 2008). See also Bauer et al (2012) in Australia, Doll (2012) in the US and Villar et al (2014) in Catalonia/Spain). Despite an emerging international scholarship on ageing sexuality, on rare occasions when the subject has been acknowledged in the professional practice literature, it has largely been framed as counterintuitive, inappropriate, or a threat or problem to be managed (Doll, 2012). This applies especially to individuals affected by a dementia/loss of cognition (Drakeford, 2006). Recognition as an older sexual being seems rare. At best, there appears grudging respect for if not pathologisation of the predatory, middle-aged, middle-class 'cougar' (Kaklamanidou, 2012) and the 'randy old goat' still interested in sex despite advancing years (Simpson et al, 2017). Yet, pressures towards what I would call 'compulsory non-sexuality' can have serious ramifications for the mental health/self-esteem and quality of life of older people (Hinchliff et al, 2019).

The stereotypical thinking outlined earlier is damaging not just because it demeans but also because it obscures understanding of the realities of older people's lives (Simpson et al, 2018). Older people's accounts range from elected or compulsory non-sexuality, to a desire for sexual opportunity, through to continuation of sexual relations (Bauer et al, 2012; Simpson et al, 2018). Indeed, it is possible that sexual experimentation may be more available to older people with more time and leisure than younger people with jobs, caring responsibilities and various social demands. It is also worth remembering that today's older people represent a generation that protested in the 1960s over rights to bodily autonomy (Simpson et al, 2017) and may now want to assert rights to sex and intimacy, whether living independently or in care. That said, older people differ markedly and ability to claim validity as an older sexual being may differ according to class among other things.

In light of ageist erotophobia, and taking an intersectional approach (involving age, class and gender), this 'think-piece' chapter will examine the literatures on ageing and classed sexuality respectively (generated from within the 'western' academy) and the few overlaps between them. (For accounts of differences of older African American women and older gay men, see the chapters in this volume by Harley and Robinson respectively). While not wanting to replicate imperialist hegemony, neither do I wish to dilute the focus, as class may be even more complex in societies where it could intersect with different conceptualisations of ageing and different status orders, for example an outlawed but persistent caste system in India. Such complexity calls for separate analysis.

As far as could be determined, there is a paucity of scholarly work focusing on class in relation to sex in later life, which is surprising given that the former influences a sense of entitlement and access to ideas that legitimate an ongoing erotic life (Jackson, 2011). Appreciation of the co-influences of age and class are critical in advancing understanding of diverse accounts of sexual relations in later life. Given that class is neglected in studies of ageing sexuality, I hope to contribute to knowledge by highlighting how theorising by Bourdieu (1984, 2005), which involves recognising class as both structuring influence *and* cultural process, could begin to address this knowledge gap.

Having outlined what is at stake in the politics of older people, sex and class, class will be defined as prelude to examining themes within the literature. For details of the literature search strategy, see the note at the end of the chapter.

Defining social class

The terms 'older' people, 'sex/sexuality' and 'intimacy' have been defined in the Series Introduction section. It is essential to acknowledge that social class, a highly contested subject, has been theorised in various ways. For reasons of space, I review three main explanations of it.

There is a tradition of theorising based on social stratification, which reflects the idea that society is hierarchised broadly in line with relationship to the means of production that is required to maintain life but that social actors can be meaningfully attributed to 'social strata' beyond Marx's dualism of capital and labour. Such analysis (which draws on the theorising of Max Weber) is represented in the work of Goldthorpe (1960) and Goldthorpe et al (1987), which argues, contra Marx, that stratification reflects labour market positioning and opportunities that affect income and wealth accumulation. For instance, there are intermediate or intra-class strata: compare the skilled member of the labour aristocracy ('upper' working class) with the labourer or the clerical worker/junior manager (lower middle class) with the middle-level manager (middle middle class). While the plumber and labourer may share a broad class position and the clerical worker and a middle manager alike in relation to (non-)ownership and control of the means of production, the plumber and middle manager will earn considerably more and experience a more enhanced quality of life than the labourer and clerical worker respectively. Indeed, the middle (or junior) manager will generally experience better opportunities for mobility and will be better placed than the clerical worker to provide opportunities for social mobility to their children. The same principle may apply to the plumber and the labourer.

While the stratification approach recognises the finely grained composition of class, its economistic focus largely ignores class reproduction as cultural process as well as forms of resistance to class disadvantage. Indeed, the cultural theorising of class by Hall and the Centre for Contemporary Cultural Studies (1982), which involved examination of the intersections of race and class, and that of Boggs (1976), recognise class less in reified form as layered and conceive of it more as processual and relational. Indeed, drawing on Gramscian neo-Marxism, Hall/CCCS and Boggs start from the premise that class relations are not forever fixed or rigidified. Rather class relations of dominance and subordination are more dynamic and require the constant winning and re-winning of consent to be ruled (secured by key social institutions like education and workplaces as well as the agenda-setting function of the media, all of which help delineate what is thinkable). The process just described exemplifies what Gramsci called 'hegemony'. The UK general election in December 2019 could provide an excellent case study of this concept. This is evident in media demonisation of the left-leaning party leader (who failed to dislodge the governing Conservative Party), who offered a social democratic programme of reforms to bolster public services, more welcoming attitudes towards asylum seekers and migrants in the context of British exit from the European Union. For a thorough analysis, see Jones (2020).

However, both the understandings of social class discussed can extend our understanding. Further, theorising by Bourdieu (which draws on Marx and Weber) suggests a possible solution in providing a wider-ranging explanation that combines considerations of hierarchy with considerations of culture through examination of class relations via forms of distinction between social actors. Furthermore, Bourdieu grounds class relations of differentiation or 'distinction' in particular social spaces ('fields of existence'), which are subject to their own classed norms/tacit rules of the game. If the former explanation of class indexes its objective elements (hierarchy based on income and wealth), the latter indexes its subjective ones (articulation of status through embodied, habitual 'taste'/cultural activities).

Following Bourdieu (1984, 2005), social class could then be usefully understood as multidimensional and relational in terms of its mutually constitutive economic, social, cultural and reputational resources. An individual's economic position (and its display in taste – appearance and behaviours) co-influences opportunities for social and cultural participation and especially status/reputation as an older sexual being (and in particular contexts). For instance, we could compare the 'cougar' with the older working class woman labelled a 'cradle-snatcher'. (See also the discussion of Bourdieusian theory in the later section on older people, sex and social class).

Older people and sex/intimacy: an incompatible relationship?

The comparative lack of attention to sexual activity/practice or enjoyment in later life, indicating that being old/er and sex are incompatible, suggests another instance of ageist erotophobia. Yet, people do not automatically cease desiring when pronounced old (Gott, 2005). Intimacy remains important until the end of life to maintain self-esteem and to keep people with a dementia connected with their routines (Kuhn, 2002). Whether living independently or needing care, older people express diverse responses towards sex, intimacy and sexuality that range from denial of interest (a valid choice), to nostalgia (a yearning for experience no longer available) through to continuing sexual relations (Bauer et al, 2012).

Arguably, the leitmotif of the body of work on older people and sex/intimacy concerns anxieties about classed expressions of sexuality. Indeed, much of this literature reflects sex in later life as problematic in various ways. For various reasons, from fears of loss of inheritance, ageism to jealousy, the children of older people can also oblige restraint on an older parent considering a new relationship following bereavement or separation/divorce. Just as consequentially, older people themselves come to see decline in desire and sexual activity as a natural, inevitable part of being older (Hinchliff et al, 2019). Even where individuals continue sexual relations, they may have to contend with anxieties and constraints attributable to discourses of 'successful ageing', which over-focus on certain forms of sexual functioning that measure performance against youthful, heteronormative standards. Such standards tend to prioritise penetrative sex to orgasm (Ayalon et al, 2019). It is also significant that scholarship addressing old/er people and sex appears primarily located within pragmatic concerns about health (itself no bad thing) but this body of work seems largely devoid of references to actual pleasure, which would advance thinking beyond the all-too-common, reductive misery narrative of later life.

As just indicated, the subject of ageing sexuality concerns achievement-oriented, sexological approaches that emphasise continuing, coital functioning and orgasm (see, for example, Trudel et al, 2000)). While such therapeutically based endeavours usefully highlight the health- and well-being-related benefits of continuing sexual experience, the focus here is commonly on a coupled, heteronormative, sexual 'book-keeping' approach that concerns who is still having sex in circumstances of reduced mobility and how often, and without much consideration of the emotional content of relationships.

However, this kind of reporting ignores the transformational possibilities of ageing as gain rather than automatic loss. For instance, such studies neglect consideration of how reduced physical capacity can encourage thinking and experimentation beyond reduction of sexual pleasure to genitalia and obsession with penetrative sex to orgasm as 'real' or 'successful' sex (again, on youthful terms). It has been observed that reduced capacity can engender creative rethinking of sex for older heterosexual women (but less so older heterosexual men), the former being freer from the genitocentric, coital (and possibly orgasm–obsessed) imperatives that enable exploration of other possibilities (Ayalon et al, 2019). It could be argued that genitocentrism and orgasm-focused sex also risk shoring up internalised erotophobia whereby older people feel they are no longer sexy, sexual or equipped for the 'proper' sex they were once used to. It is also worth bearing in mind the reactions of some older gay men to 'erectile dysfunction', which can lead to exploration of the more cerebral aspects of sex (involving negotiated play around limits in relation to bondage, domination and sadomasochism) and/or forms of sex where the whole body becomes a field of erotic possibilities. Such reflexive thinking, suggestive of the 'resources of ageing' (Heaphy, 2007), marks limits to the concept of sexual dysfunction (Simpson, 2015).

Anxieties about the sexuality of older people can have serious ramifications in terms of the erasure of older people's sexual histories and especially those thought to embody non-normative sexual identities. Indeed, regardless of identification, sex, sexuality and intimacy are commonly seen as irrelevant to ageing identities and older individuals' sense of belonging and citizenship (Gott, 2005; Hafford-Letchfield, 2008; Doll, 2012; Bauer et al, 2014; Villar et al, 2014). It has also been suggested that such thinking could be influenced by an underlying fear of mortality (Hodson and Skeen, 1994). This appears to be a curiously neglected topic in itself and could reflect that old age can be understood as 'abject'. Such thinking has concluded that the oldest, frailest citizens are substantively lacking in agentic capacity and thus have little chance of recuperating a viable sexual identity. This is linked to an over-association not just with dependency, but crucially with death, both physical and social (Gilleard and Higgs, 2014, 2015). However, the idea of the 'fourth age' (the oldest old) as hopeless and devoid of agency seems rather overstated and is challenged by evidence of sexual continuity and personal autonomy at least by some of the oldest individuals (Simpson et al, 2018). See also the chapter by Rennie in this volume.

The earlier observations concerning the creative reconfiguration of sex and intimacy are suggestive of a more sociologically informed, critical theorising that is also in tune with intersectional thinking. This kind of work has highlighted the problem of ageism and gerontophobia (ageing/old age as something to be feared) (see Simpson, 2015) and ageist erotophobia (see Hafford-Letchfield, 2008; Simpson et al, 2018). While acknowledging older people's exclusion from the sexual imaginary, these contributions highlight how the entwined differences of age and class and so on affect expression of sexuality, opportunities for sex and older people's sexual agency. Some of these contributions offer solutions at the level of social policy and practice (see Hafford-Letchfield, 2008; Bauer et al, 2012; and Villar et al, 2014). For example, in a UK context, Hafford-Letchfield (2008) and Simpson et al (2018) recommend that policy and practice at the level of the care system, and practice at the level of the institution and at an interpersonal level, should address various intersections. These contributions argue for the need to consider in practice complex needs in relation to sexuality and intimacy given the combined influences of ageism, classism, ethnocentrism, sexism, heteronormativity and cisgenderism (belief that a valid gender identity aligns with the gender ascribed at birth or into which individuals have been socialised).

As intimated, in an effort to avoid homogenising older people and their experiences, more critical approaches to later life sexuality have drawn attention to the intersecting influences of identity difference. Later life sexuality appears highly gendered in various ways. A national survey in Britain concluded that older men are more likely than older women to remain sexually active and, consequently, are more likely to report sexual problems or dissatisfaction later in life, commonly related to erectile dysfunction (Lee et al, 2016). As Ayalon et al's (2019) interview-based study in Israel has identified, gender differences in sexual activity in later life reflect dominant, enduring, 'traditional' gender ideologies. They reason that such ideologies reflect greater constraints on the sexual citizenship of older women (which drives them to invest more in disguising the signs of ageing) and a 'hegemonic masculinity' (see Connell, 2005), based on a vigorous, classed (economically successful) and status-inflected ideal that informs older men's sexual dissatisfaction. Ironically, few men of any age actually embody or 'achieve' such hegemonic status, (which may be more difficult with age) but it can act as the gold-standard of masculinity by which older and working class men especially may tacitly judge themselves.

While informative and thought provoking, much of the critical literature tends to veer towards constraint. Although sexuality itself (especially in later life) will be subject to practical, circumstantial, socio-economic, legal-institutional and discursive constraints, we would be doing older people a disservice if we failed to recognise the realities of their lives and where physical change (even decline) need not be an automatic bar to sexual engagement (DeLamater, 2012). Perhaps more importantly, we should not deny or obscure older people's capacities to challenge ageist erotophobia (Simpson et al, 2018).

Indicating a more nuanced portrayal of sexuality in later life, Fileborn et al (2017) have drawn attention to older men's reflexive use of varying narrative resources that defy binary thinking of 'decline or success' in relation to sexual experience. The authors point towards a more ambivalent understanding that can involve simultaneous use of traditional (hegemonic) and more contemporary narratives of sex as part of a more egalitarian shared intimacy. Similarly, and reflecting a more complex if contradictory understanding, Gerwitz-Meydan and Ayalon (2019) have identified how sex in later life is related to accounts of self-recuperation on rather youthful terms ('feeling young again') alongside more genuinely age-valuing accounts that involve converting lust into love over time. However, the influences of class are often missing or only implicitly apparent in much of the scholarship on older people and sexual practice.

Sex/uality and class: the working class other

If the literature addressing sex/sexuality/intimacy has largely ignored class, the literature on class experience has often ignored sex/intimacy and sexuality (as sexual difference/identity) (see Taylor, 2009). This lack of dialogue is not just surprising but also compartmentalises complex identities, indexes a reductive notion of (ageing) sexual subjectivity and represents a failure to appreciate how accounts of sexual experience are produced intersectionally and where class is crucial to understanding. Also, class is important not just in understanding the discursive constraints and entitlements regarding a sexual/erotic life and sexual self-actualisation; it can also explain the material constraints on ability to afford the prerequisites that can aid sexual pleasure such as pharma-technologies (for example Viagra), erotica, sex toys (Brents and Sanders, 2010) and the means to socialise in order to develop sexual relationships.

The marginalisation of class in studies of sex/intimacy and sexuality could be attributed to the 'cultural turn' in social sciences and especially sociology since about the late 1980s. This concept indexes the shift in emphasis on the effects of class structure on identity and lived experience to emphasis on culture as mediator of accounts/ experience (Jacobs and Spillman, 2005). It also represents a move away from materialist-structuralist (often Marxian/socialist) understandings of (sexual) subjectivity towards neo-idealist thinking as apparent in the individualisation thesis of Giddens (1992) and Foucauldian/ post-structuralist or 'queer' theorising (Lim, 2017). While Giddens' analysis emphasises the role of reflexive, culturally resourced post-class agents in negotiating a more egalitarian, democratised intimacy, post-structuralist analysis de-emphasises hierarchy and stresses instead the narrative/linguistic construction of a more contingent, mutable (yet still determined/constrained) sexual subjectivity. As Binnie and Skeggs (2004) and Skeggs (2003) have counter-theorised, such ways of theorising overlook that the resources (economic, cultural, and epistemic) necessary for fluidity, physical mobility and value in Manchester's 'gay village' (marked as 'cosmopolitan' space) are not equally available and are denied to working-class women especially: 'The value attributed to working-class women's bodies in this space marks them as the ground of fixity from which others can become mobile but also highlights who can be propertized, appropriated and attributed with worth.' Indeed, Skeggs goes so far as to say that middle-class patrons (regardless of sexuality) define themselves in this space against the sexuality/displays of 'gangs' of women in the form of hen parties. Such women are not only seen as bodies out of place and incongruent with the classed norms of the space, but are also subject to a consuming (appropriating), judgemental gaze of those who assume greater entitlement to be there and who consider that they know how to behave.

Despite denial or de-emphasising of social class by politicians, academics and people, as Skeggs reminds us, there is no getting away from the enduring, class-inflected character of sexuality. Indeed, an intriguing exploration of spatial and semiotic differences between 'sex shops' directed at women (up-market, stylish and empowering) and at men (seedy, down-market and disempowering) suggests further evidence of its classed and gendered character (Crewe and Martin, 2017). As noted, what is at stake here is not just the reputational resources that entitle older selves to a sexual/erotic life. It is likely that older working class people, and women in particular, experience a lack of economic resources and possibly knowledge. Besides, some older women may experience personal or recreational time poverty given their disproportionate caring responsibilities to partners and grandchildren (Carmichael, 2011).

Moreover, 'material queer' and hybrid forms of theorising have begun to recognise how material reality (including class structure and institutions) and ideas/language/discourse are inextricable if complexly enmeshed and, as such, are co-constitutive of (sexual) subjectivity/identity. Although not situated within this school of thought, the work of Skeggs (2003), addressing age-inflected, classed and gendered sexuality of younger people, has deployed structuralist and post-structuralist conceptual tools to recognise the combined structural-economic and cultural influences at play here. A similar theoretical move is visible in work by Heaphy (2007) and Simpson (2015) in relation to older gay men's differentiated experiences of ageing.

Arguably, the lynchpin of the literature on sex and class concerns the pathologisation of working-class sexuality and culture (McKenzie, 2015; Skeggs, 2003). McKenzie has drawn attention to classed (and racialised) state surveillance of so-called welfare mothers' sex lives. Of particular note were studies addressing sex/sexuality that focused on problems in relation to working-class people, indicating that they represent an excess of sexuality and the marked part of the class binary where middle and 'elite' class individuals represent the invisible norm or benchmark of propriety (see also Jackson, 2011). Skeggs' thinking already cited (2003, p 25) relating to Manchester's gay village serves as an example of this process. Further, as Heaphy (2011) has contended in relation to gay men/cultures, working-classness is commonly constructed as oppositional to gay male identity and thus involves dis-identification from such a label alongside strong claims of identification with middle-classness in terms of taste and behaviour.

Indeed, examination of class relations reveals a long history of anxiety over excessive, animalistic working class sexuality defined against the civilised standards of bourgeois self-restraint (necessary for economic success). Hogarth's iconic 1851 print, *Gin Lane*, portrays not just the ravages of gin in an impoverished London district, but also a related sexualised abandonment (O'Malley and Valverde, 2004) where an aged, drunken mother, bearing both breasts and dropping a baby, is foregrounded. Such representations find echoes in contemporary media moral panics that involve prurient, class-inflected 'slut-shaming' in the media of young, scantily clad, drunken, and 'touchy-feely' working class women at Ascot (for example, Stroud, 2018).

Older people, sex and class: theorising a way forward

The discussion in this section indicates a concerning lack of texts directly addressing older people, sexual experience *and* social class. It appears that older people are commonly addressed as if homogeneous and thus undifferentiated along lines of class and ethnicity (see Gibson, 2013). On rare occasions when class was indexed, it was incidental, implicit or subordinate to considerations of sexual activity and health or of experiences of being older. Class could also be addressed more obliquely in acknowledgements that maintaining a sex life can be difficult for practical reasons such as lack of available partners for working class, heterosexual women given that working class heterosexual men tend to die younger (Simpson et al, 2017; Hinchliff et al, 2019). In sum, class was seldom explored beyond acknowledgement of the potential to dis/advantage individuals' possibilities for a sex life (see Hafford-Letchfield, 2008).

Although concerning, the lack of scholarly attention indicated provides an opportunity to explore a possible solution to the knowledge gaps identified. It may then be worth outlining the value of theorising by Pierre Bourdieu (1984, 2005) to extend understanding of older people, sexual practices and social class. Essentially, in Bourdieu's analysis, class is formed by four interrelated forms of resource or 'capital', which are: economic; symbolic (reputation); social (networks/connections that can facilitate economic gain or enhance status); and cultural (related to education and socialisation). Cultural capital also refers to knowledge of society and of the tacit rules that structure particular contexts or 'fields of existence' where individuals are differently able to strategise (or not) to secure advantage or dominance. The class-inflected capitals differentially affect our sense of autonomy and influence in the various fields or arenas of contention that are undergirded by unspoken norms, which themselves sanction or encourage/discourage certain forms of behaviour/action. In daily life, we engage more often subconsciously in and can move across different social arenas (fields of existence), deploying different combinations of capitals/resources that involve distinguishing ourselves and making claims to value along class (and gendered lines). Again, the sexually active, middle-class older woman involved with a younger male partner might feel encouraged to distinguish (and thus distance) herself from the common, working-class 'pram-snatcher' and ditto the older 'gentleman' from the 'grubby old man' and so on.

Taken together, the capitals/resources structure what Bourdieu calls 'habitus' or embodied, deeply ingrained habitual thought and practice: sets of classed (and gendered) dispositions that largely unconsciously shape thought, practice and relations. Habitus may be entrenched but is not eternal and can change due to exposure over time to new experiences. One can be re-acculturated. For instance, one has to learn how to become old and discount one's sexual status but the economic and reputational means and cultural capital and connections required to resist pressures to comply with a normative aged (sexual) identity may be more available to middle class people. Nevertheless, habitus accommodates both endurance and the potential to change, which sidesteps determinism/reproductionism whereby actors are forever trapped in never-ending cycles of practice and social relations (McNay, 2000; Bourdieu, 2005).

Extension of Bourdieusian theory in relation to ageing, gendered sexuality has come from feminist usage and the sociology of non-normative ageing. For instance, Dumas et al (2005) have described how classed and generationally inflected habitus and 'age capital' animate older women's efforts to remain youthful and thus still desirable. However, 'age capital' can also serve as a resource in enabling individuals to transcend class to claim value on their own terms. 'Age capital' is similar to my use of 'ageing capital' (Simpson, 2015). This multivalent concept appeared in my study of older gay men's accounts of ageing and variously indexes emotional strength, self-acceptance and confidence born of knowledge of gay culture and wider society. It too is influenced by class, gender and sexuality and so on. Ageing capital could compensate for 'deficits' in education or credentialised 'cultural capital' and equip older gay men, regardless of class, with the emotional, epistemic and political resources to challenge both (age-inflected) gay ageism as well as homophobia. Simultaneously, it can operate in contradictory ways and even 'fail' when overwhelmed by ageist discourse or when implicated in ageism towards younger gay men. Older gay men's 'self-empowerment' can be articulated through distinction from and derogation of younger scene queens deemed superficial and self-obsessed (Simpson, 2015). For an account of classed relations and how distinction and social distance by class and age are achieved and deployed in gay culture and gay-coded spaces, see Simpson (2013).

From the earlier discussion, we could conclude that Bourdieusian theorising could be productively used to extend and deepen understanding of the under-researched subject of older people, sex and social class in various ways. As noted earlier, it recognises the objective and subjective constraints and possibilities with regard to claiming legitimate sexual citizenship in later life. Simultaneously, such theorising accommodates how age/generation and class can intersect with other forms of difference (such as gender, sexuality, race and disability) to create uneven possibilities in relation to sexual opportunity (Heaphy, 2007). As such, it allows appreciation of ageing and classed sexuality as relational: the product of various forms of distinction (and the mechanisms through which classed social distance is secured) with all manner of consequences. Finally, it can be deployed in a way that opens up phenomenological understanding of constraint, contradiction and agency, which sidesteps the binary of older people's sexuality as either passive and conformist (as post-sexual) or completely agentic or without constraints. Indeed, such a move portends examination of ambivalent experiences involving negotiation with ageing, classed sexuality (Simpson, 2015).

Concluding thoughts

This chapter has examined two main bodies of work and an emerging intersectionally informed scholarship from within the 'western' academy in relation to older people and sex/intimacy that contains mostly more oblique references to social class. I have also explored why class is overlooked in studies of ageing and sexuality yet it is central to understanding diverse experiences in later life sexuality. Such a theoretical move would avoid homogenising older people and thus would account for unequal sexual status and material opportunities for sexual and erotic pleasure. It also avoids homogenising older people as inevitably and inherently non-/post-sexual.

I have also drawn attention to the paucity of literature and some of the problems arising from existing socio-cultural attempts to explain ageing sexuality, for example in terms of how both popular and academic understandings of later life sexuality are often framed as health-related or therapeutic problems (see Taylor and Gosney, 2011; Gibson, 2013). Such factors themselves are often missing from or reduced to genitocentrism and ability to orgasm by a medicalised, therapeutic analytical gaze. In response to the problems identified and the lack of scholarly focus, I have highlighted the emergence of a more critical body of work that challenges ageist erotophobia (or compulsory non-sexuality). Related to this, I have sketched a theoretical agenda, where Bourdieusian class analysis is central, that could undergird further research on classed sexuality (and its intersections with other influences) in later life.

In the context of such lack of research on later life, sexual relations and social class (and the various 'intersections' with gender, ethnicity and sexuality), we might consider what a broader research agenda might look like. Indeed, critical theorising from social geography, feminism, anti-racism, post-structuralism and postcolonialism (which deconstructs the terms old age and ageing) could all contribute to a richer knowledge-scape. Furthermore, 'assemblage theory' of Deleuze and Guattari (1993) could be particularly useful in extending understanding. This theorising draws upon post-structuralist methodology (concerning how internalised narratives result in regimes of representation) and could also be used to address how relationships between actors, ideas, material artefacts (for example sex toys) and environments (care homes) co-produce classed and differentiated experiences of later life sexuality.

Raiding the more distant past, Mannheim's (1970) temporally oriented theorising on generations, which concerns a cultural zeitgeist that allows of variations from a dominant theme (which Mannheim termed 'entelechy'), would also appear useful in opening up understanding of a general trend towards resexualisation of older selves but conducted in different ways and from different subject positions. Simultaneously, this theorising could enable identification of specific obstacles and opportunities related to difference/social positioning and different routes towards reclaiming validity as an older 'sexual citizen' (see Plummer, 2002).

Finally, there is much at stake in the politics of later life sexuality and social class. If we continue to ignore this set of issues, we may fail to challenge stereotypes that hinder some older people's enjoyment of a sexual/erotic/intimate life. In so doing, we risk perpetuating inequalities concerning who experiences entitlement to a sex life. In effect, specific studies of class (with gender, ethnicity and sexuality and so on) could lead to better understanding of who is/not able to reclaim some measure of sexual agency and why. It may also help us think about how to challenge general and specific stereotypes of later life non-sexuality and differentiate campaigns and services that could encourage the sexual self-empowerment of diverse older people and especially those who may lack the sense of self, knowledge and status.

References

Ayalon, L., Gewirtz-Meydan, A., Levkovich I. and Karkabi K (2019) 'Older Men and Women Reflect on Changes in Sexual Functioning in Later Life', *Sexual and Relationship Therapy*. DOI: 10.1080/14681994.2019.1633576

Bauer, M., Fetherstonhaugh, D., Tarzia, L., Nay, R., Wellman, D. and Beattie, E. (2012) '"I Always Look under the Bed for a Man." Needs and Barriers to the Expression of Sexuality in Residential Aged Care: The Views of Residents with and without Dementia', *Psychology and Sexuality*, 4(3): 296–309.

Bauer, M., Fetherstonhaugh, D., Tarzia, L., Nay, R. and Beattie, E. (2014) 'Supporting Residents' Expression of Sexuality: The Initial Construction of a Sexuality Assessment Tool for Residential Aged Care Facilities', *Bio-Medical Geriatrics*, 14(1): 82–8.

Binnie, J. and Skeggs, B. (2004) 'Cosmopolitan Knowledge and the Production and Consumption of Sexualised Space: Manchester's Gay Village', *Sociological Review*, 52(1): 39–61.

Boggs, C. (1976) *Gramsci's Marxism*, New York, NY: Urizen Books.

Bourdieu, P. (1984) *Distinction: a Social Critique of the Judgement of Taste*, London: Routledge.

Bourdieu, P. (2005) *The Social Structures of the Economy*, Cambridge: Polity.

Brents, B.G. and Sanders, T. (2010) 'Mainstreaming the Sex Industry: Economic Inclusion and Social Ambivalence', *Journal of Law and Society*, 37(1): 40–60.

Carmichael, F. (2011) *Informal care in the UK: Constraints on Choice*, University of Birmingham Working Paper, Birmingham: University of Birmingham, http://www.birmingham.ac.uk/Documents/collegesocialsciences/business/crew/working-paper-carersresearch-aug-201.pdf

Connell, R. (1995/2005) *Masculinities*, Cambridge: Polity.

Crewe, L. and Martin, A. (2017) 'Sex and the City: Branding, Gender and the Commodification of Sex Consumption in Contemporary Retailing', *Urban Studies* 54(3): 582–99. DOI: 10.1177/0042098016659615

DeLamater, J. (2012) 'Sexual Expression in Later Life: A Review and Synthesis', *Journal of Sex Research*, 49(2–3): 125–41.

Deleuze, G. and Guattari, F. (1993) *A Thousand Plateaux: Capitalism and Schizophrenia*, Minneapolis, MN: University of Minnesota Press.

Drakeford, M. (2006) 'Ownership, Regulation and the Public Interest: the Case of Residential Care for Older People', *Critical Social Policy*, 25(4): 932–44.

Doll, G.A. (2012) *Sexuality and Long-term Care: Understanding and Supporting the Needs of Older Adults*, Baltimore, MD: Health Professions Press.

Dumas, A., Laberge, S. and Straka, S. (2005) 'Older Women's Relations to Bodily Appearance: the Embodiment of Sociological and Biological Conditions of Existence', *Ageing and Society* 25(6): 883–902.

Fileborn, B., Hinchliff, S., Lyons, A., Heywood, W., Minichiello, V., Brown, G., Malta, S., Barrett, C. and Crameri, P. (2017) 'The Importance of Sex and the Meaning of Sex and Sexual Pleasure for Men Aged 60 and Older Who Engage in Heterosexual Relationships: Findings from a Qualitative Interview Study', *Archives of Sexual Behavior*, 46(7): 2097–110.

Garrett, D. (2014) 'Psychosocial Barriers to Sexual Intimacy for Older People', *British Journal of Nursing*, 23(6): 327–31.

Gewirtz-Meydan, A. and Ayalon, L. (2019) 'Why Do Older Adults Have Sex? Approach and Avoidance Sexual Motives among Older Women and Men', *The Journal of Sex Research*, 56(7): 870–81.

Gibson, H.B. (2013) *The Emotional and Sexual Lives of Older People: a Manual for Professionals* (Vol. 7). New York, NY: Springer.

Giddens, A. (1992) *The Transformation of Intimacy: Sexuality. Love and Eroticism in Modern Societies*, Cambridge: Polity.

Gilleard, C. and Higgs. P. (2014) 'Frailty, Abjection and the "Othering" of the Fourth Age', *Health Sociology Review*, 23(1): 10–19.

Gilleard, C. and Higgs, P. (2015) 'Social Death and the Moral Identity of the Fourth Age', *Contemporary Social Science*, 10(3): 262–71.

Goldthorpe, J.H. (1960) 'Social Stratification in Industrial Society', *The Sociological Review*, 8(1) (supplement): 97–122. DOI: 10.1111/j.1467-954X.1960.tb03655.x

Goldthorpe, J.H., Llewellyn, C. and Payne, C. (1987) *Social Mobility and Class Structure in Modern Britain* (second edition), Oxford: Clarendon Press.

Gott, M. (2005) *Sexuality, Sexual Health and Ageing*, London: McGraw-Hill Education.

Hafford-Letchfield, P. (2008) 'What's Love Got to Do with It? Developing Supportive Practices for the Expression of Sexuality, Sexual Identity and the Intimacy Needs of Older People', *Journal of Care Services Management* 2(4): 389–405.

Hall, S. and Centre for Contemporary Cultural Studies (1982) *The Empire Strikes Back: Race and Racism in 1970s Britain*, London: Hutchinson.

Heaphy, B. (2007) 'Sexualities, Gender and Ageing: Resources and Social Change', *Current Sociology* 55(2): 193–210.

Heaphy, B. (2011) 'Gay Identities and the Culture of Class', *Sexualities*, 14(1): 42–62. DOI:10.1177/1363460710390563

Hinchliff, S., Tetley, J., Lee, D. and Nazroo, J. (2018) 'Older Adults' Experiences of Sexual Difficulties: Qualitative Findings From the English Longitudinal Study on Ageing', *The Journal of Sex Research*, 55(2): 152–63.

Hinchliff, S., Carvalheira, A.A., Štulhofer, A., Janesen, E., Hald, G.M. and Traeen, B. (2019) 'Seeking Help for Sexual Difficulties: Findings from a Study with Older Adults in Four European Countries', *European Journal of Ageing*. DOI: 10.1007/s10433-019-00536-8

Hodson, D. and Skeen, P. (1994) 'Sexuality and Aging: The Hammerlock of Myths', *Journal of Applied Gerontology*, 13(3): 219–35.

Jackson, S. (2011) 'Heterosexual Hierarchies: A Commentary on Class and Sexuality', *Sexualities*, 14(1): 12–20.

Jacobs, M. and Spillman, L. (2005) 'Cultural Sociology at the Crossroads of the Discipline', *Poetics*, 33(1): 1–14. DOI:10.1016/j.poetic.2005.01.001

Jones, O. (2020) *This Land: The Story of a Movement*, London: Allen Lane.

Kaklamanidou, B. (2012) 'Pride and Prejudice: Celebrity versus Fictional Cougars', *Celebrity Studies*, 3(1): 78–89.

Kuhn, D. (2002) 'Intimacy, Sexuality and Residents with Dementia', *Alzheimer's Care Quarterly*, 3(2): 165–76.

Lai, Y. and Hynie, M. (2011) 'A Tale of Two Standards: An Examination of Young Adults' Endorsement of Gendered and Ageist Sexual Double-standards', *Sex Roles*, 64(5–6): 360–71.

Lee, D.M., Nazroo, J., O'Connor, D.B., Blake, M. and Pendleton, N. (2016) 'Sexual Health and Well-being among Older Men and Women in England: Findings from the English Longitudinal Study of Ageing', *Archives of Sexual Behavior*, 45(1): 133–44.

Lim, J. (2017) 'Queer Critique and the Politics of Affect', in *Geographies of Sexualities*, London: Routledge, pp 67–82.

McKenzie, L. (2015) *Getting By: Estates, Class and Culture in Austerity Britain*, Bristol: Policy Press.

McNay, L. (2000) *Gender and Agency: Reconfiguring the Subject in Feminist and Social Theory*, Cambridge: Polity.

Mahieu, L., Anckaert, L. and Gastmans, C. (2014) 'Intimacy and Sexuality in Institutionalized Dementia Care: Clinical-ethical Considerations', *Health Care Analysis*, 25(1): 52–71.

Mannheim, K. (1970) 'The Problem of Generations', *Psychoanalytic Review*, 57(3): 378–404.

O'Malley, P. and Valverde, M. (2004) 'Pleasure, Freedom and Drugs: The Uses of "Pleasure" in Liberal Governance of Drug and Alcohol Consumption', *Sociology*, 38(1): 25–42.

Plummer, K. (2002) *Telling Sexual Stories: Power, Change and Social Worlds*, London: Routledge.

Sandberg, L. (2013) 'Just Feeling a Naked Body Close to You: Men, Sexuality and Intimacy in Later Life', *Sexualities*, 16(3–4): 261–82. DOI: 10.1177/1363460713481726

Simpson, P. (2013) 'Alienation, Ambivalence, Agency: Middle-aged Gay Men and Ageism in Manchester's Gay Village', *Sexualities*, 16(3–4): 283–99.

Simpson, P. (2015) *Middle-Aged Gay Men, Ageing and Ageism: Over the Rainbow?* Basingstoke: Palgrave Macmillan.

Simpson, P., Brown Wilson, C., Brown, L., Dickinson, T. and Horne, M. (2016) 'The Challenges of and Opportunities Involved in Researching Intimacy and Sexuality in Care Homes Accommodating Older People: a Feasibility Study', *Journal of Advanced Nursing*, 73(1): 127–37.

Simpson, P., Horne, M., Brown, L.J.E., Dickinson, T. and Torkington, K. (2017) 'Older Care Home Residents, Intimacy and Sexuality', *Ageing and Society*, 37(2): 243–65. DOI: 10.1017/S0144686X15001105

Simpson, P., Wilson, C.B., Brown, L.J., Dickinson, T. and Horne, M. (2018) '"We've Had Our Sex Life Way Back": Older Care Home Residents, Sexuality and Intimacy', *Ageing & Society*, 38(7): 1478–501.

Skeggs, B. (2003) *Class, Self, Culture*, London: Routledge, doi.org/10.4324/9781315016177

Stroud, C. (2018) 'Horse Play. Boozy Ladies' Day Punters at Ascot Knock Back the Champers and Get Touchy-feely on Sun-soaked Day: Raucous Scenes as Alcohol Gets the Better of Some Race-goers'. *The Sun* (online), 22 June, https://www.thesun.co.uk/news/6597205/ladies-day-royal-ascot-2018-champage-touchy-feely/

Taylor, A. and Gosney, M.A. (2011) 'Sexuality in Older Age: Essential Considerations for Healthcare Professionals', *Age and Ageing*, 40(5): 538–43.

Taylor, Y. (2009) 'Complexities and Complications: Intersections of Class and Sexuality', *Journal of Lesbian Studies*, 13(2): 189–203, https://doi.org/10.1080/10894160802695361

Trudel, G., Turgeon, L. and Piché, L. (2000) 'Marital and Sexual Aspects of Old Age', *Sexual and Relationship Therapy*, 15(4): 381–406.

Villar, F., Celdrán, M., Fabà, J. and Serrat, R. (2014) 'Barriers to Sexual Expression in Residential Aged Care Facilities (RACFs): Comparison of Staff and Residents' Views', *Journal of Advanced Nursing*, 70(11): 2518–27.

Literature search strategy

The search strategy involved word combinations based around 'older people, sex and social class'. The combinations were entered into academic search engines: the multidisciplinary Academic Search Premier; PsycINFO; and the Web of Science. These search devices were chosen to yield disciplinary variety across health studies, social sciences, social gerontology and the humanities while providing focus and manageability.

12

Final reflections: themes on sex and intimacy in later life

Paul Simpson, Paul Reynolds and Trish Hafford-Letchfield

This volume was curated to launch the book series *Sex and Intimacy in Later Life* and aims to provide a coherent, critical overview of scholarship focused on the identitarian and intersectional experience of age, sex and sexuality. As identified in the Series Introduction, it forms part of a broader intellectual project that aims to put sex back into sexuality. With such considerations in mind, we wanted to produce a text that demonstrates that this emerging field of knowledge (covering a relatively neglected set of cross-cutting concerns) contains some vibrant scholarship and is starting to set an agenda for further and future research. Our hope is that such an agenda can be articulated into policy and practice that, in time, could help validate, support and enrich the sexual and intimate lives of older sexual agents.

In effect, this volume has showcased a variety of work by emerging and established scholars based in Europe, Australia and the US, who are interested in later life sex and intimacy in various ways. As such, it has featured a mix of theoretical and theoretically informed empirical work that has variously drawn on a wide vista of thought. This theoretical purview encompasses thinking mainly from social gerontology, structuralism, poststructuralism, anti-racism and various feminisms. For example, the chapter by Debra Harley productively draws on feminism and anti-racist theory and would add to knowledge in social gerontology, where accounts of the obstacles and opportunities for agency for older black women as quotidian sexual agents seem lacking. Generally, the chapters in this volume are very much part of an uncovering of the intersecting influences that help to make up later life sexuality as it enmeshes with other forms of difference. The character of a volume that foregrounds diversity in later life sexuality inevitably commits itself to an identitarian focus and, if more 'savvy', an intersectional one in various ways.

The main foci of this volume (the recuperative and intersectional projects) rest on a threefold justification. First, it is important both to dispel the stereotypes, pathologies and prejudices that impose upon ageing sexualities and to understand some of the complexities of older people's sexuality, sexual desires and pleasures. Second, understandings of the complexity of sexuality and intimacy in later life will be limited if not exclusionary if they simply mine the intersections between age and sex/sexuality without recognising the gender, racial/ethnic, disability and class-related (and other) identity characteristics that constitute the lived experiences of older people, and how these influences impact on older people's sexual desires and pleasures. Third, it is necessary to recognise that older sexual agents (who should be free to make informed choices with the contingencies and constraints that are present for others) work within particular cultures and environments. Hence, the mix of UK, European, US and Australian contributors give a flavour of the impact of diverse cultures and there is recognition of some of the specific environments that older people encounter such as care contexts. This is apparent, for example, in the chapter on sex and the oldest citizens (aged 75 and over) by Karen Rennie.

While we would in no way claim that the volume presents a comprehensive survey of identities, intersections and their contexts and environs, we believe that the text does provide the reader with considerable insight, useful reviews of the state of current scholarship and extant and emergent questions to prompt further research. With such forward-looking considerations in mind, it would be wrong to regard the concluding remarks to this volume as an end-point or conclusion *tout court*. Any engagement with a text necessarily constitutes an open-ended exercise or dialogue and we wish to preserve this characteristic by providing some meditations on the themes and issues raised in the chapters. They reflect the influences of our different (and sometimes overlapping) disciplinary foci and different intellectual trajectories, which converge on the intersections of age and sex (and other influences).

To avoid a simple, pedestrian recap of the contents of individual chapters, this end-piece attempts a synthesis of overarching themes and issues that the chapters point to, though, inevitably, we refer to individual authors where necessary. Subsequently, we move to discuss what this volume indicates about the state of scholarship in the emerging field and, finally, how this suggests an agenda for research and as a way of signposting to a forthcoming volume on desexualisation that will address some gaps in extant knowledge.

Overarching themes on sex and intimacy in later life

Reading across the ten substantive chapters that make up this volume on diversity in sex and intimacy in later life, several overarching themes become evident. These themes range from broader ontological issues that relate to how sex and intimacy are constituted, to include those that concern the impacts and influences of complex webs of relations, of differentiation and socio-cultural positioning that in turn affect constraints on sexual and intimate self-expression. Such concerns also have epistemological ramifications in terms of how differences and constraints are understood by differently located social actors. Indeed, how actors attach meaning to phenomena (consciously or pre-consciously) becomes more relevant when we consider the countervailing forms of resistance to constraint and discourses that contribute to the desexualisation of older people – or what Simpson et al (2018) have termed 'ageist erotophobia'. This concept was elaborated in the introduction to this volume and is at least implicit in all chapters within. Nevertheless, almost as much as we see constraint in this volume, we see intimations of creative agency that involve positive articulations of diversity and practices that transcend and offer critique of dominant societal expectations related to heteronormative and penetrative/genitocentric sex.

In addition to the theoretical issues just mentioned, there is a theme that concerns (theoretically informed) policy and practice, which are necessary to undergird support for an ever-increasing social group. Ironically, older people living longer and in greater numbers in more affluent 'western' regions, which are considered 'ageing societies', often find their sexual needs, wishes and desires marginalised if not mocked, derided or denied. Yet, such forms of support are necessary if older people are to claim a more legitimate sexual citizenship on terms more convivial to them.

The bases of later life sexuality/intimacy

Many chapters address issues that concern the bases of sex and intimacy in later life as a distinct set of accounts of experience. Drawing on a range of theories from those grounded in thinking about structural hierarchies to those more concerned with the operation of discourses (influences of narrative and language), various contributors have drawn attention to how sex and intimacy as practices and pleasures are formed at the confluence of a range of influences that variously span the social-cultural, psychological, socio-economic, political and biological domains. Indeed, some chapters are based on a notion that sex and intimacy are products of the dialectic between various structural-hierarchical and cultural-discursive influences.

The kind of insights just described are particularly visible in chapters by Harley, Hafford-Letchfield and Simpson. Further, the chapters by

David Lee and Josephine Tetley and by Laura Scarrone Bonhomme all invoke biopsychosocial theory, which involves the interarticulations between three related forms/levels of experience (bodily and health-related issues, psychological and social influences) in shaping accounts of later life sexual practices. The chapter by Ela Przybylo, which draws on feminist and at times poststructuralist thinking, adopts a particularly original stance in that one of its central arguments is that ageing female sexuality, or rather the harmful desexualisation that older women experience, is bound up with a form of aesthetics, arising from ageist, sexist and colonialist notions of beauty where the bodily changes of ageing are associated with disgust. Przybylo's critical project has also usefully distinguished between desexualisation (where one is rendered sexless and unsexy) and a later life asexuality, which can involve a more agentic choice and include non-sexual forms of intimacy.

These complex formulations and critical ways of thinking are indicative of the value of theories that recognise the multiform character of how sex and intimacy are produced in different ways in relation to diverse older people.

Influences of relationality and differentiation

We would also argue that essential to any understanding of sex and intimacy are the interlinked issues of relationality and social differentiation in later life. Indeed, ways of differences in relating reflect the diversity and forms of divisions portrayed in this volume. As Bourdieu (1984) observed, 'who says differentiation, says inequality' and inequalities both help to constitute and are reflected in social networks.

The webs of relationships in which one is enmeshed with known and unknown others (even if an individual describes themselves as alone and isolated) can mediate opportunities to express desire or pleasure as well as to engage in sexual activity (Simpson, 2021). While relations with significant others or peers, known or unknown, do not always and automatically involve constraints on sexual expression, the emphasis in this volume is that, with regard to older people, more often than not they involve multiple constraints. Older people's sexual relations tend to be more subject than those of younger adults to control and influence by significant others and by broader social prohibitions (resulting from ageist erotophobia), which older people themselves can internalise and absorb (Simpson et al, 2018).

Constraint and repression of older people's sexuality are dominant themes throughout. Of course, later life itself is differentiated in terms of age and there is a difference between 50, 70 and 90 and so on. In this respect, Rennie's chapter draws attention to the particularities facing the 'older old' residents or those aged 75 and above in care environments. Rennie reminds us of the 'specialness of sex' for a group whose members may also be preparing to face the end of life, where sexual and intimate experience may take on a particular intensity as feelings, sensations and pleasures can feel particularly vital.

The notion of constraint also takes on a particular intensity in the chapter by Harley. Here, the author identifies the multiple and contradictory sexual stereotypes of older black women – as invisible yet hypervisible in certain ways – as a distinctly historical project, stemming from colonial experiences that involved the enslavement of black peoples. This chapter also points up the historical mutability of age-inflected stereotypes of black women from the sexless, older motherly 'Mammie' to the hypersexualised younger 'welfare queen', which have, along with the influence of religion, had considerable success in policing sexuality by encouraging muted or even non-expression of sex and intimacy among this social group. In such a context, it comes as no surprise to hear that older black women can come to discount themselves as sexual beings and therefore may be deterred from seeking help to achieve or extend pleasurable sexual and intimate lives. Similar themes are advanced in Przybylo's chapter focusing on women and asexuality in later life, which variously recognises how ageing femininity is shaped by the influences of ageism, sexism, heterosexism, racism and ableism. Indeed, age, gender, race, sexual identification and bodily capacity are central to regulatory narratives of 'successful ageing' that are modelled on and privilege older, able-bodied, white (and middle-class) heterosexual people. By implication, successful ageing discourse can position older asexual individuals, and women in particular, as the antithesis of 'successful' ageing, though Przybylo amply shows how older women can resist such regulatory narratives.

Continuing the theme of constraint, chapters by Hafford-Letchfield and by Lee and Tetley indicate respectively how the sexualities of older heterosexual *solo* women and older heterosexual men are differently policed. The chapters by Megan Todd and by Peter Robinson (who draws on a small, but international, Anglophone sample) indicate how the more public expressions of youth-oriented lesbian and gay cultures, as particular spheres of existence, police the sexuality of older lesbian-identified women and older gay men respectively. The same principle could apply to the chapter by Scarrone Bonhomme, who addresses the constraints on trans individuals experiencing gender dysphoria. Each author just mentioned indicates that the policing of older individuals, thought to represent non-normative forms of gender and sexuality, serves to intensify their devaluation and results in a strong sense of marginalisation if not exclusion from the sexual and intimate imaginary.

With similar considerations in mind, Hafford-Letchfield highlights the silence around, if not virtual invisibilisation of, the sexuality of older heterosexually identified solo women, given dominant expectations concerning ageing femininity. Both this chapter and that of Lee and Tetley draw attention to how older heterosexuals may find themselves more subject to the youth-coded, achievement-oriented discipline of, and sense of failure that can attach to, maintaining the ability to engage in penetrative sex to orgasm. The arrival of erection-promoting and maintaining pharma-technologies (such as Viagra) may have been a mixed blessing for older solo women (see Hafford-Letchfield) and older heterosexual men (Lee and Tetley). Pressure to embody youthful masculinity may now also be prolonged for older men (gay, bisexual queer or straight) and sex as a marital/partnership duty may be prolonged for older women desiring other forms of intimacy such as cuddling, affection and companionship over genitocentric, penetrative sex.

Despite the shift towards greater tolerance of sexual difference (still a power asymmetry) in some European and Anglophone liberal democracies over the past 20 years or so, it is instructive to reflect on the chapters by Todd on older lesbians and by Robinson on older gay men. The chapter by Todd illuminates the complex and multiple invisibilisation of older lesbians both as identifiable subjects and as sexual beings, which applies even more to those who give accounts of sexual abuse. It seems that abuse is unthinkable to many women within UK lesbian cultures given gender parity, which seems to involve forgetting that lesbian-identified women embody other differences and thus occupy diverse and unequal social positionings. The same dynamic is relevant to Robinson's discussion of different older gay men's mobilisation of the resources of ageing as a means of resisting conforming to desexualising discourses.

Further, Christopher Wells's chapter is significant for highlighting how monosexuality (the idea that one is either straight or gay) not only polices, but also erases older bisexual subjects, who themselves can come to internalise and rationalise their own silencing and invisibilisation. Drawing on Foucauldian theorising, Wells intimates how myths, stereotypes and mistaken assumptions about bisexuality follow subjects through the life course and act discursively in later life to render older bisexual subjects unthinkable and hard to authenticate.

The final substantive chapter by Simpson shows how social class can significantly influence who is more likely to enjoy sex in later life and to be able to claim valid sexual citizenship. Indeed, as this chapter argues, since the Enlightenment, the sexuality of the most socio-economically disadvantaged has been defined as an animalistic if infra-human excess against which more affluent and 'cultivated' others have defined themselves. The chapter also intimates at how policing works along lines of social class and how middle-class actors (and more likely men) might be considered or be more able to assert themselves as legitimate, older sexual beings.

In sum, this volume (and the book series in which it is situated) aims to add to a significant body of work on intersectionality, which grew out of the concerns of black feminism in response to the silences and elisions within white, middle class feminisms in the 1980s and early 1990s. The intersectional theory of Crenshaw (1991) articulated the confluence of gender, race and class in producing multiple disadvantages. The chapter by Harley is particularly apposite here. We hope to have extended this established intellectual project variously by considering the enmeshments of *age* (often the missing variable) with other influences that shape, but never fully determine, older people's sexual and intimate lives.

Later life as a position from which to challenge social expectations

As intimated, identity influences, social structures and discourses can never fully determine what people think and do. We have also hinted at how relationships and forms of differentiation/identity do not just help constitute sex and intimacy, but also inform how we *understand* sex and intimacy at any age.

Moreover, the chapters in this volume attest to bell hooks' thinking (1994) that the experience of disadvantaged social positioning can encourage critical insight into the operation of the social structures and discourses that secure oppression. For instance, the chapter by Harley addressed agency and the potential for social critique as a distinctly inter-subjective or collective enterprise between (older) black women who have learnt to reject the bodily discipline of dieting and so on, to embody a different aesthetic. Similarly, Przybylo argues that an agentic later life asexuality can disrupt ageist narratives of successful ageing that legitimate older people insofar as they emulate youth, as well as associated pressures towards full and vigorous sex lives as an ageist form of validity. Further, the potential of bisexuality to destabilise the identity categories 'gay' and 'straight' is not lost in Wells's chapter on bisexual ageing. Although subject to constraints, the author reminds us that ageing bisexuality can occupy an uncomfortable yet productively contradictory space for agency to critique mononormative discourse in relation to (ageing) sexuality.

The insights of Harley, Przybylo and Wells, albeit from different perspectives, are broadly suggestive of the knowledge that can come with ageing. Such thinking is also represented, in a LGBT context, in the work of Heaphy (2007), which has referred to 'the resources of ageing', a concept and theme that is specifically taken up in Robinson's chapter. This reversal of the usual discourse is welcome because the value of ageing and its gains are often eclipsed by misery narratives of ageing and later life as loss, decline and the slide towards abjection (Simpson, 2015). For Heaphy, the resources of ageing can serve as prerequisites for acts of resistance to dominant discourses that undergird and normalise a sense of compulsory non-sexuality. Indeed, such resources represent not just general epistemic gains, but also particular gains in political, emotional, cultural and social understanding, that is of the norms governing particular realms of existence.

Moreover, Heaphy's theorising makes clear that LGBT later life is simultaneously produced by factors suggesting constraint and autonomously deployed resources. There is no reason why this principle should not be extended to other groups of older people who might practise this in similar and distinct ways according to their positioning and context. Implicit within such thinking is that sexual and other forms of autonomy in later life are contingent on the dialectic between structural and discursive constraints and the opportunities that actors can create for agency. That said, Heaphy (2007) is also clear that the resources of ageing that enable such creative agency are 'unevenly distributed' and along lines of established social inequalities, for example the intersecting influences of gender, sexuality and class. Such a caveat is borne out particularly in the chapters by Harley, Hafford-Letchfield, Lee and Tetley, Robinson, and Simpson respectively.

However, it has been observed that the resources of ageing have relative independence from the more objective influences of class. They can also function in ways that compensate for differences of class and education to show how some older gay men can be defiant of specific and wider cultural expectations while delivering insightful critique of the constraints of (gay) ageism (Simpson, 2015). Such capacities appear not necessarily restricted to older gay men and we have already referred to the collectively derived forms of agency highlighted in Harley's chapter. Also, in this volume, Hafford-Letchfield observes how older heterosexual, 'solo' women question or even subvert approved forms of ageing femininity to engage in cybersex. Similarly, Lee and Tetley have observed how some older heterosexual men have questioned more hegemonic, youthfully coded forms of masculinity, as represented by genitocentric forms of sex, to articulate preferences for other (perhaps more feminine-coded) forms of intimacy. These contributors speak to the diversity of practice beyond heteronormative and penetrative sex and, along with Robinson (on older gay men), refer to how health or condition of the ageing body itself can limit opportunities for and enjoyment of sex and intimacy. Simultaneously, they invoke the creative adaptations (pharmacological, technological, emotional and psychological) that individuals deploy in response to a felt 'loss' of capacity.

The idea of ageing as enabling the development of understanding also applies to the chapter by Rennie on the 'older old' in care settings. Indeed, Rennie has observed a rich vein of thinking within social gerontological scholarship, which details how older people develop narratives of sexual continuity in the face of dominant expectations concerning later life sexlessness. Such a status can be linked to assumptions about health, especially as it relates to dementia, and how the oldest citizens are thought of. Rennie also points out that certain aspects of care environment design and furnishing actually prohibit sex and intimacy (single beds and single seating). In effect, such work has drawn attention to how older people have learnt, through experience of loss, to question genitocentric sex involving penile erection and have resignified what sex consists of, which can result in broader sexual repertoires that can invoke mutual understanding and relational longevity. Such thinking obliges us to recognise the discursive character of erectile dysfunction while questioning whether it automatically represents a loss for older people.

Finally, in this section, age and non-normative gender when combined might also encourage advancement of critical studies of age, gender and sexuality in quite different and unique ways. Trans and non-binary expressions of gender do not just unsettle the rigidity of a bifurcated schema of gender with its origins in eighteenth-century Enlightenment rationality and science (McIntosh, 1981), they also disrupt the very notion of normative time as strictly linear, as well as its regulatory effects. The chapter by Scarrone Bonhomme illuminates how middle-aged and older trans individuals often recount experiencing the liberating effects of a 'second adolescence' when adapting to living within their 'new' and chosen gender.

The need for policy and practice to support older people's sexuality

Although the theme of policy and practice will be addressed more specifically in the next volume in the book series on desexualisation, there are some important recommendations in this one that concern support for older people who choose to continue sex lives. Of particular note here is thinking in the chapter by Przybylo, who offers a challenge to residential care environments that 'design out' and virtually prohibit by neglect the sexual and intimate needs of older people to rethink their assumptions, prejudices, policies and practices. The author indicates a need for a paradigm shift in the care industry from viewing older people as needing to be preserved from harm to thinking of them as the loci of rich and diverse forms of subjectivity and bearers of rights to sexual and intimate and asexual experience.

A similar theme is taken up by Rennie, who maintains that the sexual and intimate needs of those in care (or receiving care at home) affected by a dementia, the oldest citizens and those nearing the end of life should not be discounted. With this guiding principle in mind, the chapter recommends that care practitioners examine their values and beliefs about the sexuality and intimacy needs and wishes of the oldest individuals receiving care. In more practical terms, Rennie recommends that care planning should be more truly holistic to cover sex and intimacy in line with differentiated and personalised support, led by the wishes and feelings of the older individual.

Implicit within Scarrone Bonhomme's chapter is much information of use to counsellors and other clinical professionals supporting trans individuals. Similarly, several other contributors, such as Hafford-Letchfield and Lee and Tetley, point up the need to provide emotional and psychological support to older heterosexual women and men respectively, which should involve peer-run services as well as advice and support related to physical health, including age-inclusive sexual and emotional health services. Of course, mental and physical health are not entirely unconnected. It has been observed that mental health difficulties can be just as consequential if immobilising of older people's sexual and intimate lives as physical ill-health or loss of capacity (see Hafford-Letchfield in this volume).

The kinds of provision and practice just outlined could help address stereotypes of inevitable or compulsory non-sexuality and stigma, which, according to Hafford-Letchfield, can prevent older women in particular from seeking help to maintain a pleasurable sexual/intimate life. One can easily imagine, though, how such a principle would apply to older men who need a good 'listening to' but who have endured a lifetime of messages, which convey that proper masculinity rests on emotional self-control. Such thinking has likely involved pressure to deny or keep in check 'feminine' emotions that acknowledge vulnerability and thus would risk compromising masculine status (Seidler, 2013).

The state of research in the field and whither a progressive approach to ageing, sex and sexuality in research and policy?

The book series of which this is a first contribution was inspired by the resolution that there is a paucity of research on older people's sexual and intimate lives. Certainly, a cursory look at the development of sexuality studies suggests that this wide and august body of work has not really given substantial focus to older people whether in terms of sexual identifications or as sexual agents/beings. (See, for example, the relative paucity of references to older people in major edited collections such as Herdt and Howe (2007), Hall et al (2012), and Fischer and Seidman (2016)). The focus has been on sexuality as a subject, itself previously neglected, and particularly non-heterosexual sexual identities given their recent (late twentieth-century) legitimation, is understandable. The correspondence of sexual to gendered and later ethnic- and disability-related structures of prejudice, pathology, oppression and pathways to emancipation has encouraged explorations of these various intersections. Again, we recognise that age has been less visible as a variable, partly reflecting a mainstream predisposition towards focusing on the legal, social and cultural issues in relation to younger people's sexuality. Leaving aside the irony of reproducing unexamined prejudices and stereotypes within critical studies, the omission of considerations of later life has seriously restricted possibilities for engaging older people as sexual agents.

Further, there has been proportionally far less research on older people's sexual health needs, the spread of sexually transmitted diseases among older people and the patterns of older people's desires in comparison with youth and young adults. Even when later life has been addressed in sexuality studies (that is largely in lesbian and gay studies), it features rarely in the more visible LGBT community spaces. Consider the case of older gay men in Manchester who have developed an 'alternative Pride' to the official one because of claims about exclusion from the latter, which is understood as a youth-oriented festival. Ironically, this alternative Manchester Pride has taken place in the seaside town of Blackpool, in the north-west of England, about 55 miles from Manchester.

What is evident in these chapters is that there is a paucity (comparable to other sociological identity-focused studies) of empirical studies that address the intersections of age and sex/sexuality. Only recently has this begun to change. That said, the chapters in this collection and some of the literatures they invoke, speak to that research being conceptually sophisticated and theoretically informed. Wells's exploration of older bisexual lives employs a Foucauldian framing to theorise the 'bitopic' writing out of bisexuality by mononormative sexual discourse and then reminds us that this is overlaid by the presumption that older people are less or non-sexual. Todd, on older lesbians, Robinson, on sexually active older gay men and Harley on older US black women all speak to an amplification of what Hafford-Letchfield and Tetley and Lee describe as the limiting effects of age on presumptions around sex and sexuality. Such effects underline why, as series editors, we sought to curate a collection on desexualisation of older people as the next volume in order to understand better the constraints on their sexual and intimate self-expression.

Finally, we consider the research and policy agendas the volume indicates for a more progressive approach to ageing, sex and sexuality. The keen reader will already have intuited a plethora of possibilities within the chapters, whether in terms of recommendations or absences, which are issues that we have not (so far) been able to address but would recognise as important.

Perhaps most evident are issues that concern healthcare policy and practice and the need for the education of practitioners (as per the Lee and Tetley and the Rennie chapters in particular). The chapter by Todd calls attention to the invisibility of lesbian domestic violence and we plan to invite further work on the invisibility of older lesbians as sexual subjects. Very much to the fore in practically all chapters was a need to understand better the agentic capacities for resexualising the older self. This process might also be linked to class, which, according to Simpson in this volume, is under-researched with respect to ageing sexuality. In respect of the issues just mentioned, we might think of uncovering the specific means by which, and under what conditions, different social actors can challenge if not resist discourses that would otherwise desexualise them.

In terms of absences from this volume, a productive research and policy agenda could address *discretely* and centrally the obstacles to sexual and intimate citizenship faced by older disabled people, those affected by a dementia and the oldest old or 'fourth age', whose identities have been described as rendered abject (Gilleard and Higgs, 2014). We are glad to say that such issues will be explored in more detail in the next volume on desexualisation.

A broadening out from accounts of experiences of later life sex and intimacy in Western contexts, like Harley's chapter, is likely to reckon with the historical forces of imperialism and colonialism that have misunderstood and helped secure the lesser value and oppression of 'non-western' others. Indeed, we intend that planned volumes on HIV, sex and later life, and accounts of later life sex in global regions obscured by the western hegemonic gaze might help destabilise established meanings of age, ageing and what constitutes sexual and intimate activity. These are likely to include postcolonial and social anthropological lenses, and could also trouble simple binaries of East/West, North/South and the sexually progressive and regressive labels that have become attached respectively to the West and East and particularly the Muslim other (Butler, 2008; Puar, 2018).

Thinking about diversity and respect also brings us to consider our very engagement with older people as scholars (and some of us *as* older scholars). It will be vital to consider in future volumes innovative methods of working *with* older people and their significant others and in ways that include strategically planned co-produced research (Willis et al, 2018). Such approaches should help ensure that we minimise inequalities of voice and representation and acknowledge and negotiate productively the shifting relations of power in empirical work. These kinds of approaches may ensure that we do the kind of research on sex and intimacy that older people would recognise and associate with their lives, which captures the complexities of experience and helps claims to sexual status on their terms. As Plummer (1995) might argue, the time has come to tell particular stories about sex and intimacy in later life. We consider that if a poll were to be taken today concerning the experience of sex and intimacy in contemporary life, most older people (aged 50 and over) would, rightfully, feel offended if they were excluded. Sadly, in Britain, the next National Survey of Sexual Attitudes and Lifestyles is to stop at age 59. Arguably, the most important question (and very much answered in this volume) should be, what is at stake if we neglect the sexual and intimate needs of older people? We think the short answer is that older people need and are worthy of much better than this!

References

Bourdieu, P. (1984) *Distinction: a Social Critique of the Judgement of Taste*, London: Routledge.

Butler, J. (2008) 'Sexual Politics, Torture and Secular Time', *British Journal of Sociology* 59(1): 1–23.

Crenshaw, K. (1991) 'Mapping the Margins: Intersectionality, Identity, and Violence Against Women of Color', *Stanford Law Review*, 43(6): 1241–99.

Fischer, N.L. and Seidman, S. (eds) (2016) *Introducing the New Sexuality Studies*, New York, NY: Routledge.

Gilleard, C. and Higgs, P. (2014) 'Frailty, Abjection and the "Othering" of the Fourth Age', *Health Sociology Review*, 23(1): 10–19.

Hall, D.E. and Jagose, A., with Bebell, A. and Potter, S. (eds) (2012) *The Routledge Queer Studies Reader*, New York, NY: Routledge.

Heaphy, B. (2007) 'Sexualities, Gender and Ageing: Resources and Social Change', *Current Sociology* 55(2): 193–210.

Herdt. G. and Howe, C. (eds) (2007) *Twenty-first Century Sexualities: Contemporary Issues in Health, Education, and Rights*, New York, NY: Routledge.

hooks. b. (1994) *Teaching to Transgress: Education as the Practice of Freedom*, New York, NY/London: Routledge.

McIntosh, M. (1981) 'The Homosexual Role', in Plummer, K. (ed) *The Making of the Modern Homosexual*, London: Hutchinson.

Plummer, K. (1995) *Telling Sexual Stories: Power, Intimacy and Social Worlds*, London: Routledge.

Puar, J.K. (2018) *Terrorist Assemblages: Homonationalism in Queer Times.* Durham, NC: Duke University Press.

Seidler, V. (2013) *Unreasonable Men: Masculinity and Social Theory*, London: Routledge.

Simpson, P. (2015) *Middle-Aged Gay Men, Ageing and Ageism: Over the Rainbow?* Basingstoke: Palgrave Macmillan.

Simpson, P. (2021) *'At YOUR Age???!!!': The Constraints of Ageist Erotophobia on Older People's Sexual and Intimate Relationships*, in Simpson, P., Reynolds, P. and Hafford-Letchfield, P. (eds) *Desexualisation: The Limits of Sex and Intimacy in Later Life*, Bristol: Policy Press.

Simpson, P., Wilson, C.B., Brown, L.J., Dickinson, T. and Horne, M. (2018) ' "We've Had Our Sex Life Way Back": Older Care Home Residents, Sexuality and Intimacy', *Ageing & Society*, 38(7): 1478–501.

Willis, P., Hafford-Letchfield, P., Almack, K. and Simpson, P. (2018) 'Turning the Co-production Corner: Reflections from a Community-based Action Research Project to Promote LGB&T Inclusion in Care Homes for Older People', *International Journal of Environmental and Public Health*, 15(4): 695–711. DOI: 10.3390/ijerph15040695

Index